MANCHESTER
UNITED

THE QUEST FOR GLORY

1966 ———————————— 1991

TOMMY DOCHERTY

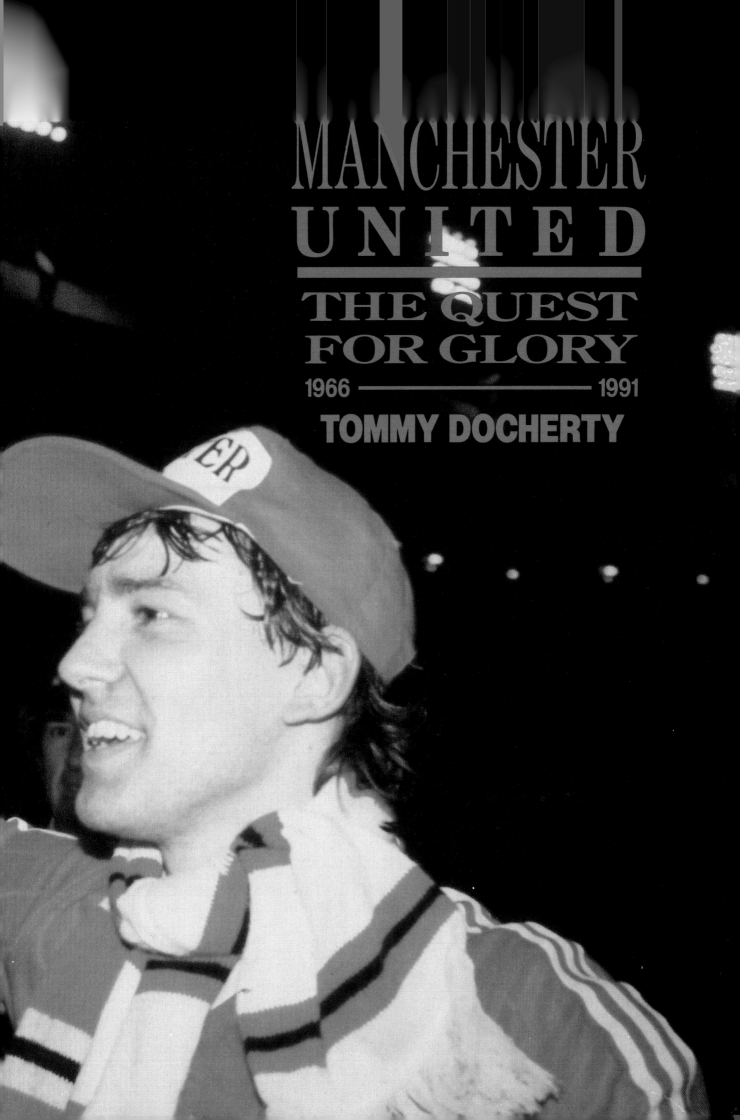

MANCHESTER
UNITED

THE QUEST
FOR GLORY

1966 ——————— 1991

TOMMY DOCHERTY

First published in Great Britain in 1991
by Sidgwick & Jackson Limited

© Copyright 1991 Brown Packaging Limited, 257 Liverpool Road,
London N1 1LX

Editorial and production by Brown Packaging Limited
Design by Allister Cordice Design Limited

ISBN 0-283-06105-7

Printed in Great Britain by Eagle Colourbooks Limited, Blantyre,
Scotland for Sidgwick & Jackson Limited, 18-21 Cavaye Place,
London SW10 9PG

BIBLIOGRAPHY

The Manchester United Football Books [numbers
1-15], edited by David Meek, published by Stanley Paul
Manchester United: Barson To Busby, by Eric Thornton,
published by Robert Hale and Co.
United I Stand, by Bryan Robson, published by
Pelham Books
On Top With United, by Pat Crerand, published by
Stanley Paul
Alex Stepney, by Alex Stepney, published by Arthur
Barker Limited
George Best: Where Do I Go From Here?
published by Futura
United — We Shall Not Be Moved, by Lou Macari,
published by Souvenir Press
Touch and Go, by Steve Coppell, published by
Collins Willow

United To Win, by Ron Atkinson, published by
Sidgwick and Jackson
Gordon Strachan: An Autobiography, published by
Pelham Books Limited
Denis Law, An Autobiography, published by
Queen Anne Press
Soccer At The Top, by Sir Matt Busby, published by
Weidenfield and Nicholson
Manchester United Football Club Official Annuals
[1978, 1979, 1980, 1981 and 1982], published by
Circle Publications Limited
Manchester United: The Betrayal Of A Legend, by
Michael Crick and David Smith, published by
Pelham Books
Manchester United My Team, by Sammy McIlroy,
published by Souvenir Press

PICTURE ACKNOWLEDGMENTS

The publishers would like to thank the following for
their permission to reproduce the material listed
below. Every effort has been made to trace the
copyright holders of this material and we apologise
for any omissions.

Chilton Collection: 18 (ticket), 40b (programme), 52
(newsletter), 84b (newspaper), 99, 112t
Colorsport: Title page, 12, 14, 16, 22b, 25, 28, 30,
34, 36, 37, 40t, 45t, 45b, 46, 48, 49t, 49b, 50, 53t,
53b, 54, 56, 57, 62, 63, 64, 66t, 66b, 68, 70, 72, 73,
74, 76, 78, 80, 82, 86, 87, 88, 90t, 93, 94, 100,
101t, 108, 113t, 113b

Camera Press: Back cover
Dawn Cover Productions, 27 Ashfield Road, Davenport,
Stockport SK3 8UD: 101b (first-day cover), designed
and produced by Stuart H. Renshaw
John Davies Photography: 58/59
Express Newspapers: 106
John Frost Historical Newspaper Collection: 18, 47t, 101b
Rex Features/News International: 114
Syndication International: 8, 10, 23, 26, 32, 35, 42,
47b, 60, 67, 71, 81, 84t, 98, 103t
Bob Thomas Sports Photography: Cover, 7, 44, 69, 81,
90b, 96, 97t, 97b, 102t, 102b, 103b, 105, 107, 109,
111, 112b, 115
Letter 47, courtesy Tommy Docherty

**Front cover: Steve Bruce and Mark Hughes celebrate
after Manchester United's 2-1 victory against
Barcelona in the 1991 European Cup Winners' Cup
Final in Rotterdam on 15 May 1991.**

CONTENTS

PREFACE

My time at Manchester United was the greatest experience of my managerial life. My career at Old Trafford was tremendous, and it was capped by a Second Division Championship triumph and two FA Cup Final appearances. I'm proud of my achievements at United: building a young side that filled stadiums throughout the world, playing such exciting, attacking football — and in a sportsmanlike fashion.

Manchester United is the most popular and glamorous football club in the world, and the last 25 years at Old Trafford have been dramatic, traumatic and filled with wonderful moments. I hope this book gives an accurate and vivid picture of that story.

I would like to thank Sharon Hutton for her diligent picture research. I should also like to thank Barney Chilton for the monumental task of compiling the statistics. Many former Manchester United players, and many people within the game, have helped with their insights and information: I should like to thank, in particular, Chris Turner, Steve Coppell and the England Assistant Manager Lawrie McMenemy.

Finally, I should like to thank especially Martin Chilton for his efforts in writing, editing and producing the final manuscript.

My proudest moment as manager of Manchester United was leading them to victory against League champions Liverpool in the 1977 FA Cup Final. OPPOSITE: Here, I have just been crowned with the lid of the FA Cup after our memorable 2-1 victory.

THE LEGACY OF SIR MATT BUSBY

Under Matt Busby, there were countless glory days for Manchester United, when several trophies, including the European Cup, were won in great style. Six successors have struggled to live up to Busby's wonderful heritage — but under Alex Ferguson, the days of European glory have returned.

For millions of people throughout the world, the name of Manchester United is inextricably and joyfully entwined with its greatest manager, Sir Matt Busby. His 24-year reign at Old Trafford was one of the most glorious and successful ever seen in football. United is still the most popular club in Great Britain — more than a million people attended Old Trafford in the 1990-91 season — and the club has retained a splendid aura of prestige. The glory days have returned to Old Trafford in the 1990s — with an FA Cup victory and the wonderful European Cup Winners' Cup triumph against Barcelona in Rotterdam in May 1991 — yet the club's success in the 20 years after Matt Busby retired was limited to just three FA Cup wins, and 1966 remains the last year in which a Manchester United team started a triumphant League Championship campaign.

For United fans, bred on a diet of fantastic football and regular success, the lean years since 1970 have been hard to swallow and the club remains, to an extent, trapped by its past, as Bryan Robson explained: 'Wherever you go at Old Trafford there are reminders of their great past. The Busby Babes of the 1950s, the Championship and European Cup winning days in the 1960s. Names such as Duncan Edwards, Bobby Charlton, Denis Law and George Best seem to hang in the air. Some United players have felt intimidated or haunted by the club's golden image. Supporters are quick to compare players and teams with those of yesteryear and there's no doubt about it — United and its supporters expect nothing but the best.'

The course of history changed for Manchester United in February 1945, when the Board appointed Matt

LEFT: Look at the joy (so well deserved) on Matt Busby's face as he brings back the European Cup to Old Trafford, after United's 4-1 victory against Benfica in May 1968. Winning the trophy was Matt's ultimate ambition, as he said: 'Frankly, ever since my wife, Jean, had told me in the Munich hospital that she felt sure that the lads who died would have wanted me to carry on, I had become increasingly obsessed about United winning the European Cup. It was almost as if this glittering trophy were the Holy Grail.'

Busby as manager. This modest, determined and kindly man transformed a struggling football club into one of the greatest and most revered in the history of the game. Under Matt Busby, they won the Championship five times — and finished as runners-up on seven occasions — won the FA Cup twice and made two losing appearances in the Final, reaching the semi-final in five other seasons. Most memorably, they became, in May 1968, the first English club to win the European Cup.

As soon as he took over at Old Trafford, Matt Busby began to revolutionise the club, as he recalled: 'I was determined to manage the team as I felt players wanted to be managed. To begin with, I wanted a more humane approach than there was when I was playing. Sometimes, lads were just left on their own, and the first team hardly recognised the lads underneath. There never seemed to be enough interest taken in players. The manager was at his desk and you saw him once a week. From the start I tried to make even the smallest member think he was part of the club.'

Millions of supporters were thrilled by the dazzling 'Busby Babes'

Busby began to reap almost immediate success. Within three years, United had twice finished as League runners-up, and in 1948 they beat Blackpool 4-2 in the FA Cup Final. During that year, Busby declined lucrative offers from Manchester City, Tottenham Hotspur, and turned down an offer to manage the Italian national team. Busby knew that he was well on the way to making Manchester United the foremost footballing force in Europe — and his brilliant young team of the 1950s (based around the superb 'Busby Babes', who had won the FA Youth Cup five times in succession) would, but for a fateful day in 1958, have been unstoppable. It was on the journey home from their European Cup quarter-final match against Red Star Belgrade, during a refuelling stop at Munich, that tragedy struck. In the air crash on that fateful day, 6 February 1958, eight of the finest players ever to wear United shirts perished, including the boy maestro Duncan Edwards.

ABOVE: Wilf McGuinness (right, in a maroon tracksuit top), with Busby just to the right, takes charge of his first training session with the first team, in July 1969, after being appointed Chief Coach. Sadly, the appointment was not a popular one with all of the players.

That tragic day in Munich somehow set the seal on Manchester United not merely as a professional football club, but as a romantic phenomenon. The story of the rise and destruction of Busby's brilliant young team, and the subsequent remarkable re-birth of the club under Busby — right down to the epic European Cup win — is the stuff of glorious myth. Yet it wasn't just the scale of Busby's achievements, it was the scintillating style in which they were forged that inspired such devotion to the club. Millions of people were thrilled by the dazzling Busby Babes of the 1950s and their superstar counterparts of the 1960s: George Best, Bobby Charlton and Denis Law. Over two decades, United were synonymous with attacking, daring football — and a graceful, shrewd manager.

Under Busby, the team went through indifferent periods, but the club always seemed to be developing and heading towards a fresh, achievable aim. From 1958 until 1968, this goal was the European Cup. New players were immediately struck by this all-consuming passion, as Pat Crerand explained: 'Everything was geared towards winning that Cup. When I joined in 1963 there was this great underlying wish to win it. I think that was the main aim all the time I was there.'

In May 1968, they achieved Matt Busby's heartfelt ambition by beating Benfica 4-1 in the European Cup Final. Yet the joy was mixed with other emotions, as Bobby Charlton explained a couple of years later: 'Winning the European Cup was the greatest moment the club has had, but it has not been quite the same since. We strived so long to win this particular prize that my ambitions since have been an anti-climax.'

Busby believed that the best hope for success lay in appointing from within

That European Cup win, and the 1966-67 title triumph, proved to be a turning point for the club. Busby's Champions were a team of tremendous flair, but they also possessed a steely professionalism that has been missing from United teams ever since. United's penultimate game in their title winning season was at Upton Park, and they hammered West Ham 6-1. Nobby Stiles recalled: 'Just after we had scored our sixth goal, I trotted over to Bill Foulkes and said: "Congratulations on your fourth Championship medal," but all he did was give me a rollicking and tell me to concentrate on the game.' This singlemindedness, however, has given way to inconsistency.

Busby's decision to relinquish the managerial throne, in 1969, was more like an abdication than a resignation, so associated was he with the ruling of United. Busby was aware of the problems that his long, successful reign had set his successor. Many clubs have found that appointing managers with close experience of the club is the best policy. Liverpool did that with Kenny Dalglish, and Arsenal won the Championship twice within three years under George Graham, who was a vital member of Arsenal's 1970-71 League and FA Cup 'double-winning' team.

Busby believed that United's best hope for continued success lay in appointing somebody who knew and was loyal to the club, and for this reason he picked a former Busby Babe, Wilf McGuinness — who was a coach at United — to succeed him. Unfortunately, this didn't work out. Many established players found it hard adjusting to working with a new, young manager and they withheld their respect and wholehearted co-operation from Wilf McGuinness, whom they continued to address by his christian name. Busby, meanwhile, was still called 'boss'.

Many supporters would like to have seen Bobby Charlton as manager

This failure made it very hard to appoint from within the club's ranks again, and there were no automatic choices from among the great players of the 1960s. George Best and Denis Law were not interested in management, and of the players who tried it, there were no startling successes. Nobby Stiles (at Preston North End), had a reasonably successful time, but found his real niche in coaching, while both Paddy Crerand (who lasted just six months as boss of Northampton Town) and Bobby Charlton (who was also at Preston) had unsuccessful apprenticeships.

Many supporters would like to have seen Bobby come back to United as manager, but it was not a role he was cut out for. He took over at Preston in May 1973 — bringing former United colleagues David Sadler, Francis Burns and Nobby Stiles with him to Deepdale — but a year later, after a run in which the team had won only two out of 18 games, Preston were relegated from Division Two. It remains to be seen whether, if they do eventually decide to replace Alex Ferguson — and it won't be for a few years — United try again the policy of appointing a former player, such as Bryan Robson or Steve Coppell, for example.

'The club was rife with petty jealousies, an unfriendly, almost hostile place to be'

Without the possibility of continuity in 1971, United appointed an outsider. Although Frank O'Farrell was a good manager, by the time he took over the club was already in a deep slide and he was faced with insurmountable problems. The youth policy was in decline, and he inherited a team that was splintered and demoralised. Ted MacDougall, the striker whom O'Farrell signed from Bournemouth, said of his unhappy stay at Old Trafford: 'While I was there the foundations of a once great club were eaten away by internal squabblings. Team spirit vanished and players went into revolt. The club was rife with petty jealousies, an unfriendly, almost hostile place to be. There were players who hardly bothered to talk to me, or acknowledge that I was around the place — Bobby Charlton and George Best, for instance. They were great performers, but I lost respect for them. They wouldn't talk to each other off the park, and during the game seldom passed the ball to each other.'

For everyone involved with Manchester United, these years were intensely depressing ones. Shortly before Frank O'Farrell was fired in December 1972, Matt Busby said: 'We are having a rough time. It hurts us even more than it hurts our supporters. Everywhere I go, I am asked: "What's wrong with United?" A poor run for us seems to be an international disaster, let alone a national one.'

It had been very hard for Matt to detach himself completely from the running of the club, particularly in the years just after he had retired as manager. After all, the job had been his whole life for a quarter of a century. Busby once said: 'Let me say here and now that I was largely responsible for the appointments of Wilf McGuinness, Frank O'Farrell, Tommy Docherty and Dave Sexton in turn. Never, at any time, did I interfere in their management of the team. Since I stepped down from the managerial chair, I have not tried to run Manchester United as a Matt Busby show.'

'We were convinced we could bring back the glory days to Old Trafford'

When Frank O'Farrell was sacked, I think the Board realised that the new manager had to be given more independence. For years, the club had been run with the heart and not the head, and United was stagnating. However, Busby never interfered when I was in charge, and always gave me his help and encouragement. As manager, I put the emphasis on attacking play and a strong youth policy. United had failed to bridge the gap from the fabulous era of the 1960s to the necessities of football in the 1970s. The game had changed, and United had stood still. My one regret was that we couldn't avoid relegation, but there were still grounds for optimism, because it was accepted that we had to rebuild, and it made for an exciting time. There is something so special about United. The club has millions of followers all over the world — and, in Old Trafford, a stadium that is one of the most impressive and atmospheric in the world.

In the Second Division, Tommy Cavanagh and I worked furiously to salvage the situation. We plotted the rise of Manchester United, and we were convinced that we could bring back the glory days to Old Trafford playing the sort of attacking, inventive football that had made the club so popular. We achieved this, thrilled supporters everywhere we went, won the Second Division Championship and reached the semi-final of the League Cup. Back in the First Division, we pushed hard for the title, went to two FA Cup Finals in succes-

Alex Ferguson, who took over United in 1986, had a difficult start at the club, but has since become the most successful manager since Busby. In 1990, he led United to an FA Cup win, and in 1991 he guided the Reds to victory in the European Cup Winners' Cup Final against Barcelona.

ish as also-rans while their arch-rivals Liverpool have won trophy after trophy (Manchester City, who were the team United's fans wanted to beat most during Busby's reign, have long since faded as serious rivals, having not won a major trophy since 1976).

'Our followers have been very patient. Like us, they have taken the insults'

United fans desperately want to see the club win the Championship, and they have grown frustrated and cynical about the long, barren years United have spent as also-rans. They have done their part — supporting the team week in and week out — and in the early part of the 1988-89 season, during a particularly dour game, a chorus of: 'Will We Ever Win The League?' rang out from the Old Trafford faithful. The players are certainly aware of the frustration for their supporters, as Mark Hughes commented after his superb performance in Rotterdam in May 1991: 'Our followers have been very patient. Like us, they have taken the insults and jibes about us being one-off merchants. It's about time we wiped that stain off United's record, and laid the ghost about us being Championship busters for all time.'

Yet United's past successes should be put in historical context. Certain clubs have dominated particular eras. Aston Villa have never equalled their conquests of the 1890s; Huddersfield ruled the 1920s, and Arsenal the 1930s — much as Liverpool did from 1977 until 1990. Manchester United's golden period lasted roughly 16 years — from the title winning success in 1951-52 to 1968, when they fulfilled their dream of winning the European Cup. I don't think United will ever get near the levels of performance and results that they achieved under Matt Busby.

Manchester United have become the champion cup team in Britain

Despite their failure to win the League in the past quarter of a century, there have been glory days at Old Trafford as United have become the champion cup team in Britain — winning the FA Cup four times in 15 years, reaching the Final a further two times; reaching the League Cup Final twice and winning the European Cup Winners' Cup — and the marvellous players who have graced Old Trafford during those years have continued to bring magical times to the club.

Just as Matt Busby was a hard act to follow for managers, George Best, Bobby Charlton and Denis Law, were hard to follow on the pitch. Although it would have been impossible for any manager to replace three of the greatest players ever to grace a football pitch, there have been a lot of players who have pulled on the famous red jersey during the past 25 years who weren't good enough — and I signed some of them myself!

Although no one has come near to matching Best,

sion and were exemplary sportsmen into the bargain — we won the Fair Play League two years in a row!

All of Busby's successors have struggled with the legacy of following one of the greatest managers in the game, but this sense of living up to his image has weakened as the years have rolled by, and each of his six successors have tried different methods to bring success to Old Trafford. Wilf, Frank, Dave, Ron, Alex and I have experienced the tremendous pressure that the United manager's job brings. Interestingly, the style of play of United teams has switched dramatically during the past 20 years, in tune with the character of the managers. The flamboyant and expansive attacking style of my team was followed by a cautious and tactical approach that reflected the introverted nature of Dave Sexton. Likewise, Ron Atkinson's flamboyancy was mirrored by his teams — who played great football — and Alex's blend of austerity and courage has, to a certain extent, shaped the team's playing style.

All Busby's successors have been faced by one common problem: the high expectations of the supporters. Ron Atkinson once wrote about this factor: 'The brutal truth is that Manchester United and its supporters were living in a fool's paradise and had been doing so for some considerable time.' United's supporters demand success, and they have become frustrated during the past quarter century having to watch United fin-

who could tackle, shoot and head like a master and beat opponents on either side using methods that nobody could thwart, United teams in the past 25 years have had their fair share of glorious players: Sammy McIlroy, the last of the Busby Babes (and worthy of the title), who could dribble and distribute like a master; Martin Buchan, an ice-cool, world-class defender; Steve Coppell and Gordon Hill, the wizards of the wing; Stuart 'Pancho' Pearson and Jimmy Greenhoff, two fantastic inside-forwards, who had an almost telepathic awareness of each other's strengths; Lou Macari, a skilful, unflappable player; Arnold Muhren, a midfield maestro; Paul McGrath, that cultured and self-possessed player; Norman Whiteside, an aggressive, bold, match-winner; Bryan Robson, one of the most inspirational players in the club's history; Mark Hughes, who possesses remarkable strength and technique, is one of the world's finest volleyers and has come good for United in so many important matches; and right up to winger Lee Sharpe, who is sure to be one of the most exciting players of the 1990s.

Under Ron Atkinson there were a series of wonderful cup games

Although United have not experienced anything in the League comparable to that tremendous win at West Ham United in 1967 — they have finished as Division One runners-up just three times since their last title win — the glory has come in some fantastic cup games. When I was manager, there were two great FA Cup semi-final wins, and our thrilling 1977 FA Cup win over Liverpool, depriving them of the 'treble'; Dave Sexton led United to a fine win against Liverpool in the 1979 FA Cup semi-final, and the dramatic Final against Arsenal.

Under Ron Atkinson there were a series of wonderful cup games: the stunning wins in the two legs of the League Cup semi-final against Arsenal in 1983 — and the FA Cup semi-final win against the Gunners that year; the 1985 FA Cup semi-final win against Liverpool; the 1985 FA Cup Final, when United, down to 10 men after Kevin Moran had been sent off, beat League Champions Everton; the fantastic 3-0 victory against Barcelona in the 1984 quarter-final of the European Cup Winners' Cup, when Bryan Robson, who scored twice that night, outclassed his opponent Diego Maradona and helped United overcome a 0-2 deficit to reach the semi-finals against Juventus.

During Alex Ferguson's first five years, United's marvellous cup tradition has been maintained — and extended — in glorious games such as the 1990 FA Cup semi-finals against Oldham Athletic, and the Final against Crystal Palace; the 3-1 destruction of Liverpool in the Rumbelows Cup and the subsequent 6-2 drubbing of champions Arsenal in that competition in the 1990-91 season. And, of course, there were the dramatic European victories in 1991: the spirited 2-0 defeat of Montpellier in March; the superb 3-1 win against Legia Warsaw in April and the victory in the Final against Spanish Champions, Barcelona — capped by Sparky's magnificent, determined winner.

Ferguson embarked on a massive spending spree to bring success

Despite these successes, the burden of bringing success back to Old Trafford has proved to be too demanding for some managers (and scores of players), and the situation is worsened by the prevalence of the view, a somewhat naive one, that there is a sleeping football supremacy at Old Trafford that is waiting to be awakened. For all its size, wealth and status, if United are to match Liverpool's record of success, it will take ceaseless work and shrewd planning — and Alex can do it!

To that end, in 1989, Ferguson embarked on a massive spending spree to try and bring success to Old Trafford, and the 1990-91 season showed that his policy — of buying top players and nurturing youngsters — is paying off. Ferguson made his first contribution to bringing back the glory days to United when they won the 1990 FA Cup Final. It was the seventh time United had won the FA Cup, and equalled the record held by Aston Villa and Tottenham. The pressure Ferguson had been under — when he came perilously close to getting the axe — revealed how much bigger the stakes are at Old Trafford in the 1990s than they were 20 years ago.

'The longer the quest for the title goes on, the more the manager bears the brunt'

Although Matt Busby did not enjoy unbridled success, there was never any question that he would have the time and support to get things right again when United were in a lull. Indeed, United's form in 1962-63 was so disturbingly erratic that they came close to relegation, and Busby came in for a lot of criticism. Yet the FA Cup win of 1963 marked a turning-point. Maurice Setters, Jack Charlton's assistant with the Republic of Ireland team, was a member of the cup winning team, and he said of Alex Ferguson, just before the 1990 FA Cup Final: 'The omens are good for United. I've said that to Alex. The situation is remarkably similar to 1963, when we were terrible in the League and struggled to beat Southampton, a Second Division team, in the semi-finals. That Final was a significant match in United's history, because it turned things around and two seasons later they were Champions again.'

It remains to be seen whether 1991-92 will bring the League Championship back to the Old Trafford trophy room, but until it does, no United manager will be deemed to be a complete success and the the club will remain trapped by the grandeur of its glorious past. In 1989, Kevin Moran, who had played under United's last three managers, expressed the dilemma which Busby's legacy has created: 'There is a tradition at United that you feel so proud to be part of. And I suppose the way the tradition weighs so heavily is with regard to the League Championship. That's why I feel sorry for every manager, because the longer the quest for the League title goes on, the more he bears the brunt. Ferguson may be in charge only three years, for example, but as far as United fans are concerned it's *his* fault that it's 23 years since they won the League Championship.'

United's managers have been held responsible for the lack of success, and rightly so. All six successors have wanted to emulate Matt Busby's achievements, and to do that they have to *start* by winning the title.

Alex Ferguson brought Mark Hughes back to Old Trafford in June 1988, after the Welsh striker, who is a product of United's junior system, had been abroad with Barcelona and Bayern Munich. Hughes has been a magnificent player for Ferguson. In the 1990 FA Cup Final, his predatory instincts were on full, brilliant show. In the 63rd minute of the game against Crystal Palace (below), Hughes took a pass from Neil Webb, gave himself room and fired a ferocious left foot drive past Palace 'keeper Nigel Martyn, as a stranded Palace defender, Gary O'Reilly, and Brian McClair raced in.

The Championship has now become a complete fixation with the club, to such an extent that I believe that even if they do actually win it within the next few seasons, it won't answer the nagging questions about the club. If United do, for example, win it in 1992, on current form, they would go until the year 2017 before they won it again! The acid test is consistency — the way for example the title has gone to Anfield with monotonous regularity, and the way Busby chalked up success after success — and United would have to retain the League title (or capture the European Cup), or at least win it again within the next few years, to show that they had truly re-established their pre-eminence.

Matt Busby was such a marvellous manager, and his achievements so awesome, that the legacy he created has made it extremely hard for his six successors. Under Busby, as he himself said when he retired, Manchester United had become an institution, but they had failed to keep pace with the changing world of football — and while the Board have transformed United into a major money-making business, including floating the club on the stock exchange, the club haven't performed as well as they should have done on the park.

United's cup runs of the past 15 years have been lovely. Enjoyable for the fans, managers and players, but I believe and hope that Alex Ferguson is starting to turn the club around to make them the top team of the 1990s. Ferguson has spent lavishly during his five years as manager, but he has also rebuilt the youth programme. United's great success of the past was built on their youth policy, and although United's is now in good shape, the real test of a youth system is the first team: Arsenal's title winning squad of 1991 possessed seven homegrown players. I would like to see the brilliant crop of youngsters at Old Trafford given their chance in the first team.

The biggest and the best is what Manchester United is all about

After the epic 1968 European Cup triumph at Wembley, United's supporters had a wait of 23 years for a taste of European glory, but they got it in real style in Rotterdam on 15 May 1991. When Mark Hughes fired United to victory over Barcelona in the Cup Winners'

Cup Final, he signalled that United were back in the big time. Alex Ferguson has assembled a young squad — with an average age of 26 — with a few key players of exceptional talent and great experience. Those players have tasted real success now and will want more of it. As Alex himself said after the game: 'Hopefully, we can use this as a platform. Having experienced this tonight, you need it all the time now. It becomes a drug.'

Alex Ferguson knew when he took over Manchester United in 1986 that it would take a few years to rebuild the club, but he has done it well. Now, he must use the foundations and take the club even further. After that European triumph, Alex was given a new, long-term contract, which means that unlike any of his five predecessors, he will have *time* — and financial backing — to achieve the most important goal. Alex knows that the biggest test of any club is to win their League *and* the European Cup — which was Alex's stated aim when he joined Old Trafford. The Champions Cup is the greatest prize in club football, and the biggest and best is what Manchester United is all about. The quest for glory from 1966-91 has been a dramatic one — and at times a frustrating one — but the future looks very promising.

FATHER OF FOOTBALL

When the Manchester United directors appointed Matt Busby as manager in 1945, they made the most important and far-sighted decision in the club's history. In a glorious reign, which spanned a quarter of a century, Busby built United into one of the greatest football clubs in the world.

Sir Matt Busby's greatest moment in football — 'the crowning glory of my days in football and the fulfilment of my personal dream', as he put it — came at Wembley on a May evening in 1968, when the whistle ended extra time in the European Cup Final. Busby's beloved Manchester United had just beaten Benfica 4-1 to win the trophy which Busby coveted above all others.

United's players certainly knew how much winning the trophy meant to him. Goalkeeper Alex Stepney later described how: 'The man we all made for when the final whistle was blown was Matt. It was his hour. He was, and still is, the heartbeat of Manchester United. Through his vision and enterprise, United became a worldwide institution, and this was his reward.'

That evening, at a celebratory banquet at London's Russell Hotel, Busby was presented with the 'Manager of the Year' award. John Aston, Bobby Charlton and Pat Crerand, who were too overcome by the emotion of the night to appear at the banquet, missed a moving moment, when, late in the evening, an ecstatic Busby stood up and sang *What A Wonderful World*. Nobody would have denied him that triumph.

Matt Busby, sporting a hat, and his right-hand man, Jimmy Murphy (below right), concentrate intently on the 1958 FA Cup Final, which United lost 0-2 to Bolton Wanderers. The game at Wembley was the first Busby attended after his release from hospital, following his treatment for near-fatal injuries suffered in the Munich air crash in February 1958.

The first time I met Matt — the son of a Scottish miner, he was born in Orbiston, Lanarkshire, on 26 May 1909 — was in October 1958, when, as manager of the Scottish national team, he selected me to play against Wales at Ninian Park. All my team-mates were aware of the tremendous work he'd done at Old Trafford — and of his feat in leading a Great Britain team to the semi-finals of the Olympics in 1948 — but it was actually working as a player for Busby that brought home his inspirational character. We won that match in Cardiff 3-0 (a young Denis Law scored on his international debut), and playing for Matt Busby is an experience I will remember forever.

Busby was certainly not in the pocket of Gibson, an autocratic Chairman

His achievements with United are awesome. He took a struggling club and transformed it into one of the most successful and revered in the world. After the Second World War, Busby had been forced to choose between Liverpool and Manchester United, and after considerable soul-searching with his late wife Jean, he opted for Manchester, which was his first home after leaving Scotland in 1928.

Busby was offered a three-year contract by United's Chairman James Gibson, but he held out, successfully, for a five-year one. He also showed the steel in his character at one of his first matches. During the first half, United director Harold Hardman criticised Busby's selection of Johnny Carey. Busby waited until they were alone and warned him never to speak like that in public again. An item on the agenda for the next Board meeting read: 'Interference by Directors'. Matt Busby was certainly not in the pocket of Gibson, who was an autocratic Chairman. Gibson backed down when Busby refused to sign a player he'd recommended from Newcastle United. Busby warned him: 'I will not sign him, and I will remind you of two things, Mr Gibson. I am here to manage the club, and part of the management is giving you advice. And the second is that I lived long before I ever saw you.' There was never any question again that Busby was in complete control of the team.

Matt Busby was the original tracksuit manager

When Busby arrived in 1945, United was in a decrepit state. The club was in debt, and Old Trafford was still in ruins because of war-time bombing. Busby knew the club had to be rebuilt from the very foundations — and that included establishing the manager's position. Jack Crompton, who was a player when Busby arrived, and who later became a trainer under Busby in the 1960s, recalled: 'When Matt first took charge he had to fight to make his presence felt, and he had still to win the great respect that exists for him today.'

Yet he soon stamped his mark. He resolved a strike among the players over money, sold the popular Johnny Morris to Derby County and bought Celtic's Jimmy Delaney — who'd been written off as 'old brittle bones', because insurance companies, mindful of his injury record, were reluctant to issue policies for him. Busby later said that Delaney, who cost £4000, was one of the main reasons for United's emergence after the war. He made over 200 first-team appearances, and continued to win caps for Scotland, although his international career was more than a decade old.

Busby had mapped out his plans for the future, and he established new patterns immediately. Whereas his predecessor, Scott Duncan, had been an aloof figure — dandyish in his polished spats and three-pieced suit — Busby made real contact with his players a priority. He was the original tracksuit manager, training with the players, devising new practice games, explaining different playing systems, moves and ways to use the ball. Busby, more than anyone, was orchestrating their development as a team.

Jimmy Murphy and Matt Busby were a perfect partnership

In 1946, Jimmy Murphy became Busby's first, and most important, signing when he joined the club as Busby's assistant. Murphy, who died in November 1989, was one of the cornerstones of United's empire, and a tremendous asset, personally, to Matt. Jimmy didn't get the credit he deserved for his part in United's success. He and Matt were a perfect partnership, and Jimmy, who was a marvellous buffer for Matt, played his full part in the coaching.

Jimmy Murphy was a boisterous man, who never minced his words. He would drive the players on, and if he ever went over the top, then Matt would calm things down. At the same time, however, Matt was always rock solid. In the end, he never left you in doubt about who was boss, and of the consequences if you stepped out of line. Players thrived under their joint care, including Denis Law: 'While Matt Busby gave United their subtlety and sophistication', said Law, 'it was Jimmy Murphy who put a little bite into our play.'

One of Busby's finest achievements was the way he developed a family atmosphere at Old Trafford. At Christmas, the players were presented with National Savings certificates. There were frequent trips out, including annual summer outings. Matt was a wonderful family man, and he wanted Manchester United to have a family spirit. Matt believed that the groundsmen, the laundry ladies and the administrative staff, were every bit as important as the players. The spirit he created was unique. 'If you've a happy family, you'll have success,' was his motto. Denis Law is one of hundreds of players who have testified to Busby's marvellous character: 'Matt seemed to care about your life off the field, as well as how you performed on it. Were your

League debut on 4 April 1953, aged 15 years and 285 days. Edwards was a colossus, immensely powerful and a beautiful passer, a splendid tackler and wonderfully effective when he went forward. As Matt Busby put it: 'He inspired by his sheer presence, by his sheer enthusiasm. If ever there was a player who could justly be called a one-man team, that man was Duncan Edwards. He was the most valuable member of one team I ever saw anywhere.'

Edwards wasn't the only great discovery. When I was with Preston North End, we played against the Busby Babes several times, and all of them — including Eddie Colman, Dennis Violett and Jeff Whitefoot — were stupendous. Busby later recalled: 'The team grew in stature and they were dubbed "The Busby Babes" by the press. It wasn't a title I particularly liked, but it certainly stuck.'

The 6 February 1958, was the blackest day in the history of the game

What happened subsequently dismayed the world. On 6 February 1958, I was at Preston, and working for Lancashire County Council on a coaching scheme for schoolboys organised by the Football Association. I remember vividly doing some coaching near Wigan, and while I was travelling home to Preston, I saw a newspaper billboard which said: 'United in Plane Crash!' My first reaction was that it was probably the press exaggerating, but when I got home, the devastating news was confirmed. I was absolutely stunned, and dreadfully worried about Matt. Great players, and some good friends in the press, had been killed in the crash. It was the blackest day in the history of the game. Twenty-three people, including eight glorious players, died on the tragic runway at Munich.

I firmly agree with the former Liverpool manager Bob Paisley, who said that had the team not perished they would have set records no team would ever have matched. I'm certain that if the crash had never happened, United, and not Real Madrid, would have won the European Cup five years in succession. They were that good. The tragedy is that they were kids, nowhere near their full potential.

'Tom,' Matt Busby told me, 'we tried very hard to get you'

Busby knew it would take years to build another winning team. Facing this task, after the trauma of Munich, was a severe test, as there was no simple way of replacing players of such special quality. Ironically, I was one player he had in mind for this rebuilding programme. Joe Armstrong, a United scout, told me that United were interested in buying me. However, Cliff Britton, manager at Preston, wouldn't let me transfer to a 'local' team, and I went to Arsenal. Soon after, I was at a match at

The *Daily Mirror* reports the tragic events of 6 February 1958, when eight United players, and 15 other passengers, were killed when their plane crashed after stopping to refuel in Munich. United were returning from their European Cup quarter-final game against Red Star Belgrade (INSET: a ticket from that game, the last the Busby Babes ever played).

digs alright? Your family? Your wife? Your children? It got through to me that here was a man who cared. It made players run through brick walls for him, because they knew he had their personal interests at heart.'

This communal spirit produced an almost immediate turnaround in the club's fortunes. United had really struggled in the 1930s, but Busby transformed Old Trafford. In his first five years, United were runners-up in the League three years in a row (1946-47, 1947-48, 1948-49), and in 1948 they beat Blackpool 4-2 in the FA Cup Final. I saw that match, and while United were obviously a great side — with Johnny Aston, Allenby Chilton, Jack Crompton, Jimmy Delaney and Jack Rowley — once they had achieved their ultimate triumph (winning the League Championship in 1951-52, United's first League title win for 41 years) that team had to be disbanded.

Busby acted decisively, and comprehensively rebuilt. He had anticipated the decline of players well before the end, and had initiated a revolutionary youth policy — which bore prodigious and startling fruit. United's youth team won the FA Youth Cup five years in a row from 1952, and these youngsters were gradually introduced into the first team. They blossomed, especially the pick of the crop: Duncan Edwards. He made his

Blackburn Rovers, and Matt was there. 'Tom,' he said, 'I just want you to know, that we tried hard to get you.'

Bobby Charlton was emerging as an outstanding player, and Busby soon moved to bring in fresh faces. In August 1960, he bought Tony Dunne from Shelbourne for £5000. Dunne was a long-term buy. He made his debut in October 1960 — the first of 415 League appearances for United, fourth highest in the club's history, behind Bobby Charlton (606), Bill Foulkes (567) and Alex Stepney (433) — and was at Old Trafford a further 13 years, during which time he also won 32 caps for the Republic of Ireland.

Matt Busby made two brilliant signings in Pat Crerand and Denis Law

Although Busby was gradually assembling a great team, the early 1960s were a turbulent time for the club. In 1961, stories that United players were involved in fixing matches were investigated by newspapers, and their League form was very poor. For two seasons running, they scrambled to hold on to their First Division place. In 1961-62, they finished 15th, and in 1962-63 they finished 19th, narrowly avoiding relegation.

The foundations for the future were being laid, however, and Busby made two brilliant signings in Pat Crerand and Denis Law. I was coach at Chelsea in 1963, and I went up to Glasgow with our boss, Ted Drake, to try and sign Crerand. However, Pat was fixed on going to United. Denis Law, who'd been unsettled in Italy, was snapped up for a British record fee of £115,000 from Torino, and was perhaps Busby's best buy. In this pair, Busby had bought two players of genuine international class, but — just as importantly — he signed two stars who genuinely wanted to be United players.

'Every aspect of ball control was perfectly natural to George Best'

Law and Crerand were an integral part of the FA Cup winning team of 1963, who salvaged a terrible season. That win signalled the beginning of Busby's third burst of success, and it was the most sustained and glorious yet. United's 3-1 victory at Wembley (which included a goal by Law) seemed finally to release them from the doom-laden post-Munich era. Winning the Cup also put United back in Europe for the first time in five seasons.

United had also found their most exciting discovery yet. Belfast-born George Best, who joined United as a shy teenager in August 1961, made his debut in September 1963 against West Bromwich Albion — the first of 361 League appearances for United. I saw Best play at 17, and he was frighteningly good. He was quiet in some early games, but the moment he was on the ball he was electric. Matt Busby believed that Best was the most talented player he had ever seen, as he later explained: 'George Best was gifted with more individual

ability than I have ever seen in any other player. He had more ways of beating a player than any other player I have ever seen. Every aspect of ball control was perfectly natural to him from the start. He even used his opponents' shins to his advantage by hitting the ball on to them so accurately that it came back to him like a one-two pass. He had more confidence in his ability than I have ever seen in any other sportsman.'

That confidence was infectious, and Best helped improve United's fortunes dramatically. That season after the FA Cup win, they finished runners-up in the League to Bill Shankly's Liverpool, reached the European Cup Winners' Cup quarter-final and the FA Cup semi-final. By the start of the next season, when he had become a regular first-team player, he attracted enormous attention. On 30 September 1964, United beat Chelsea 2-0 at Stamford Bridge. Best ran the game, scored and in the process tormented Chelsea's full-back Ken Shellito. Paddy Crerand joked after the game that: 'Shellito was taken off suffering from twisted blood.' Best scored 10 of United's 89 League goals (Law netted 28), as United won the League title ahead of Don Revie's Leeds United on superior goal average — a mere 0.686 goals better.

Denis Law went where angels wouldn't even poke their toes

As reward for winning their first title for seven years, Busby received a £4000 bonus and £500 of shares in the club. Not only was United's success deserved, it had been achieved in scintillating style. With the 'Great Triumvirate' of Best, Charlton and Law, fed by Crerand and Foulkes, United had wonderful attacking zest. In the five seasons from 1963-64 until 1967-68, United scored 436 goals in 210 games (the Babes had managed 458 in 210 games from 1954-55 to 1958-59). Busby had taken the game of soccer and orchestrated it into an art form.

There were five absolutely great United players in the 1960s. Pat Crerand was a tremendous passer of the ball. He wasn't a good ball winner, but he possessed great vision, and as soon as he received the ball he knew exactly where to dispatch it, and he would always do so with deadly accuracy. He wasn't the fastest player on the pitch, but he made up for his lack of physical speed by his speed of thought and elegant, fluent play. In addition, he was a great enthusiast and remains to this day a United fanatic.

Paddy linked up well with Denis Law, who was such a splendid finisher. He was great in the air, and tremendously brave (maybe too brave); you just couldn't intimidate him. If he had the sniff of a chance, it was in the back of the net. He had everything a striker needs; he was explosively quick over 20 yards, his balance was impeccable and he went where angels wouldn't even poke their toes. Law also possessed an almost telepathic flair for knowing where to be in the goalmouth.

The midfield linchpin was Bobby Charlton. Bobby was the provider, who would run at people, beat them, put them out of the game and lay on chances for Best and Law. He had two tremendous feet, and could shoot with immense force and accuracy from anything up to 35 yards. He was also beautiful to watch when he had the ball. Charlton in full stride, about to unleash one of his thunderbolt long-range drives, was one of the greatest sights in football. When he surged forward he was so graceful, like a gazelle. He would jink, changing his feet and direction in the twinkling of an eye, accelerate away and play a marvellous pass. Added to these prodigious talents as a player was his character: Bobby was a model professional.

In midfield, too, Nobby Stiles epitomised the spirit of the club. Nobby was about five foot six, and reputedly had worse eyesight than Mr Magoo, but very few players ever got past him. He won the ball by hook or by crook, and set the attack in motion. As Matt Busby put it: 'Set Nobby Stiles a job and he would do it if it killed

him. No opponent was too big for him. He was as brave a warrior as ever trod a pitch.'

Finally, there was the incomparable George Best, who was, for Sir Matt, the pick of these wonderful players, as he wrote: 'Of all the truly great players who passed through my hands as a manager, George Best was the one who gave me most enjoyment — as a *footballer*.' Not only was there a charisma about him, he had wonderful reflexes, his balance was exquisite, he could shoot powerfully with both feet and he was immensely dangerous in the air. Best was a genius.

'The whole beauty of our game was its simplicity'

These five were the outstanding ones, but they also had wonderful support from others such as Willie Morgan, a superb dribbler and a marvellous athlete, Bill Foulkes (who wasn't a great player, but he stopped great players from playing), Tony Dunne, who was skilful and cool, David Sadler, who was defensively sound and a good reader of the game and John Fitzpatrick, who was like a little tiger when he tackled.

Busby's genius lay in the way that he knew how to make all these disparate talents work as a single unit, and how to tick as individuals. He made them believe, and act on the belief, that individually and collectively they were better than the teams they went out and played. 'Let them worry about you,' Busby would say in his team talks.

This team was sometimes criticised for playing 'off the cuff' football, but their style wasn't just arbitrary. When Law and Best first linked up, if they were being tightly marked, then they would switch wings and positions to confuse their opponents. It took a couple of seasons before managers started telling defenders to simply pick up the man who was nearest to them. But it would have taken about 30 players to mark that calibre of player out of the game.

When Manchester United played against teams which employed man-to-man marking, such as Arsenal, United retreated towards their own half. As Denis Law explained: 'Once defenders got too near to the halfway line they weren't sure what to do. Then we'd have Bobby Charlton breaking quickly from deep positions. The whole beauty of our game was its simplicity: skilful players using their heads and playing within the framework of a broad tactical plan. Regimentation is by definition predictable, and in the end the truly skilful players will always find a way to beat it.'

All Matt's team had played with this unconventional, attacking freestyle manner. Busby wanted his players to express themselves on the pitch, and there was a

LEFT: George Best, football's first 'pop idol', found the pressure of his celebrity status difficult to handle. Although his career with United ended prematurely, at the age of 27, he had played 466 first-team games, and scored 178 goals.

glamour and panache to United in these years that distinguished them completely from other leading First Division teams. While Don Revie's Leeds United relied on solid formations and breaking in strength, United could utilise individual players — who were the finest in their positions in the world — winning games using their individual skills.

'We are as alive to the need for tactics as any other team'

United's freestyle play — which was so popular with the fans — aroused jealousy within the game, and Busby was stung by criticism that United's style was haphazard. As he said in 1966: 'When things go wrong for us there always seem to be critics who like to dwell on the fact that I once said our forwards were given free expression. From that it is deduced that United are not a "method" team and that they play it all by ear, relying on the brilliance of individuals. Nothing could be further from the truth. Our achievements in reaching the FA Cup semi-finals five years in succession, winning the Cup and carrying off the League Championship is the reward for playing soccer in a methodical manner. We are as alive to the need for tactics as any other team; and I submit that no team can achieve our measure of success over the years without some sort of method. But I mean what I say about freedom of expression, too. For when a team has international players such as Denis Law, Bobby Charlton and George Best in the attack they have their own ideas, and it's a waste of talent to subject them to a list of do's and don't's.'

United, unbeaten in their last 20 games, brought the title back to Old Trafford

Matt's evaluation is fair, but it would also be true to say that with the talent his team had during those years, if they had been a bit better organised at times they would have won *more* trophies. That team was great to watch, but there were times when complacency crept into their game, when players would become slightly lackadaisical. Yet look at what they did achieve without being really well-drilled. When United did go through some bad patches, it was usually because some of their brilliant players weren't working as hard as the opposition. When they did, not a team in the world could touch them.

United's Championship success in 1964-65 was followed by a rather disappointing year, but Busby was determined to continue the run of success. In September 1966, Busby bought Chelsea's 'keeper, Alex Stepney, for £60,000. I was manager at Chelsea at the time, and Peter Bonetti was my first-team goalkeeper. While he was in the England World Cup party in 1966, I learned that Peter had been approached by West Ham, and was keen on going to Upton Park, so I

bought Alex from Millwall as insurance. My intention was to play them alternately, but I soon realised that wouldn't work. Soon after, Matt Busby inquired about buying a 'keeper. I said: 'Who do you want?', and he said: 'Whoever is for sale, I want'. I've a sneaking feeling that he really wanted Peter, but he didn't show it. When Matt and Jimmy Murphy came to see me at Stamford Bridge, I told them they could have Stepney. Matt was delighted and Alex never looked back.

At the start of the season, United sold John Connelly, who'd been with the England World Cup winning squad, to Blackburn Rovers. New players Jimmy Ryan and John Aston were pushing for places, and full-back Ray Noble, who had come up through the juniors, played 29 games before his career was ended by a car crash.

BELOW: George Best's lightning reflexes in action, as he leaps high, with eyes open, to head past Liverpool's Tommy Lawrence — who was known as 'The Flying Pig' — in United's 2-0 victory at Old Trafford in October 1965.

United were leaders by November, and a marvellous run of results — they were unbeaten in their last 20 games — ensured that the Championship returned to Old Trafford. Busby praised his new goalkeeper, who had kept 16 clean-sheets that season in the League: 'Without Stepney', said Busby, 'I don't think we would have won the Championship.' More than a million people had watched United's home League games — the highest total since the Second World War — and they were treated to some scintillating football. As George Best said of that season: 'Even if we were several goals down it never occurred to us to stop playing our natural attacking game.'

United's last Championship win was earned in real style (above, a report and programmes from their last two games). BELOW: Denis Law lifts the trophy at Old Trafford, with, to his right, George Best, David Sadler and Bobby Charlton. OPPOSITE: Nobby Stiles (far left), Charlton (centre) and Bill Foulkes celebrate the 1968 European Cup win.

United won 6-1 away against West Ham United to clinch the Championship

United were unbeaten at home in 21 games (losing only six away, scoring 84 goals for the loss of 45), and the whole season had gone according to Busby's plan — winning at home and trying to get at least a draw away — a cast-iron method under the old system of two points for a win.

When United won 6-1 away against West Ham United on 6 May 1967 to clinch the title, they swept into a 3-0 lead within the first 10 minutes. Busby had been held up in the dressing room, and he reached his seat just

as Bill Foulkes's goal, United's third, was hitting the back of the net. However, nobody had told Busby that there had been two goals before then, and he suffered for a long time thinking that the Hammers needed only one goal to equalise. He needn't have fretted. It was a decisive and stunning way to win a Championship.

For Matt Busby, winning the European Cup was 'the quest for the Holy Grail'

In the following season, United finished as runners-up in the League, but their real ambition that year was to win the European Cup — a goal which Busby had described as 'the quest for the Holy Grail'. It was United's obsession. Having sampled Europe, and with the memory of Munich hanging over the club like a black cloud, it was always burning inside Matt that he *must* win that trophy.

Many people outside United, however, did not rate their chances highly as the campaign kicked off. Although Brian Kidd had emerged at the start of the season, many players, including Law, struggled with severe injuries. United knocked out Hibernians (Malta), Sarajevo, Gornik Zabre and, in a memorable semi-final, they put out Real Madrid in a two-legged marathon in which a brilliant United forced a 3-3 draw at the Bernabeu Stadium after trailing 1-3 at half-time. The decisive goal was scored by 36-year-old Bill Foulkes, to set up a Final against the Eagles of Lisbon.

Some people claimed that Benfica were over the hill, but they were still a good team. However, I felt United's name was on the Cup that year, even though a lot of players were past their best, and knew it was a case of 'now or never'. Indeed, Bobby Charlton once said: 'Without being disrespectful to the players involved, the 1968 team was not our best. Manchester City had won the League and we had faded. A lot of us were past our peak. I knew I wasn't going to get another chance and about half the team were in the same boat.'

'Alex Stepney had stopped Busby's dream from shattering around him'

That momentous Wednesday night of 29 May 1968, was the climax of Sir Matt's (and, it has proved thus far, Manchester United's) story. Busby used all his tactical knowledge to win the game, shrewdly playing John Aston to wear down the right-back Adolfo. With the game tantalisingly poised at 1-1, Alex Stepney made a world-class save from Eusebio moments before the final whistle. Eusebio's shot was like a bullet. 'Bang!', the crowd froze, but Stepney held on to it even though it nearly bored a hole in his chest. Stepney had stopped Busby's dream from shattering around him.

During extra time, the emotion and strain was tremendous. 'If it hadn't been played at Wembley, I don't think United would have won it. The place was full of 'Reds',

and it carried them through. Yet at this heart-stopping moment, Busby proved what a great manager he was. As the players waited on the pitch before extra time began, Busby inspired them, as Pat Crerand recalled: 'Everyone knew how he had set his heart on winning this Cup, yet after 90 minutes of ups and downs, he still looked completely composed. He walked around talking quite quietly, and saying: "You're giving them the ball too often. We must keep possession. It's easy to play on Wembley when the ball is at your feet!"'

United played with control and passion in extra time, and a thrilling 30 minutes was capped by a marvellous goal from Best, and one each from Charlton and Brian Kidd (celebrating his 19th birthday). At the final whistle, the players showed how important the victory was. Bobby Charlton, overcome with emotion, said that they'd won it for the lads at Munich. I've never seen such emotion on players' faces in all my life.

Matt began to run the club with his heart and not with his head

Busby's financial rewards — his Rover was replaced by a Mercedes, his salary increased to £10,000 — were nothing compared with the satisfaction he felt at having achieved his life's ambition. Yet for Busby, and United, dangerous rapids lay ahead. Bill Foulkes said of this critical time: 'In my opinion, Matt should have started to break up our side as soon as we had won the European Cup.' Yet Busby remained loyal to the men who had helped him achieve his dream, and there were no new signings.

Two vicious encounters with Estudiantes for the World Club Championship christened the 1968-69 season, and heralded another lacklustre season in which United finished 11th in the League. Busby should have given promising youngsters a chance, and he certainly should have brought some fresh faces into the club. The problem was that Matt was running the club with his heart and not his head. He had such deep affection for some players — who had, after all, given him such excellent service — that he found it impossible to tell them that their time was up. Busby wasn't good at saying to players: 'On your bike!', especially great players who were also close friends. It is a difficult part of a manager's job, but it has to be done.

A lot of the players at United then weren't interested in how they played, only in continuing playing, and Matt's generosity made this easier. Between 1964 and 1968, Matt Busby bought one player — Alex Stepney — at a time when he should have been rebuilding. Nevertheless, United still tried with all their heart to defend their European crown. On 18 September 1968, United began their campaign against Waterford of Dublin. In the second leg at Old Trafford, Law scored his 14th goal in the competition — a club record. United then put out RSC Anderlecht and Rapid Vienna to reach the semi-final against AC Milan. The Italian

Champions won the first leg, at home, 2-0, and although United won the return game at Old Trafford 1-0, with a goal from Bobby Charlton, it was not enough to secure another European Cup Final appearance.

'Manchester United have become rather more than a football club'

It had been a bad season for injuries (John Aston broke a leg, Bobby Charlton was out for two months with knee ligament damage, and Nobby Stiles and Francis Burns had cartilage problems) and a deep and pervading air of anti-climax hung over Busby's final season in charge. He obviously sensed this, as in January 1969 he said: 'For some time now, and largely since our victory in the European Cup, I have been looking towards the future. I feel it is time for someone in a tracksuit to take over the players out on the training pitch. I am finding less and less time to give to the thing I consider paramount, which is the playing side.'

As a manager, when you stop going on to the training field with your players you lose contact with them, and when this happens you lose your grip on a team. Even if you're just out there supervising while someone else takes the training sessions, you're still able to hold the reins effectively, but in the latter years, Matt was seldom out with the players and that was the beginning of the slump. That was definitely the case when he took control again in January 1971 after Wilf McGuinness's

sacking. Matt had lost his way a bit, and it's something which happens to every manager in the game who loses contact with his players.

In April 1969, at the age of 58, Busby retired from the direct running of the team's affairs. His influence at the club remained, however, and he is a central character in the subsequent history of Manchester United. He will be remembered forever as the father of modern-day United. 'Manchester United have become rather more than a football club. They are now an institution,' he said after announcing his retirement at a press conference, and it was Busby, more than anyone else, who was responsible for the pre-eminence of the club.

During his illustrious reign, Matt Busby created some of the greatest teams ever to grace the world of football. He won five League titles, won the FA Cup twice, led United to two other Final appearances, and netted the club a vast profit. The European Cup win of 1968, at the fourth attempt, 12 years after entering the competition — was a brilliant and fitting conclusion to his story. Unfortunately, the Busby story had one final, and rather depressing, chapter left to unfold.

Matt Busby's retirement in 1969, marked the end of an era for Manchester United (below, he accepts the applause of a devoted Old Trafford crowd before his last home game as manager). Busby hadn't been in the best of health for a while then, and he was paving the way for his successor, Wilf McGuinness, a former Busby Babe and a coach at the club, to ease himself into the 'hot seat'.

MATT'S TROUBLED HEIRS

When Matt Busby retired, Manchester United stood at a crossroads. Busby's two immediate successors, Wilf McGuinness and Frank O'Farrell, had a legacy of glory to live up to, but they never succeeded in becoming masters of the Old Trafford empire, and were both doomed to an early exile.

When, in 1969, Wilf McGuinness succeeded Sir Matt Busby as Manchester United's manager, he inherited a football club which had been successful for more than 20 years, and a team that included some of the greatest players the game has produced — players whose magical skills had made them world stars.

Although the legacy Busby left seemed perfect — Bobby Charlton was 31, but still a key member of the England team; Denis Law and Pat Crerand were only 28; Francis Burns was a Scottish Under-23 international and George Best could have been good for another decade — many of the players, although still able to play wonderful football, were reluctant to give their all for a manager other than Matt Busby.

The result was that the first three years of the 1970s were the most traumatic in Manchester United's history. The club lost respect, Wilf McGuinness suffered enormous stress during his brief managerial stint — all his hair fell out after leaving the club — and Frank O'Farrell lost his faith in Matt Busby as a person. Busby's two successors certainly didn't find glory at Old Trafford, and Frank O'Farrell once remarked bitterly that his treatment at Manchester United: 'Was a death by a thousand cuts'.

Former Busby Babe Wilf McGuinness (below), who had been a coach at the club since 1959, when injury ended his playing career at the age of 22, was appointed to succeed Matt Busby. McGuinness's traumatic reign lasted 18 months.

Busby was an extraordinarily hard act to follow, because he was, in a very deep sense, Manchester United. Busby's long-term friend, then Manchester City manager, Joe Mercer said in 1968: 'I would hate to be the man who had to follow Matt Busby as manager of United. It is virtually impossible for anyone to take over the Old Trafford throne and rule with as much glory and success as has befallen Matt Busby. His reputation and tremendous place at the top of the managerial tree makes the job of a successor almost impossible.'

The uncertainty ended with the appointment of Wilf McGuinness

There was enormous speculation about who would succeed Busby, and the rumour fever even reached the players, as Alex Stepney said: 'Stories about the future of the club were tossed about as wildly among the players as they were on the streets of Manchester.'

One account said that the former Republic of Ireland boss Noel Cantwell, then managing Peterborough United, was being considered for the job, but was dropped when Johnny Aston (chief scout), Jack Crompton (first-team trainer) and McGuinness threatened to leave if Cantwell was appointed. I don't think this story has any credibility, because Matt just wouldn't have stood for that sort of nonsense. Ironically, I think Cantwell, who captained United in the 1963 FA Cup Final, would have been an excellent choice to replace Busby. He knew the way United worked, and he was a wise student of the game.

The uncertainty, if not the acrimony, ended on 9 April 1969, when Louis Edwards announced that Wilf McGuinness had been appointed chief coach, 'responsible for team selection, coaching, training and tactics'. 'Busby,' said Edwards, 'will be responsible for all other matters affecting the club and players and will continue as General Manager and club spokesman.'

Some players were shocked and bitter that McGuinness had been given the job

McGuinness, at 32, became the youngest coach to lead a First Division team, but he did not have the title of manager. Busby explained that it was just a case of McGuinness learning the ropes, and United certainly had good reasons for selecting McGuinness: they wanted someone who knew the United set-up and who wouldn't rock the boat, and the concept of promoting from within was a sound one.

There was no doubting McGuinness's commitment to United. He'd started under Jimmy Murphy, playing for Manchester Boys, and had graduated to the first team, playing 83 times for United. In 1957, he'd won a League Championship medal, but on 12 December 1959, when he was only 22 years old, he broke his leg during a reserve game against Stoke City, and the

injury had ended his playing career. United had then appointed him assistant trainer with the reserves.

When he was promoted to running the first team, his problem was always going to be his relationship with the players. Although he is a strong and aggressive character, some of the players — who were older than their new boss, and who'd achieved more in the game — were shocked and bitter that McGuinness had been given the job, and they did not hide their displeasure at the decision. Too many players had mixed with him in his former role, and resented his new status.

On 1 June 1969, McGuinness officially took up his appointment at a salary of £4000 a year, and in that pre-season period, there was already an underground current against the new manager. There was a hint of trouble in store in Bobby Charlton's assessment (before the season actually started) of McGuinness's prospects as manager: 'Some people think that an ex team-mate could not command the necessary respect and authority. It may not be easy; there *will* be problems,' he warned. It was not clear how much authority McGuinness had been granted when he took over.

When Wilf played 'Matt's team', he put a nail in his own coffin

United got off to a terrible start in August 1969, and straight away the atmosphere at the club began to deteriorate. First-team players stopped talking to the juniors. Then, as the results started getting worse, the first-team players stopped talking to each other, and cliques started to form. Busby's vision of a united, family club was melting away.

United won only one of their first eight League games under McGuinness, and suffered a humiliating 1-4 home defeat to Southampton. Following that defeat, McGuinness dropped five players for the match at Everton, including Bobby Charlton and Denis Law. It created a sensation in the football world, and Charlton complained that: 'Wilf's manner of telling players that they were dropped often rubbed them up the wrong way. The way he did it meant that they lost their confidence.' The decision also dented, for the first time, Busby's confidence in his successor. He later remarked: 'I did not agree with Wilf's dropping Bobby and Denis on the same day. I do not wish to say that I would not have dropped Bobby or Denis, or anybody else if I thought it was the right thing to do. I did not think it was the right time to do it.'

Busby has repeatedly denied that he interfered with the decision-making of his successors, but there seems to have been a thin line between interference and intervention. United lost that match at Everton 0-3, and four days later, on 23 August 1969, United were due to play at Wolves. Busby recalled that: 'Wilf asked my advice. We had been through one unhappy spell of non-success and Wilf came to me and asked: "What team would *you* play on Saturday?" I gave him my team

and he selected it. We went to Wolves and made a draw and did not lose for 10 matches.' The team which Busby 'gave' McGuinness included two reinstated players: Charlton and Law. When Wilf McGuinness played Matt's 'team', he put a nail in his own coffin as manager of Manchester United.

'That dilemma you've got is what I pay you for,' the Chairman said

When it comes to picking the team, a manager's decision-making powers are sacrosanct. That's the heart of his job. When I was Chelsea's manager, Graham Moore picked up a cartilage injury and was out for two months. I introduced Terry Venables, who was then 18, and he was outstanding. When Moore was fit again, we were away to Grimsby Town. Before the game, our Chairman asked why I was looking tense. 'Between you and me', I said, 'I've got a dilemma. Graham's fit again, but I don't know whether to leave Venables in.' When he inquired if I was asking his advice, I told him: 'No. It's just a dilemma I've got.' He said: 'Well, that dilemma you've got is what I pay you for. I'm sure you'll come to the right decision.' I kept Terry Venables in, and we won 3-1. In Wilf's case, he showed that when it came to the crunch he allowed someone else to make the decision. Once you've done that, you leave it wide open to happen again in the future.

'Not even the Berlin Wall could have stopped George Best in that form'

McGuinness wasn't helped by the way in which certain players, used to being feted as the finest players in the world, resisted attempts to make them change their style, as former United full-back Tony Dunne recalled in 1991: 'The problem was that there was no one to come in and replace Busby. Nobody could come in and change his standards, and I think the senior players felt that deep down. I realise that now, though I didn't at the time.' Complaints about Wilf McGuinness's managerial style were being voiced — one senior player even went to Louis Edwards's home to voice his concern — and Denis Law said that McGuinness coached with the blackboard 'all the time', adding that: 'Our general attitude to the game was being changed from an attacking one to a defensive one.'

This criticism was particularly hard, because Wilf, being so young and so enthusiastic about getting the job, wanted to introduce fresh ideas. And his own methods, whether the players liked it or not, involved using the blackboard to teach tactics. McGuinness may even have been trying to correct some of the organisational flaws of the team — and the game was beginning to change tactically. Many players, especially the established ones, were so used to Matt's genial management that they dug their heels in against change. They should have listened to Wilf and tried to work through his ideas. That's what they were paid to do, after all.

The players grumbled that McGuinness was failing with his man-management, as Alex Stepney put it: 'Wilf McGuinness had moments of frightening indecision. He could not stand up and administer the kind of discipline that would gain him our respect — adult discipline. Something was missing in his make-up; perhaps it was simply experience. He was just not up to it. When he stepped up from the second-team dressing room he was moving out of his depth.'

United's poor results were highlighted by the success being enjoyed at Maine Road, and it was Manchester City who knocked United out of the League Cup semi-final in December 1969. George Best, who was beginning to go off the rails, was sent off for knocking the ball out of referee Jack Taylor's hands.

United's only hope of a trophy that season was the FA Cup. George Best, returning from a one-month suspension, took the opportunity, in the fifth round match at Northampton Town, to give one of his finest displays. United won 8-2, and Best scored a marvellous double hat-trick — with shots, headers and a beautifully cheeky goal in which he waltzed round the 'keeper. Northampton's goalkeeper, Kim Book — the brother of Manchester City captain Tony Book — said: 'We hadn't an earthly with Best in that form. Not even the Berlin Wall could have stopped him. He was brilliant, fantastic, fabulous. It got to the stage where I thought he was going to score every time he got the ball.'

For the third successive season, over a million fans had visited Old Trafford

It was a tragedy for McGuinness, United and football that the club's slump was marked by the decline of George Best. If he had maintained his commitment and form, United might have continued winning trophies. Even up to the end of McGuinness's reign he was producing splendid football, as Paddy Crerand described: 'George's range still made him absolutely special. He could do things better than anyone else playing. He was a magnificent distributor of the ball, and he could beat a man on either side using methods that no one ever thought possible. He could shoot, he could tackle, he was competitive and yet cool under pressure. And courage? I have never seen a braver player.' Sadly, that performance against Northampton Town was to prove a watershed for Best and Manchester United.

The FA Cup run ended in failure, with United losing in the semi-final (over three very tight matches) to Leeds

LEFT: Pat Crerand challenges Reading's Tony Wagstaffe in the Watneys Cup match at Elm Park on 1 August 1970, which United won 3-2. Crerand's clever passing always took the eye, and although he favoured using his right foot, he was also excellent with his left. In 1970, Crerand was appointed as the coach of United's youth team.

United. For the third successive season, more than a million fans had watched United's home games, and although their League form had been poor, McGuinness remained optimistic. In the summer of 1970, he was promoted to team manager, and he proclaimed: 'Great things are in store for Manchester United.'

'Another winter of reserve-team football will kill all the talent there is in me'

However, the rumblings of discontent in the dressing room continued. United hovered close to the relegation zone, and crowds began to fall for the first time in 25 seasons, reminding the Board about the need for success. A host of important players — such as John Aston, Francis Burns, John Fitzpatrick, Steve James, Jimmy Rimmer and Nobby Stiles — were resentful at being on the sidelines. John Aston said: 'Another winter of reserve football will kill all the talent there is in me.'

Matters reached a head in a disastrous period in December. Within 12 days, United were beaten at home twice in the League (1-4 by Manchester City and 1-3 by Arsenal) and were knocked out of the League Cup semi-final, in a replay, by Aston Villa. Before that evening match at Villa Park, George Best walked off with a girl just hours before the match began. Best had a terrible game, and the players, who believed that

Best should have been immediately dropped, blamed McGuinness for his lack of control (although Wilf told me that he wanted to drop Best, but was stopped by Busby). United did win a trophy under McGuinness that month (the *Daily Express* Five-a-Side Championship), but this success was not enough to save McGuinness.

The Board moved speedily, and five days after the match at Villa Park, on 28 December, Wilf's reign was terminated. Busby suggested that McGuinness should make a public statement asking for his old job back, as reserve-team boss, but McGuinness told him: 'If you want me to go, you'll have to sack me!' The Board relieved him of his duties as manager, and he reverted to training the Central League team, turning down an offer to manage Bolton Wanderers.

Wilf's situation was muddied by the way that Busby kept his hand on the button

It was a terrible turnaround in fortunes for Wilf McGuinness. By January 1971, he was back packing the boots of players over whom he had recently been in command. He lasted two months before leaving for Greece to manage Aris Salonika. McGuinness later said that he was convinced it would have come right: 'I was on a contract which had 18 months to run when I got the sack. I thought I had time,' he said.

At an impromptu press conference after the decision was announced, McGuinness said: 'I would bleed for Manchester United, although this is disappointing. Managers are judged by results, yet with a bit of luck we might have been in three cup finals.' He had piloted United to three cup semi-finals within 12 months. At most clubs, this would have been regarded as a fine achievement, but not at United. He later complained of Busby that: 'I thought we were doing the job together. I was wrong. I was on my own.'

Unfortunately, Wilf didn't sort out his position from the start. Used in the right way, Busby would have been his greatest asset. When I was manager of Chelsea, I used to ring Matt (and Bill Nicholson) for advice. I didn't always use it, but it was always given. Now, 15 yards down the corridor, McGuinness had a man with all that experience; why not use it? That's what I did, although Busby never interfered when I was manager. I think Wilf's situation was muddied by the way that Busby kept his hand on the button.

Following his sacking, there was widespread sympathy for Wilf. In an abrasive newspaper article, headlined 'You've Bungled It, Sir Matt!', Derby's manager, Brian Clough, wrote: 'It is a long time since we stopped offering sacrificial lambs in this country, but McGuinness was virtually one. From the day he took over he never

LEFT: Willie Morgan jinking on the wing. Morgan, who won 21 Scottish caps, had deft footwork at speed, and was an excellent crosser of the ball. He could cover a tremendous amount of ground, because he was such a fine athlete.

WILF McGUINNESS

SOUVENIR TESTIMONIAL PROGRAMME — Price £1.00

BURY
versus
MANCHESTER UNITED
WEDNESDAY, 1st AUGUST, 1990

Wilf McGuinness, who became the physiotherapist at Bury in 1980, has renewed ties with Manchester United, who played in his testimonial in August 1990 (left). Wilf's son, Paul, signed professional forms with United in July 1989.

Under Busby, United improved. When they beat Tottenham 2-1 on 6 February 1971 (the 13th anniversary of the Munich disaster), it was their first home win for three months. Busby brought back several players (Crerand, Gowling, Morgan and Stepney) dropped by McGuinness, and United clambered up to finish eighth.

In March 1971, United advertised the manager's job for the first time in the club's history. Although the team were pulling away from relegation, there was a suspicion that Busby had lost his way. When Busby dropped Brian Kidd for United's game at Crystal Palace on 17 April 1971, Kidd lambasted Busby: 'Is Sir Matt trying to humiliate me altogether? Does he think he can trample all over me until a new manager takes over? Everyone knows that he doesn't want me at Old Trafford. I only wish he would come out in the open and say it. A move is the only solution for me. Sir Matt has completely washed all my feelings for Manchester United out of me, and I can tell you that takes some doing.' Kidd was restored to the team two games later, but Busby's happy family seemed to have disintegrated.

had a chance.' I don't agree with Brian Clough here, and, incidentally, it was this sort of comment that stopped him from ever becoming United's manager, because United's Board would have held it against him.

Busby believed that he'd done the right thing by appointing from within the club, and he did find it difficult to let go of the reins, but the real problem was the players. There were too many who were at the stage in their careers when they didn't want a young manager. Some were absolutely green with jealousy that McGuinness had been given the job, and they did everything possible to destroy his confidence.

'The side, as a whole, did not give 100 per cent effort for McGuinness'

Sometimes, directors don't sack managers, players do, and they achieve this by refraining from giving their full commitment. Indeed, David Sadler has stated that certain players just did not pull their weight: 'Not everyone, sadly, would play for Wilf. The side as a whole did not give 100 per cent effort for him. It was as simple as that. As soon as Sir Matt returned to the scene it changed at once,' he said.

For Busby, it was a heart-rending time. He felt responsible for making a major blunder as he later said: 'It was our fault for choosing Wilf. He was too close to the players. He had played with most of them and knew their habits and this they resented. Disharmony developed and team discipline waned. They resented Wilf and it did harm to the club.'

United offered the manager's job to Celtic's boss Jock Stein

There was intense speculation about who would be the new manager. Dave Sexton, Don Revie and Sir Alf Ramsey were all reputed to be in the frame, but United in fact offered the job to Celtic boss Jock Stein. In April 1971, Stein and Busby met secretly at a petrol station off the M6 near Haydock. An initial approach had been made through Pat Crerand, a former Celtic player, and as they talked in Busby's Mercedes, it seemed as though Stein would take the job. However, he rang Busby back a few days later and turned it down. Jock Stein later told Alex Ferguson that it was a decision he had always regretted.

At the end of the season, during a tour of Austria, a delegation of players, led by Bobby Charlton, implored Busby to stay on, but his mind was made up. The new favourite to replace him was Leicester City's boss, Frank O'Farrell. Leicester's chairman, Len Shipman, gave permission for United to approach their Cork-born manager (who'd led Leicester to the 1969 FA Cup Final), and the deal was signed in Louis Edwards's car.

The appointment sparked a fanfare of optimism. O'Farrell looked like an excellent choice. Frank and I were wing-halves together at Preston for seven years and we're good friends. Frank is very stern, a great family man, and in many respects not unlike the younger Matt Busby, which may have been what attracted Matt, who enthusiastically declared: 'I look upon Frank as my last great signing, possibly the *greatest* of the lot. He

31

always seems to know what he's doing, and I especially like the way he handles difficult situations.'

O'Farrell took over on 1 July 1971, and after failing to enlist John Lyall, a former team-mate at West Ham United, as his coach, he appointed Malcolm Musgrove. O'Farrell described his appointment as 'long enough to achieve what I hope to achieve'. Busby, meanwhile, in a move to allay fears of interference, stood down as general manager, and accepted a post as a director.

'Manchester United are glamour boys left behind by the legend'

United started the season playing their home fixtures on neutral grounds — because of crowd trouble — and beat Arsenal 3-1 at Anfield (probably the only time they've been cheered on by the Kop). United enjoyed one of their best starts to a season ever. By the end of 1971, Best had scored 14 goals, Law 12, and United, beaten only twice, led Division One by five points. Bookmakers made them odds-on favourites for the League Championship.

Once again, however, there were dark portents of trouble ahead. In one game, O'Farrell made Law a sub-stitute. Denis sat in the dressing room throughout the game, after having declared: 'If anyone wants me they know where I am.' Meanwhile, the defence was leaking goals, and the team weren't finding any consistency. O'Farrell said: 'Team work is vital and we are behind in it.' His worries were soon confirmed.

After Christmas, United went into steep decline. On New Year's Day, United lost 0-3 at West Ham United, and this was followed by six successive League defeats. Alex Stepney claimed that this affected their manager: 'Suddenly, from being the cheerful Irishman at the top of the heap, Frank O'Farrell stopped communicating. He started ignoring his players. He would sit behind his desk for a day at a time so that we rarely saw him. He was no longer the nice guy.'

Perhaps the most telling comment of the season came after United's humiliating 1-5 thrashing at Elland Road. Leeds United's centre-back Jack Charlton said of brother Bobby's team: 'Manchester United are glamour boys left behind by the legend.' Disappointing results

BELOW: Sir Matt Busby offers a guided tour of Old Trafford, in June 1971, to new manager Frank O'Farrell (far right), and his wife Ann. Busby described O'Farrell as: 'My last great signing, possibly the *greatest* of the lot'.

accumulated, and United's season all but ended on 22 March 1972, when they were knocked out of the FA Cup quarter-final by Stoke City. The rest of the season eked out in a dispiriting two months.

At the same time, George Best, who'd been a law unto himself under Busby, began to go completely off the rails. Best missed a week's training, and was dropped and fined two week's pay and ordered to leave his house in Bramhall and move back into 'digs' at Chorlton. In May 1972, he flew to Spain after announcing his retirement from football. However, he was back by June, when he signed a new eight-year contract to keep him at Old Trafford into the 1980s!

'George Best thought he was the James Bond of soccer'

Best's team-mates resented his behaviour. Willie Morgan commented: 'George thought he was the James Bond of soccer. He had everything he wanted and he pleased himself. He had money, girls and tremendous publicity. He lived from day-to-day. Until right at the end he got away with it when he missed training or ran away — so he didn't care. People made excuses for him; he didn't even have to bother to do it himself. People talked about pressures and depressions. It was rubbish. He just hadn't any responsibilities, nothing to worry about at all. All kinds of people covered up for him, even the press. He was lucky to get away with it for so long.'

Frank O'Farrell certainly tried to prevent George's career from disintegrating. He made Best the highest-paid player at the club, and even visited Best's parents in Belfast to try and sort out their son's future. Sadly, time was running out for both manager and player.

'The atmosphere was depressing. Law, Charlton and Best were at loggerheads'

O'Farrell realised that United needed strengthening, and in March 1972, he made two wonderful signings: Martin Buchan, bought for £130,000 from Aberdeen, and Ian Storey-Moore, who cost £200,000 from Nottingham Forest. Storey-Moore was a great player, and it was a real set-back when he had to quit the game, soon after joining, because of an ankle injury. There was also a host of players O'Farrell wanted to sell, but United's Board vetoed his plans.

As the 1972-73 season kicked off, there was a growing feeling that even major transfer changes could not paper over a deep malaise at Manchester United. Alex Stepney said: 'The atmosphere at the club was depressing. The big three, Law, Charlton and Best, were at loggerheads. There were long days when they simply did not speak to each other.' Any manager's job can be made impossible when there is such deep disharmony between key players.

United started the season badly, failing to win any of their opening nine games, and soon sunk to the bottom of the table. O'Farrell bought two strikers to revive the team — Ted MacDougall from Bournemouth for £200,000 and Wyn Davies from Manchester City for £65,000 — but they could not alleviate the air of despondency about the club. Matt Busby said: 'I have tried to keep out of Frank's way, but I hear whispers that things have gone sour in the dressing room. As for the buying, I am concerned.'

After an initial honeymoon phase between O'Farrell and Busby, a creeping hostility had developed between them. It had irked O'Farrell that he had not been given the use of the manager's office at Old Trafford (which Busby continued to occupy), and Busby told O'Farrell's wife, Ann, at one club function that Frank was 'too independent'. In his autobiography, *Soccer at the Top*, Busby claimed that: 'Frank O'Farrell was brought to the club to manage players. It seemed as if he wanted to manage the Board, too', but Busby didn't explain what he meant by this.

Some United players were just going through the motions

I don't think Frank wanted to run the Board. All he would have wanted was the same authority that Matt had been granted when he was the manager. Frank tried to work directly with the Chairman on the buying and selling of players, in the same way that I later did. Louis Edwards and Frank O'Farrell were on good terms at the start, but gradually Frank began to feel aggrieved about his lack of authority.

O'Farrell's buying had helped plunge United into debt (to the tune of £234,000) and the new players were not gelling. On 16 December 1972, United travelled to Selhurst Park and the result, a 0-5 defeat, settled O'Farrell's future. I was Scotland's manager at the time, and in that capacity I'd gone to the game to watch Crystal Palace's left-back, Tommy Taylor. Ironically, Frank O'Farrell gave me my ticket in the director's box for the game, and I was sitting just behind him.

It didn't take great perception to see that quite a few United players were just going through the motions. Alex Stepney later wrote: 'I have never played in a team that was so lacking in spirit and fighting quality. We lost 0-5, and the scoreline could easily have been double that.' I went into the Boardroom after the game, and Busby came over and said: 'What did you think, Tommy?' I told him it was a disaster, and that clearly half of United's team weren't trying. Busby said: 'I think something will be happening on Tuesday, will you be interested?' I said: 'Yes, of course, I would.' The following day, a newspaper headline said: 'Frank O'Failure!', but he'd been failed by certain players.

Two days later, at a club banquet in Manchester's

Midland Hotel to celebrate the end of Bobby Charlton's testimonial year, O'Farrell, although present, was not invited to the top table. His time was up. The following morning, United's directors met at the Collyhurst offices of Chairman Louis Edwards. They decided to sack O'Farrell and his backroom team. 'A nice day for an execution,' Frank remarked on his way to the meeting. In a public statement, Busby said: 'The team had lost all fight. There were observations by a number of senior players that there did not seem to be a close relationship between manager and players.'

Frank blamed the 'Old Trafford mafia' for influencing the Board

O'Farrell was told that results during his period in charge (24 wins in 64 League games) were unacceptable. O'Farrell still had three years and six months of his contract left to run and, after a lengthy legal battle, he was given a pay-off of more than £50,000. Malcolm Musgrove was given three month's pay, and coach John Aston a year's salary.

Matt 'phoned me at home and said that Frank had been dismissed, and asked if I would like to apply for the job. I told him that I wouldn't, but that I'd be delighted to accept the job if it was offered. Louis Edwards rang Willie Allen at the Scottish Football Association for permission to talk to me, and I flew to Manchester on the Friday. Louis and Matt met me at the airport and it took about 10 seconds to agree terms.

O'Farrell, who went on to manage Torquay — and the Iran national team — did not believe he had been given a fair crack of the whip at United. He blamed a fringe element, which he called 'the Old Trafford mafia', for influencing the Board. These people were not a figment of Frank's imagination. Tommy Cavanagh, who worked under me and under Dave Sexton, dubbed them the 'junior board'. They are a group who would like to be directors, but have to make do with being 'hangers-on' at the club. They try to influence decisions at the club — some are shareholders — and they hold everyone

Manchester United's 0-5 defeat at Crystal Palace, on 16 December 1972, sealed Frank O'Farrell's fate, and persuaded me that Wyn 'the leap' Davies (below, heading the ball) and Ted MacDougall (to the right of Davies), two recent signings, would soon be packing their bags again.

(apart from themselves) in moral judgment. They make life difficult if you don't socialise with them. They're like a cancer, but the treatment for them has been the eroding force of time, and their force is spent now.

Both Busby's immediate successors got a raw deal at United

Looking back on his time at Old Trafford, Frank O'Farrell said: 'I am only sorry the way things turned out at the end. Every successful club has a void — a period when things don't go so well — but United would not accept this. When I was there I made offers for a host of top-class players, such as Tony Currie, Peter Shilton, Mick Mills and David Nish, but they were just not available. In time, I believe I could have built up the team again, but time was the only thing I didn't have. I have never admired another man in my life the way I admired Matt Busby. But by the time I left the club I had never felt so let down by a man as I did by him.'

Frank O'Farrell has been a good friend of mine for over 30 years — he's godfather to one of my children — and I felt very sorry for him. I was told that he was quite upset that I'd taken the job. However, when I next met him, I said: 'If I hadn't have taken the job, Frank, someone else would. It shouldn't affect our friendship.' In the end he accepted that. It was the shoddy way he'd been treated that hurt Frank.

It had proved, as Joe Mercer had predicted it would, to be an impossible job to succeed Sir Matt Busby. Both his two immediate successors received a raw deal at Manchester United, more from the players than from Sir Matt. Tony Dunne said that Wilf McGuinness: 'Came as a boy and left as an old man', and in Wilf's case familiarity had definitely bred contempt.

O'Farrell 'came a stranger and went a stranger', said Denis Law

Frank O'Farrell, however, had encountered an escalating tide of resistance that he wasn't empowered to quash. Ironically, before he started, O'Farrell said: 'One of the most important things in management is communication,' but he will always be dogged by Denis Law's caustic assessment: 'Frank O'Farrell came a stranger and went a stranger.'

While McGuinness has renewed links with the club he loved so dearly — on 1 August 1990, Manchester United played in his testimonial at Bury, where he is the coach and physiotherapist, and his son Paul signed professional forms with United in July 1989 — for O'Farrell, Old Trafford is a place best forgotten.

As Manchester United prepared to start 1973, the Doc was in charge at Old Trafford. I was United's 10th manager, and I was not in the least willing to play the role of the shrinking violet. An exciting new chapter in my life was about to begin.

Matt Busby, with Secretary Les Olive in his wake, leaves Old Trafford after sacking Frank O'Farrell. There were claims by the United Board that the torn-up souvenirs strewn across the doorway were planted by reporters.

THE DOC'S TONIC

There was never a dull moment while I was manager of United, but it was certainly a period of ups and downs. We suffered the heartache of relegation, the joy of winning promotion as Champions, two contrasting FA Cup Final appearances and a controversial climax to my reign at Old Trafford.

I had always believed I was destined to manage Manchester United, and although I had enjoyed my period in charge of Scotland, the opportunity to take over at Old Trafford was something I couldn't resist — it was the fulfilment of a dream.

Manchester United was in a bad state when I took over, but my authority wasn't in question, because it was accepted that major changes were needed. There was a lot of dead wood at the club and I had been chosen to chop it away. The club had to be rebuilt, and that entailed putting out to grass the ageing remnants of the 1968 European Cup winning team.

There was an element among the players who were intent on preserving their positions, even at the expense of the manager's job. They had got rid of both

Wilf McGuinness and Frank O'Farrell, and if I hadn't dumped them, they would have got rid of me — it's as simple as that. It's never a popular job telling players that their days are numbered, but it had to be done. The whole club was stagnating.

I was fully aware of the situation at Old Trafford in December 1972. As Scotland manager I'd seen many of the players, and I had a good idea about who would be packing their bags. Ironically, two players who later fell out with me, eased my way into the club. As Denis

I always preferred watching games from the stand (below right), because I didn't think the view from the dugout was good enough. Here, my first assistant at Old Trafford, Paddy Crerand (below left), offers a fretful face to the camera.

Law described: 'When Matt Busby asked Willie Morgan and me how we got on with Tommy Docherty and what we thought of him as United's next boss, we both unhesitatingly said that he was the ideal man for the job. He had done wonders for Scotland and was the man to solve United's management problems.'

Alex Forsyth was a quick, attacking player, with a fierce shot

Within weeks of taking over, I plunged into the transfer market. My first signing was Alex Forsyth, from Partick Thistle, who cost £85,000. I'd brought Alex into the Scotland team; he was a quick, attacking player, with a fierce shot, who was great at making overlapping runs — not unlike Denis Irwin, who joined Alex Ferguson's team in the 1990-91 season. I also added a tartan trio: George Graham (£125,000 from Arsenal); Jim Holton (£65,000 from Shrewsbury Town) and Lou Macari (£200,000 from Celtic). With Denis Law, Willie Morgan and Martin Buchan already at the club, Old Trafford resembled a Scotland United.

George Graham was signed as a replacement for Bobby Charlton — who was due to retire at the end of the 1972-73 season — and I made him captain. I'd given 'Stroller' Graham his first international cap, and bought him nearly a decade before for Chelsea, and I admired his graceful skills and subtle reading of the game. Unfortunately, he didn't have a fruitful time at Old Trafford — but how could *anyone* have filled Bobby Charlton's boots?

'Six foot two, eyes of blue, Big Jim Holton's after you!', the fans chanted

Lou Macari was one of my best buys. He was an artistic ball player, who scored opportunist goals. Macari, who was unsettled at Celtic, was having talks with the Anfield Board. I was staying in Liverpool when he was down for talks, and when I got back to my room at the Adelphi Hotel, Lou called and said: 'Jock Stein's agreed a fee with Liverpool, but the deal isn't final.' Lou thought he might get a better financial package at United — if he'd been looking for medals, not money, he'd have joined Liverpool, who won the title that year — and after I'd spoken to Jock Stein we wrapped up a deal to bring 'Little Lou' to United, and he signed on 18 January 1973.

My first priority, of course, was avoiding relegation. United had won only six games out of 26 during Frank O'Farrell's last five months at the club, and morale had suffered. The introduction of 21-year-old Jim Holton into the centre of defence steadied the team, and a run of eight games without defeat kept United in Division One. Holton's start at United was certainly eventful: in his first nine games he was sent off twice, booked once and scored three times. He won instant hero-status

with the fans, who used to chant: 'Six foot two, eyes of blue, Big Jim Holton's after you!' A Jim Holton Fan Club was soon established, although it wasn't heavily subscribed to by his opponents. During the game against Birmingham City, when John Roberts was giving Macari a rough time, Holton approached Roberts and warned him: 'I'll break you in two when you come to Old Trafford for what you did to the wee dwarf today!' It was a great first season for Holton and at the end of it, United rewarded him with a five-year contract.

Among the first players to be swept out of the club were Wyn Davies (sold to Blackpool for £14,000), and Ted MacDougall, sold to West Ham for £170,000. MacDougall had endured a rather lacklustre time at United, and he later complained that: 'I once asked Bobby Charlton for the best way to the training ground, and I'm still waiting for an answer.' I had my reasons for selling Ted. He may have been a noted goalscorer, but he netted only once in nine games under me, and that

Jim Holton (below, beating Chelsea's Peter Osgood to the ball, while Arnold Sidebottom looks on), was brave, strong and unfailingly good in the air, but on the ground Big Jim would sometimes have had trouble trapping a medicine ball.

wasn't good enough. Old Trafford was too big for him, and his sour, dour personality didn't win him many friends in the dressing room. When he returned to smaller clubs he found his goalscoring touch again, and in 1975-76, with Norwich City, he was the First Division's leading scorer.

'Tommy Doc has got the ability to communicate with players'

During that first half-season the rearguard action on the pitch worked, and Matt Busby said: 'Tommy Docherty and his assistant Tommy Cavanagh have this knack of human contact and have created a good relationship with the players. They have given them spirit and the will to fight for results. Tommy Doc has got the ability to communicate with players. He makes them feel part of it. They have all responded to him, playing to win and running about to win. Before Tommy arrived it was like a nightmare. We were all under a cloud with embarrassments and headaches. I was beginning to lose hope. I thought an improvement would never come.'

Improvement had come, but there had been some hard lessons to learn as well. One of my first moves at United was to make Paddy Crerand my assistant, and this turned out to be a dreadful mistake. Matt Busby and I both thought it was a good idea at the time — Paddy had previously been running the youth team —

but after six months it was clearly not working. Paddy took umbrage at the decision (he once said: 'As an enemy, Doc was vicious, vindictive and callous'), and although I recognise that he's a United fanatic, I made my decision for the good of the club.

Of course, 1972-73 was always going to be a season of real upheavals, because it was the year when the great Best, Charlton, Law triumvirate finally disintegrated. Denis Law had been a fantastic player for United. Bobby Charlton once gave an excellent description of this acrobatic, pulsating forward in action: 'Denis Law is a powerhouse player,' said Charlton. 'He is volatile, tempestuous and colourful. In common with all great headers of the ball, he seems to hang in the air a split-second before making contact. His timing of the jump is perfect, and he contorts himself in the most amazing ways to get his head to the ball. When Denis has the bit between his teeth, he is virtually unstoppable. He is one of the few players who would have got into the pre-Munich United team.' Sadly, by 1973, Denis was in decline, he was missing a lot of training sessions and he was no longer the player he had once been, and in the best interests of the player — he needed a fresh spark and he got that in his move to Manchester City — I let him go on a free transfer.

Bobby Charlton helped me enormously when he retired. He came to me and asked for permission to announce his retirement to Matt and the Board. I'll always be grateful to Bobby for that, because the day would have come when I would have had to tell him that his time was up, and I would have been remembered as the manager who transferred Bobby Charlton. On 28 April 1973, Bobby played his last League game for United — against Chelsea at Stamford Bridge. It was his 606th League appearance, a glorious club record.

There were other players who didn't survive under my rule. I transferred Brian Kidd, who'd been in and out of the team, and I sold Tony Dunne. I felt sorry for both of them, but being sentimental only gets you the sack. I thought Dunne was past it, but he proved me wrong and went on to enjoy three excellent years with Bolton Wanderers. We needed to make room for youth players, such as Gerry Daly, Brian Greenhoff and Sammy McIlroy, even if it was just a chance to see if they *could* move up to the highest level. To make room for these youngsters, I sold Paul Edwards, Peter Fletcher, Jimmy Rimmer, David Sadler and Carlo Sartori.

During that 1972-73 season, the club was still reeling from the effects of these changes. In less than 18 months, I'd sold or released 32 players and signed 12 new ones — including Tommy Baldwin, Alan Foggon, Alex Forsyth, George Graham, Jim Holton, Stewart

LEFT: Two of my first signings were Lou Macari (left) from Celtic, and George Graham, from Arsenal. Macari had 12 excellent seasons with United, during which he scored 97 goals. Both later became managers, and Graham, who led Arsenal to two League Championship triumphs within three seasons, has been by far the more successful in this field.

Houston, Lou Macari, Jim McCalliog, Mick Martin, Stuart Pearson and Paddy Roche — and in the process the average age of the first team was reduced to 23.

There were other players I tried and failed to sign. West Brom's Asa Hartford, Derby County's Archie Gemmell and Sheffield United's Tony Currie were top of my list. Paddy Crerand and I tried ever so hard to get Currie, and United were happy to pay the fee, but Sheffield United wouldn't sell him. It was a real shame, because he was tailor-made for Old Trafford.

Alex Stepney drove his shot well wide of Peter Shilton into the back of the net

The 1973-74 season was one of ups and, most definitely, downs. Willie Morgan, the regular penalty-taker, was out with an eye injury and we found a new player to take the spot-kicks. Goalkeeper Alex Stepney would always play outfield during our eight-a-side practice matches, and he was a good finisher. At the time, the strikers — who should be deadly from 12 yards — weren't happy to take the responsibility, so I appointed Alex as our penalty-taker.

On 12 September 1973, in a home match against Leicester City, the crowd and the Leicester players — including goalkeeper Peter Shilton — were amazed to see Stepney walk from the other end of the field and line the ball up on the penalty spot. He drove his shot well wide of Shilton into the back of the net. The second penalty he scored, a month later in our 1-0 victory against Birmingham City, made Stepney United's leading goalscorer, which shows how bad things were. After he had a penalty kick saved by the Wolves's goalkeeper, Gary Pierce, I allowed Alex to rest his shooting foot, and Jim McCalliog took over the job.

Best's vision was still there, but he couldn't leave players for dead anymore

That season was also notable for another failed comeback by George Best, who'd gone to Spain a few weeks before Frank O'Farrell was sacked. By the start of October 1973, we were in such a poor state that Busby, Crerand and I agreed that Best would be an asset to the side. All I promised George was the chance to reestablish himself as a United player. I agreed that he could miss training some mornings, as long as he was producing the goods. Unfortunately, like the proverbial leopard, George hadn't changed his spots.

George Best made his comeback on 20 October 1973 against Birmingham, and he played a further 12 games (scoring twice). George, who was only 27, was still terrific when he was on the ball, and his vision and control was still there, but when he beat players he could no longer leave them for dead. Sadly, his comeback didn't last. I picked him for the FA Cup third-round tie at home to Plymouth Argyle on 5 January 1974. I

told the whole squad to report for a pre-match meal, from 11.30 until 12 o'clock, in the Old Trafford Grill Room. Best, with a girlfriend in tow, arrived at the ground at 2.40 and knocked on the dressing room door. I'll pay him the compliment of saying that a drop or two of alcohol had passed his lips. He was in no condition whatsoever to play. I told him: 'George, come and see me on Monday and we'll sort it out.' Best walked out and left Old Trafford for good. We cancelled his contract, which was not a pleasurable thing to have to do.

Two months later, we were bottom of the table and although we had a mini revival at the end of March — winning four out of five games — United, Norwich and Southampton couldn't avoid the drop. There is, however, a misconception that it was a back-heeled goal from Denis Law (the least joyful goal he ever scored), in our 0-1 home defeat by Manchester City, which actually sent us down. In fact, the result of that game was irrelevant, because even if we'd beaten City 15-0, and then thrashed Stoke City, our final opponents, we could have reached only 36 points. Birmingham City, who avoided relegation by finishing fourth from bottom, won their final two games and ended with 37 points.

Tommy Cavanagh was a great coach and a boisterous man

United were thus relegated after 36 years in Division One. For Busby, the drop was a hammer blow. As he said at the time: 'In all my 40 years as a player, manager and director, I've never been in the Second Division. It's a terrible disappointment.' I was bitterly disappointed as well. At the time, I would rather have shot myself than quit. Ever since I'd been a professional, it had been my ambition that one day I might succeed Sir Matt Busby as manager at Old Trafford, and I knew I could still bring success. Fortunately, any fears that I would be receiving my P45 in the post vanished when Matt and Louis Edwards arrived at my house with a crate of champagne, and told me my job was safe.

I was lucky in having a brilliant right-hand man in Tommy Cavanagh, who was a marvellous influence in the dressing room. He knew how to inspire players, even if it just entailed rousing their adrenalin by playing them Max Bygraves tapes on the team bus. Cav was a real character. Our Chairman, Louis Edwards, used to love to hear him sing, especially his version of *Why Don't You Come Home Bill Bailey?*, which Cav would always alter to *Why Don't You Come Home Louis Edwards?*. 'Give us a song, Cav!', Louis Edwards would always call out.

Tommy Cavanagh was even more boisterous than me at times, but he was a great coach and he wouldn't tolerate egotism from a player — he didn't care how important a player considered himself. Yet players liked him, because they respect people who are straight with them. He would never duck an issue, and Cav and I had numerous fierce rows, but we always spoke our minds

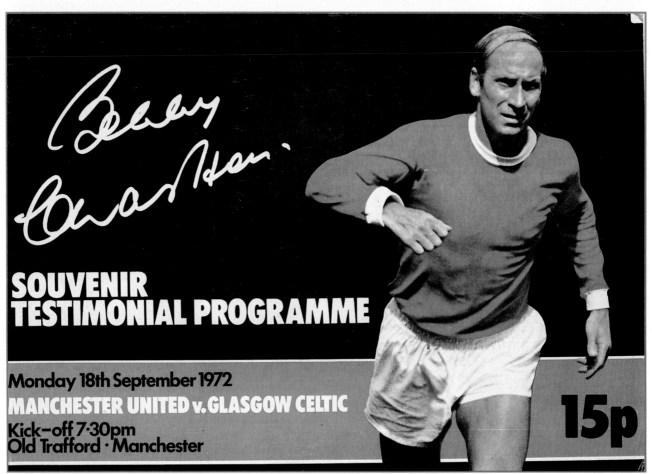

SOUVENIR TESTIMONIAL PROGRAMME

Monday 18th September 1972

MANCHESTER UNITED v. GLASGOW CELTIC

Kick-off 7·30pm
Old Trafford · Manchester

15p

Bobby Charlton made the last of his record 754 first-team appearances for Manchester United on 28 April 1973 at Chelsea (opposite above, Bobby on the ball, being jockeyed by Ron Harris and John Hollins). In 17 years at United, he collected a record 106 full England caps. His testimonial against Celtic (opposite below, the souvenir programme) on 18 September 1972, was watched by 60,538 fans and raised £46,000. In 1984, Bobby became a director of United.

and never bore a grudge. I'm still friends with him, and he's retired now and living in Hull.

Tommy Cavanagh and I shared the same philosophy about how the game should be played. As he put it: 'I can't stand negative football. I am sure that both myself and Tommy Docherty feel that there is no substitute for class. The one thing we will not do is turn the United players into robots. They will be encouraged to play football at all times.'

Manchester United's descent into Division Two had a cauterising effect. I've never been a great believer in numbers and systems. Teams should be mobile and skilful and at the heart of the team's play should be the intention to attack. During that relegation season, we'd played negative, defensive football and we had paid the penalty. From that point on I decided to manage a United team which attacked.

Stuart 'Pancho' Pearson was a beautiful striker — intelligent, subtle and brave

Entertaining, incisive football was just what United's fans wanted. Average gates at Old Trafford that season in Division Two were 48,388, the highest in the division for more than 25 years. When we played Sheffield Wednesday at Hillsborough on 7 December 1974, we were watched by a crowd of 35,067, a huge increase from Wednesday's average in their nine previous home games that season of 12,200. That day, we took around 25,000 travelling fans across the Pennines, and the crowd were treated to a glorious 4-4 draw. Everywhere we went that season, United's massive, brilliant travelling support made our games buzz with a carnival atmosphere.

The team that stormed home in Division Two was magnificent. Stuart Pearson, a bargain buy from Hull City for £200,000, scored 18 goals for us that season. 'Pancho' Pearson was a beautiful striker — intelligent, subtle, brave and brilliant with his back to goal. He was at the heart of so many of our attacking moves, because he was an expert at receiving the ball and laying it off perfectly into the path of a supporting teammate. Midway through that fantastic season, we beat promotion rivals Sunderland 3-2, after trailing 1-2, and that result was nearly as pleasurable as knocking Manchester City out of the League Cup. We were unlucky to get knocked out of that competiton in the semi-finals, by Norwich City.

One of the best players that season was Martin Buchan, who played 41 magnificent League games as captain. It was remarkable to see the way the rest of the players responded to his leadership both on and off the field. Buchan had a precociously cool demeanour on the pitch, and he was very much his own man off it — when all the players signed a contract worth £300 each to wear Gola boots and tracksuits, he signed his own individual deal with Adidas — and he could be very sardonic. A reporter once asked Buchan if he could have a quick word. 'Aye' said Buchan, without breaking his stride, 'velocity!'

'Martin Buchan was one of the most talented defenders in Europe'

Buchan was a world-class defender, and he was such a great reader of the game that he could pick up moves and stamp them out even as they were crystallising. Yet he was so quick that he used to test himself by leaving tackles to the very last moment, milking the applause of the crowd for wonderful split-second interceptions, even though he possessed the skill to be there seconds ahead of the player. Steve Coppell once said: 'In that season in the Second Division and in the next two in the First, Martin Buchan was probably one of the most talented central defenders in European football.'

Buchan also had a wonderful partner in Brian Greenhoff. When I was manager at Rotherham United, in 1968, I tried to sign Greenhoff on schoolboy forms, but he went to United. When I arrived at Old Trafford, Greenhoff was never off the treatment table. I told him: 'Brian, if I see you on that table again, I'll make you take it home with you!' His fitness improved and in no time he proved what a great player he was. He won the first of 18 England caps when he was only 23.

Sammy McIlroy was brilliant at picking up the ball and running at opponents

Neither Greenhoff nor Buchan was a recognised centre-half, they were both used to playing off a tall centre-half like Jim Holton, whose job was to win the aerial battles, but when Holton broke his leg at Hillsborough, we decided to pair them in central defence, and it was a success. They had such a great understanding, and although they weren't that tall (both were 5'10") they were exceptional in the air. In the FA Cup semi-final against Leeds in 1976, they won all the aerial battles against Joe Jordan and Gordon McQueen. On the ground, they were a revelation. Greenhoff was superb at breaking up an attack and then bringing the ball out of defence and setting up a good attacking movement.

Sammy McIlroy was a brilliant player and a dream to manage. He was splendid at picking up the ball and then running at opponents. He committed them, skipped past them and then played a deadly through-ball. He possessed the stamina to keep doing this throughout a game, and he used to bag a fair share of goals by following up the forwards.

Steve Coppell, my best signing, would run a full-back to exhaustion

McIlroy worked well with Gerry Daly, but his best partner was probably Lou Macari, who was marvellous at seeing space and running into it. He loved the middle of the park, but when he did move forward it was always into intelligent positions and he was a great finisher. One season he bagged 18 goals from midfield. It's enlightening to look at the difference between the midfield in the mid-1970s, and that of the early 1990s. In 1974-75 and 1975-76, playing a combined total of 297 games, Daly, Macari and McIlroy scored 82 goals between them. In 1989-90 and 1990-91, playing a total of 245 games, Paul Ince, Michael Phelan and Neil Webb managed 15 goals between them.

That Second Division side was brilliant, and those players helped me win the 'Manager of the Month' award twice that year. United finished as Champions, with 61 points, scoring 66 goals, while conceding only 30. Sir Matt Busby said: 'Being wise after the event, I would say that relegation was a blessing in disguise.' That was a kind thing to say, and although we were one of the best things to happen to the Second Division, I don't think we *had* to go down to turn the club around.

Another key player, whom I consider my best buy at the club, was Steve Coppell (who'd been rejected by Everton and Liverpool). He signed from Tranmere Rovers in February 1975 for £30,000, when he was 19. Coppell had been recommended by my old friend, the ex-Liverpool manager Bill Shankly, and after Tommy Cavanagh watched him play for Tranmere, he said: 'Sign him Doc, he's another Ian Callaghan!' By the end of that first season Coppell had established himself as a regular. Steve was skilful, intelligent and always showed real determination. If he was beaten nine times by a defender, he'd keep going until he'd beaten him at the tenth attempt. He would a run a full-back to exhaustion. Added to that, he is as bright as a button, and his subsequent success as manager of Crystal Palace has not come as a surprise.

Martin Buchan (left) and goalkeeper Alex Stepney, dubbed 'Steptoe' by his team-mates, parade the Second Division Championship trophy during a lap of honour around Old Trafford on 26 April 1975, after beating Blackpool 4-0.

Originally, I'd earmarked Coppell as a future replacement for Willie Morgan, but Morgan actually left the club in June 1975. Morgan had been a great player for United, but his last three years had not been his finest. On 26 October 1974, he was substituted for the game against Southampton at Old Trafford. His replacement, Stuart Pearson, actually scored the winning goal, but Willie stormed off and left the ground even before the final whistle had sounded. It was unfortunate, because I honestly think that his eye injury prevented him from performing as a top-class player.

Hill was a completely intuitive player — a master of the unexpected

Many pundits expressed doubt that United would be able to continue playing attacking football in Division One. That's just what we did, and our start to the 1975-76 season could hardly have been better. We thrashed Sheffield United 5-1 in our first home game, and I won the first 'Manager of the Month' award of the season.

In November 1975, I bought Gordon Hill from Millwall for £70,000. Hill was the piece in the puzzle I really wanted. With him, I could build a team around two wingers. Hill was very fast, skilful and a marvellous goalscorer. He was a completely intuitive player, and because he was a master of the unexpected — he'd volley from impossible angles and once scored from a corner — defenders couldn't close him down. He was slim, mobile, explosively quick and he could wrongfoot defenders at will. Together, Coppell and Hill were electrifying. They would fire in high-velocity crosses from both wings. As a result, our opponents used to concede a high number of own goals (14 in three seasons), and we would score countless goals from rebounds.

'United were a revelation with their running capacity and skill'

After six games we were top of the League, and our attacking style was being feted. Leeds United's Billy Bremner said after playing against us: 'United were a revelation with their running capacity and skill. They have all-round teamwork, plus one of the best target men in the business — Stuart Pearson.' West Ham United's Trevor Brooking was also full of praise. As he put it: 'The biggest factor in Manchester United's favour is that they attack — they came at West Ham more than any other side that has been to Upton Park. Their strength is this emphasis and belief in attack. At Old Trafford the crowd lifts them, but they still go forward away from home.'

Teams just couldn't combat our wing play. Hill and Coppell attacked the full-backs as soon as they got the ball and prevented them from coming forward. This allowed McIlroy and Pearson to exploit the holes in the middle, while being supported by Brian Greenhoff, who could bring the ball out of defence and distribute it intelligently. It wasn't harum-scarum stuff; we played to an intricate and extensive passing game, which allowed defenders such as Stewart Houston to get forward into scoring positions. Sammy McIlroy said of that season: 'People used to say we played as if we didn't even consider the possibility of defeat, and to be frank, the Doc had more or less indoctrinated us with this philosophy.'

United's success did not go unnoticed. Thirteen players earned international honours that year: Brian Greenhoff, Gordon Hill and Stuart Pearson [England]; Martin Buchan, Alex Forsyth, Stewart Houston and Lou Macari [Scotland]; Tommy Jackson, David McCreery, Sammy McIlroy and Jimmy Nicholl [Northern Ireland]; and goalkeeper Paddy Roche [Republic of Ireland].

The highlight of that season was a terrific FA Cup run, which included a thrilling quarter-final win at Molineux that went to extra time. We were 0-2 down at half-time, but we beat Wolves 3-2 with goals from Stuart Pearson, Brian Greenhoff and Sammy McIlroy. That magnificent display summed up the character of that team.

Jimmy Greenhoff and Stuart Pearson were tailor-made for one another

In the semi-final, against Derby County, Gordon 'Merlin' Hill scored both goals at Hillsborough in another fine display. After that win, it was a terrible disappointment to lose in the Final against Southampton, but Lawrie McMenemy marshalled his experienced campaigners well, and we didn't play well, or take our chances. Later that evening, Lawrie McMenemy was astonished when a waiter at Southampton's banquet said: 'Mr Tommy Docherty is on the 'phone!' Big Lawrie thought it was a wind-up, but he was touched that I'd called to offer my congratulations. Even though I was really choked at losing, I was genuinely pleased that Big Lawrie was the man who had triumphed.

At the start of the 1976-77 season, revenue from season ticket sales had reached £500,000 — a new record for a British club. We were obviously popular, and we'd been successful — as well as being FA Cup runners-up, we'd finished a highly credible third in the League — but I believed that some changes were necessary. I sold Gerry Daly to Derby for £188,000 and bought Jimmy Greenhoff, Brian's older brother from Stoke City, for £100,000. He even took a £50 a week pay cut to come to Old Trafford.

Jimmy took the weight off Stuart Pearson's shoulders, allowing Sammy McIlroy to move back into the midfield. Steve Coppell said: 'Jimmy was the best player I *ever* played with. There was no telepathy or anything like that, it was simply that whenever you needed him he was there.' Jimmy was a wonderful player, and he and Pearson were tailor-made for one another. They blended superbly, understood each other's individual strengths and they certainly disproved the theory that you have to use a hulking great centre-forward. They were subtle, skilful and sharp; splendid to play with and absolutely deadly to play against.

Greenhoff's winner had the touch of luck that helps win an FA Cup Final

I had exclaimed, more in hope than certainty, after the defeat in the 1976 FA Cup Final, that we would return to Wembley in 1977. Once again, our cup run was exceptional, and after beating Walsall and Queen's Park Rangers, it was good to exact revenge and put out Southampton in the fifth round. Then, after beating Aston Villa, we knocked out Leeds United in the semi-final. The 2-1 scoreline doesn't do justice to our total superiority that day.

The actual Final, against Liverpool, was an anticlimax. Bob Paisley's team was going for the treble, United were desperate not to lose for the second year running and I was keen to break the jinx of Wembley — I had never won there as a player or a manager. Stuart Pearson scored a cracking goal and although Jimmy Case equalised, our winner — which ricoched off Jimmy Greenhoff's chest from a Lou Macari shot — had the touch of luck that helps win an FA Cup Final. That day, Buchan was outstanding, as was young Arthur Albiston who'd replaced the injured Stewart Houston.

After the FA Cup win I was due to sign a new four-year contract, but I knew I had to make a decision about my domestic situation. My marriage to Agnes had run its course, and I had fallen in love with Mary Brown, the wife of the club physiotherapist Laurie Brown. I rang Louis Edwards, but his son Martin said Louis was still out celebrating. When I explained my decision to Martin, he said: 'Don't worry, Tommy. It's something that's been going on since Adam and Eve, and it won't

BELOW: Stewart Houston advances on the ball, in our ill-fated 1976 FA Cup Final against Southampton. OPPOSITE: Wing wizards Gordon Hill (top) and Steve Coppell (bottom).

affect your position at United.' When I got hold of Louis, he was of the same mind, and actually said: 'It's a private matter, you'll definitely be staying at the club.'

The Board and Chairman were backing me, and they agreed that I should take the youth team to Portugal. However, when I returned the Board called me in for a meeting and asked me to resign. I declined, and said: 'I am not ashamed of my actions.' They suspended me on full pay, and later that week told me I was fired.

Steve Coppell was one of many players upset at the news. As he later said: 'If ever there was a man tailor-made to be manager of Manchester United it was Tommy Docherty, and it was as though all his earlier years of management in the game had been spent preparing for this one particular job.'

Nevertheless, the Board made their decision, and it wasn't an easy one to make. I've always had peace of mind about that time, because I behaved with integrity by telling them before I signed the contract. Louis Edwards didn't speak to me for a while afterwards. I

don't think it was a decision he fully supported, and embarrassment made him reluctant to speak. He knew he'd done the wrong thing, and that he'd been painted into a corner by various people. My domestic situation was a heaven-sent opportunity for the people who were trying to get rid of me.

I gave the club the FA Cup, they gave me the sack

My love for Mary certainly wasn't a fly by night action. Now, some 15 years later, we're still together and happily married. I have a great relationship with my two step-daughters, Helen and Jane, and we have two daughters of our own, Grace and Lucy. Mary and I laugh at some of the skeletons which have since tumbled out of cupboards. When Ron Atkinson split up with his wife in 1984, it didn't cost him his job at United. Many journalists who penned holier-than-thou editorials have done exactly the same thing in their private lives. And when Martin Edwards was at the centre of front-page stories in April 1990, which alleged that he had had an affair with a woman who was trying to blackmail him for £100,000, I didn't notice him tendering his resignation. I'm not bitter about the events, because Mary and I are really happy, but if every chairman and manager of

BELOW: Stuart Pearson advances on Liverpool's goal, in the 1977 FA Cup Final. Pearson scored our first in a memorable 2-1 win. I signed him from Hull City in 1974, for a bargain £200,000, and he netted 59 goals in 139 League games for United. He possessed an outstanding physique, and played Rugby Union for Sale after retiring from football in 1982.

a football club were sacked for what I did, there wouldn't be many of them left with a job!

Despite my shoddy treatment, I still love Manchester United. It is the best club in the world, and I had a marvellous time at Old Trafford. People complain about the pressure of being manager there, but for me it was sheer enjoyment. I loved the club, and the supporters loved me. I'm still a red through and through, and when I do criticise the club nowadays, it's the response of a supporter and not an ex-manager.

The biggest tragedy about my sacking was that I had built a great young side and we were on the brink of tremendous things. Furthermore, I built the side for peanuts and balanced the books. A manager should be judged on his results and his transfer dealings. My transfer record stands up to any amount of scrutiny. We filled stadiums everywhere, playing exciting, entertaining football, and we were exemplary sportsmen into the bargain: in 1975-76 and 1976-77 we won the *Daily Mail* Fair Play League, proof that we were playing, not kicking, our way to victory.

I made the club money, entertained the supporters and gave the club the FA Cup. They gave me the sack. It was a golden opportunity to bring back the glory days and the Manchester United hierarchy threw it away. I don't think any of my successors has produced a team that was as exciting as the one which had Buchan, Macari, McIlroy, Pearson, the Greenhoff brothers and Coppell and Hill. If it had been up to the supporters, I'd probably still be there.

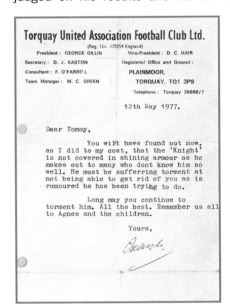

My domestic situation was a heaven-sent opportunity for the people who were trying to get rid of me. There were unseen forces at work (far left, my old friend Frank O'Farrell warned me that things were afoot in this letter sent 10 days *before* the 1977 FA Cup Final); and Alex Stepney's theory — 'I knew one group leading the attack on the Doc would be the wives of the Manchester United directors' — about the people behind my sacking was echoed by the *Daily Express* (left). However, Mary and I (below) are still together, and happily married with two step-daughters and two daughters of our own.

SEXTON SAGA

During Dave Sexton's reign, United reached a Cup Final and were runners-up in the League. Yet the style of play he produced was unpopular.

Tommy Cavanagh should have been chosen to succeed me as manager. He knew the club inside out, had played a vital part in the success of the previous three years and had a good rapport with the players. Instead, 11 days after my dismissal, on 14 July 1977, the Board appointed Dave Sexton as the new boss of Manchester United.

Sexton and I are like two sides of a coin. Sexton is tense and unassuming, and you could be with him for a year and never get to know him. United's Board wanted a 'nice man', as a reaction to the events associated with my sacking. Ironically, I actually introduced Dave into the managerial game, when I made him my youth coach at Chelsea. Then, when I left Stamford Bridge in October 1967, he succeeded me as manager.

At a press conference to announce his appointment, 47-year-old Sexton said: 'I've got to be honest and say the image of Manchester United overawed me, to a certain extent, but this job has got to be the peak of ambition for any manager. United have given me three years to do a job and with a club of their standing and quality of players, it's long enough to win something.' His anxiety was justified — the job was too big for him.

Sexton was always uneasy when dealing with the press — and the United manager's job is a very high-profile one — because it is bred in his bones to be on his guard. Reporters soon dubbed him 'Whispering Dave', because of his introverted personality, yet Sexton was aware of his image problem, as he said: 'I don't want to become a talking head. If you go around talking all the time in this game, you are bound to hurt someone. If you talk you have to criticise and someone has to be the butt of that criticism. I could do better at selling the team and the game, but it doesn't suit me. I

RIGHT: Dave Sexton, looking concerned. Dave, who became United's fourth manager in eight years when he was appointed in 1977, is a highly respected coach, and a wise student of the game, but during his period in charge at Old Trafford he found difficulties with the PR side of the manager's job. His attempt to impose a more structured, tactical playing style produced a team with an organised defensive game, but with little flair or attacking zest.

feel awkward saying: "We'll murder 'em!", and all those kinds of things. This is a dangerous game to go around boasting in. I prefer to win quietly.'

After taking over, Sexton appointed Tommy Cavanagh, who had signed a long-term contract in 1977, as his second-in command. Sexton told my FA Cup winning team: 'Let's keep it successful. Let's keep the ship going!', and he let Cavanagh continue with the same pre-season training routines.

'I felt the pressure. There is something awesome about Old Trafford'

United's first competitive game under Sexton, on 13 August 1977, was the Charity Shield match against Liverpool at Wembley. It ended, symbolically, in a scoreless draw. By the end of October, United had lost seven games and had been knocked out of the League Cup by Arsenal. They also fell by the wayside in the European Cup Winners' Cup. After knocking out St. Etienne, United went out to my old side FC Porto. United lost 0-4 in the Estadio das Antos, and a spirited performance in the home leg, which United won 5-2, was not enough to get them through.

There were some uplifting performances that season — including a fine 6-2 win away at Everton — but United fizzled out in the League, and a fourth-round FA

Cup defeat at West Bromwich Albion meant that United had squandered three chances of a cup run. United finished 10th in Division One, and Steve Coppell later summed up Dave Sexton's first season in command of Manchester United: 'It represented a shocking season. It was reflected in our attitude both on the pitch and in the dressing room. We were not as resilient, our naivety had gone and, increasingly, players began to look after themselves instead of each other.'

In the last three seasons in which I'd been manager, United had lost only five games at home in the League — Sexton's side lost six in his first season as manager of United! Little wonder that the Old Trafford faithful voiced their discontent. Sexton said of that year: 'It often takes a little time for a new manager to get to know a team in depth, and the last season has been a finding out period for me. There were disappointments and set-backs, but I think we learned from them.'

It does take time for any manager to find his feet at a new club, but after that first season some players were already expressing doubts about Sexton's motivational powers, as Alex Stepney explained: 'Something was

Dave Sexton's first two signings at Manchester United were good ones. Gordon McQueen, and Joe 'Fangs' Jordan were both bought from Leeds United. McQueen (top, using his 6'3" frame to maximum advantage), whose dad played for Accrington Stanley, made 228 appearances for the club. Jordan (left, shielding the ball from Chelsea's Micky Droy), who was capped 52 times for Scotland, was a fearsome competitor. He scored 41 times in 126 games for United.

Mickey Thomas was an industrious midfielder, who never quite settled at United — one of 11 clubs he was at in a decade. Sammy McIlroy, his midfield partner, said: 'Mickey was very superstitious. He made sure, before every game, that he sat in four different parts of the dressing room.'

wrong. The team was not fully responding to Dave. It seemed that he had not taken the dressing room by the scruff of the neck.' Whispering Dave did, apparently, have a set technique for inspiring his players, as Sammy McIlroy described: 'Dave goes round to each player and has a quiet but encouraging word; then he has a collective message for us. Five words which we have come to expect: "Come on, my bonny boys!"'

Despite this rousing oratory, Sexton was keenly aware of his communication problems. 'The tension inside me could be part of the problem,' he said. 'When Tommy Docherty was manager, I couldn't help noticing how relaxed he was — the *most* relaxed man I'd ever seen. And the team seemed to play like that. But I'm so tense and conscious of having to prove myself that I wonder whether I might be conveying that to the players. I feel the pressure. There is something awesome about Old Trafford.'

Sexton was an extremely tense man. If you asked him a question, even a simple one requiring a casual response, he would always take a deep swallow and

ponder. He was on the defensive straight away. A man's character is his fate, and Sexton's indecision and introversy began to darken the atmosphere at Old Trafford.

One of Sexton's heroes is Groucho Marx, yet his control of the club exhibited all the lightness of touch of Karl Marx. Tactics dominated team talks, and there were a host of complicated video lectures to illustrate skills. Dave is an excellent coach, but it is very difficult trying to get established players, many of them internationals, to go right back to basics. After being successful by expressing their skills and showing their attacking verve, many players resented the instruction to treat every match like a complex chessboard contest.

Martin Buchan marched up to Gordon Hill and clipped him round the ear

Faced by these problems, Sexton reached for the cheque book, and in January 1978 he paid Leeds United £350,000 for their fiery Scottish international striker Joe Jordan. A month later, former team-mate Gordon McQueen joined United for a British record fee of £495,000. I wasn't really a McQueen fan — his ability in the air was tremendous, but he sometimes looked like he was on casters when he ran — but he turned out to be a good buy. Joe Jordan was something of a battering ram, compared to Jimmy Greenhoff, but he paired up well with Lou Macari and was a real competitor.

When United reached the 1976 FA Cup Final, their commemorative record had included a B-side, called *Old Trafford Blues*, written and performed by Martin Buchan. In one verse he crooned:
'Then there's Brian Greenhoff, he's got lots of skill.
And he really needs it to play with Gordon Hill.'
During their last season together, the ill-feeling between Buchan and Hill was transferred from vinyl to grass. On 15 January 1977, during a game against Coventry City at Old Trafford, when Hill failed to come back and mark an opponent at a throw-in, Buchan marched up to Gordon and clipped him round the ear.

'You need a degree to understand the tactics at Old Trafford'

In truth, Hill's fate had been sealed when Sexton switched from a 4-2-4 formation to one of 4-4-2. Sexton said: 'Gordon is a very selfish player and to accommodate him other players have done extra work. He scored goals, but we had to pay a price for them.' Hill had not been happy working under Sexton, and he complained: 'You need a degree to understand the tactics at Old Trafford. Somehow it appears they don't want entertainers anymore at Manchester United. I'm becoming the fall guy and scapegoat at Old Trafford.'

In April 1978, as manager of Derby, I bought Hill for £275,000. One of the things that summed up Sexton's reign at United was the way he sold Hill and replaced him six months later with Wrexham's Mickey Thomas, or Mickey Mouse as I called him, who cost £70,000 more than Hill. This demonstrated Sexton's preference for workers rather than players with imagination and flair — in 30 months, Hill had scored 50 goals for United; in 33 months, Thomas managed 15 goals. And if it was graft Dave wanted, why didn't he keep David McCreery? He was probably the hardest worker and best professional I've had at any club.

'Mickey Thomas became a target for the biting humour of Lou Macari'

Hill may have not have been popular in the dressing room, but Mickey Thomas hardly seemed to win many friends, as Steve Coppell recalled: 'Mickey was not the brightest of people, by his own admission, and he became a target for the biting humour of Lou Macari, who would pursue him everywhere, until one day Mickey went missing. We found him hiding from his tormentor in the sauna.'

The 1978-79 season was United's centenary year, and it started with a 4-0 win over Real Madrid in a friendly. This was followed by a string of draws in the League, and a League Cup exit following a defeat at home to Watford. On 11 November 1978, United were thrashed 1-5 away by bottom-placed Birmingham City, and in the next weeks a glut of 'Sexton Must Go!' badges appeared on the coats of thousands of United supporters. Louis Edwards said after the game: 'I'm very concerned with recent events. I haven't, and the Board haven't, been satisfied with performances. We've got to work through this and we will do. We are right behind Dave Sexton, I will be working with him far more in the future.'

'I never want to live through anything like that ever again'

The fans, like the Chairman, weren't happy with the fare they were being offered. When United beat Queen's Park Rangers 2-0 at Old Trafford on 28 February 1979, United were booed off the pitch by the 36,085 crowd — a drop of 10,000 from the previous season's average home gate. Dave Sexton's explanation for the drop in attendance figures — 'People have got out of the habit of coming, because of all the games which have been called off' — rang pretty hollow.

Sexton was saved that season by a good run in the FA Cup. After knocking out Chelsea, Fulham, Colchester United and Tottenham, United beat Liverpool, over two enthralling matches, in the semi-final. Jimmy Greenhoff scored the winner in the replay at Goodison Park with a marvellous stooping header. Greenhoff, who had scored the winner in the 1977 FA Cup Final against Liverpool, will always be a hero at Old Trafford — it was the second time he had helped prevent Liverpool from

achieving a League and Cup 'double'. It was Sexton's finest moment at Old Trafford, and he said after the game: 'At last I really feel I belong now. I feel as though spring has finally begun.'

It would have been wonderful for United to have won the FA Cup in their centenary year, but Arsenal won a match which is remembered only for the last five exhilarating minutes. After trailing 0-2, two goals in the last four minutes put United level. Then, Sexton should have deployed his tactical strategies and killed the game stone-dead, but United lost their concentration, and the match. Sammy McIlroy, who scored United's second goal with a brilliant individual effort, said after the game: 'When Alan Sunderland scored their third goal, it was the worst moment of my football life. I never want to live through anything like that ever again. I nearly collapsed with excitement when I scored to put us level. To lose like that so near the final whistle was like winning the pools only to find that you had forgotten to post the coupon.'

Gary Bailey's coolness under pressure earned him the nickname 'Grandad'

When Alan Sunderland equalised, a lot of blame for the goal was attributed to United's young goalkeeper Gary Bailey — who was badly positioned when Graham Rix's cross came over — but this error did not detract from the excellent start Bailey had made at Old Trafford, following Alex Stepney's departure to play for Dallas Tornados. Bailey was 20 when he made his debut, and his coolness under pressure earned him the nickname 'Grandad' from his colleagues. Sexton had tried, in November 1978, to buy Coventry's 'keeper Jim Blyth for £440,000, but the deal fell through on medical grounds. Blyth would have been a bad investment, and Gary Bailey — the son of Roy Bailey, who won a League Championship medal with Ipswich Town in 1961-62 — saved United a lot of money.

In August 1979, Stuart Pearson was sold to West Ham for £200,000 after a dispute about a wage increase. Another departure was Brian Greenhoff, who went to Leeds United for £350,000. Greenhoff said of Sexton: 'I couldn't work for that man — I just didn't like him. You could say we had a minor tiff.' One by one, Sexton was getting shot of those players who had joined during my period in control.

The sale of Pearson and Greenhoff helped finance Sexton's costliest signing — Ray Wilkins, from Chelsea, for £825,000. Wilkins stepped straight into the team, but he couldn't inspire a great start to Sexton's third season in charge. United were hammered 1-4 by Norwich City in the third round of the League Cup — at the end of September — and the leading scorer in the first two months was Gordon McQueen. That season, however, proved to be Sexton's best at United, as they sought to challenge Liverpool for the title. During the year, Sexton inquired about Roberto, Brazil's striker, and he tried to buy Argentina's World Cup winning captain, Daniel Passarella and goalkeeper Ubaldo Fillol. Later Sexton said: 'The price River Plate want is too high and we have pulled out of the deal.'

Once again, Jimmy Greenhoff showed he had the Indian sign over Liverpool

One Continental player did join United, but unfortunately Yugoslavian international Nikola Jovanovic was a poor advertisement for European goods. Jovanovic, who was bought for £350,000 in January 1980, had played 359 times for Red Star Belgrade, and netted 50 goals. He couldn't speak English, cost a fortune to board in a top Manchester hotel and played just 21 times during his 34-month stay at Manchester United — at a cost of £14,000 for each performance.

In May 1980, United finished as runners-up behind Liverpool. Statistically, it was the club's best position since winning the Championship in 1967, and their tally of 58 points was the highest since that title win. Throughout the 1979-80 season, United had been very strong at home, gaining maximum points from the first seven home fixtures, but any illusions that Manchester United would be able to surpass Liverpool were shattered at Anfield on Boxing Day, when United were beaten 0-2 by their Merseyside rivals.

Three days later, at Old Trafford, United beat Arsenal 3-0, but the damage had been done, not least psychologically. United had been shown to be second-best to Liverpool. United failed to win a League game in January — and went out of the FA Cup to Tottenham

Hotspur — and suffered a major set-back when they were beaten at home 0-1 by Wolves early in February. That defeat severely dented United's Championship challenge, and the bubble burst in dramatic style at Portman Road on 1 March, when United were slaughtered 0-6 by Ipswich, and were saved from even greater ignominy by Gary Bailey, who saved two penalties!

Hopes of capturing the elusive League title were raised in April, when United beat Liverpool 2-1 at Old Trafford, and once again Jimmy Greenhoff showed he had the Indian sign over Liverpool. The 33-year-old striker — who'd been advised to retire because of a pelvic injury — scored the winner. With six games left, United had closed the gap to four points, but the title win was a mirage: while United lost their final game at Leeds, Liverpool beat Aston Villa 4-1 to take the title.

'They are the most unselfish team, on the field and off, I have ever managed'

United's position as runners-up that season belied performances which were frequently poor and often dreary. Most of the season was spent in a desperate battle to shadow Liverpool. United's players were aware of the yawning gap between their results and their performances, as Gordon McQueen explained: 'We were getting points but we were scrambling them and did not look Championship material. Frankly, I don't blame supporters who criticised us at all. If I had been watching some of our games, I would have been complaining as well. We just did not look the part and no one could fancy us. At the end, though, I think we did well to close the gap on Liverpool.'

The defence had been United's strongest asset — they conceded only eight League goals at Old Trafford in 21 games and the partnership of Martin Buchan and Gordon McQueen, ably supported by full-backs Arthur Albiston and Jimmy Nicholl, was one of the most effective of the last 25 years. Gary Bailey, in goal, had fulfilled his early promise, and he was selected as runner-up in the PFA 'Young Player of the Year' award.

At the end of the season, both Sexton and Tommy Cavanagh were given new three-year contracts. Sexton said: 'I am having one of the great experiences of my life, and I thoroughly enjoyed the battle last season, especially the last few thrilling weeks closing the gap excitingly on Liverpool. The players did wonderfully well, giving their all. They are the most unselfish team, on

There's only ONE......
U-NI-TED
THE OFFICIAL NEWSLETTER OF MANCHESTER UNITED SUPPORTERS CLUB
1968 1978
'Kop that'

LEFT: The newsletter of the Manchester United Supporters' Association celebrates Jimmy Greenhoff's headed winner in the 1979 FA Cup semi-final replay against Liverpool. The Final, which United lost 2-3 to Arsenal, had a memorable ending. United, trailing 0-2 with only four minutes left, pulled level with a shot from Gordon McQueen, and Sammy McIlroy's wonderful solo goal. McIlroy wrongfooted David O'Leary (opposite above), jinked into the box and beat goalkeeper Pat Jennings with a low drive (opposite below).

and off the field, I have ever managed or coached.'

Sexton may have been confident, but there were nagging problems under the surface. To win the League, a team needs consistent goalscorers, but nobody had scored more than 20 League goals in a season since George Best in 1967-68. Many people thought the player to break that record was Andy Ritchie. In 1978-79, he'd made 17 appearances and notched nine goals, including a hat-trick against Leeds United at Old Trafford. In the following season, Ritchie started just three games, and in one of these he scored a magnificent hat-trick against Tottenham — his 13th goal in 22 League games. Sexton, however, decided to sell this born goalscorer.

The decision to sell Andy Ritchie deeply perturbed Sir Matt Busby

The decision to transfer Ritchie, a product of the youth system, deeply perturbed Sir Matt Busby, who said: 'I had reservations about letting Andy Ritchie go — I also wasn't happy about Brian Greenhoff being allowed to leave for Leeds, but the decision was up to Dave Sexton. Dave put up a good case for letting the player have the last word. When an offer of close on £500,000 was made for Andy Ritchie, Dave felt he had to be fair to Ritchie in telling him about it and letting him decide what he wanted to do. So the decision was left that way and Ritchie said he wanted to *stay*.'

I was manager of Queen's Park Rangers at this time, and while driving to watch a midweek game, I heard on the radio that Ritchie — who'd been discovered by Norman Scholes while I was United's manager — was for sale. 'Bingo!' I said to myself, and I nearly crashed the car pulling over to get to a telephone. I rang the QPR Chairman, Jim Gregory, who was an admirer of Ritchie, and he gave me the immediate go-ahead to bid for him.

Garry Birtles, who cost £1.25 million, found the pressure was too much for him

When I rang Sexton the following morning, I had to say 'hello' about six times before he responded. Then I heard Sexton's familiar swallow. I told him I was ringing about Andy Ritchie and asked how much he would cost. When he said '£500,000', I said: 'I'll pay it!' There was another pregnant pause. 'Dave...Dave? Hello! Hello! Oh! hello, Dave', I said, 'I thought you'd dropped the 'phone.' When I told him that I'd fly up the next morning to see Ritchie and discuss terms, he said: 'Oh! That

Dave Sexton knew that Manchester United needed a player of vision and passing ability to strengthen the midfield, and he bought Ray Wilkins (opposite) from Chelsea to fill that role. Wilkins was an excellent professional, and it is a pity that he didn't give greater scope to his fine attacking game, as he scored only 10 goals in 193 appearances for United.

soon!' 'Well, *is* he for sale or isn't he?' I asked. Eventually, we fixed a meeting for the next morning. Early that following day, however, I received a message saying that the meeting was off and that Ritchie wouldn't be available to me.

Instead, Ritchie was sold to Brighton for £500,000. It was disappointing, because he was a certainty. I think Dave Sexton suddenly thought that Ritchie might be better than he realised and that if he sold Ritchie to me and he did really well, then it would reflect badly on his judgment. In the event, Ritchie did well for Brighton, then Leeds and, even after he turned 30, was still scoring regularly for Oldham Athletic in the 1990s.

Sexton's replacement for Ritchie cost £1,250,000. Garry Birtles, who was bought from Nottingham Forest, was not the right player for United. He missed his home in the Midlands (he would rush straight home after a game) and he didn't have a burning ambition to succeed — he told team-mates that on the whole he'd rather be laying carpets (his old trade) than playing football, and the pressure was too much for him.

It was one of the most depressing — and boring — seasons ever for United fans

In his first 25 League appearances for United, he failed to score a single goal. The fans were very patient with him, but there was an oft-told joke in Manchester that if Garry had aimed 12 shots at John Lennon, he'd still be alive today. Birtles just couldn't handle the transformation to a club the size of United.

In December 1980, Sexton sold Jimmy Greenhoff to Crewe Alexandra. Martin Buchan said they really missed Greenhoff: 'Jimmy is not only a very accomplished player up front, he makes everyone else in the team play.' Sexton's behaviour had perplexed the United forward, and he told me about a time when he'd gone to see Sexton at his office. Sexton turned aside and gazed at the office wall, with his back to Jimmy. A heavy silence ensued, which was broken after about three minutes by Jimmy, who said: 'You're going to drop me boss, aren't you?' Sexton gulped and replied: 'Yes, but I don't know how to tell you.'

With Birtles pursuing a shoot-to-miss policy, and the team lacking cohesion, United were in deep trouble in Sexton's last season. They were knocked out of the UEFA Cup at the first hurdle by RTS Widzew Lodz, lost in the first round of the League Cup to Coventry and were knocked out of the FA Cup in the fourth round by Nottingham Forest.

It was one of the most depressing — and boring — seasons ever for Manchester United fans. The team drew 18 games in the League (11 at home) — and a fifth of all their games that year were scoreless draws. At one stage, between 7 February 1981, until their game against Aston Villa on 14 March, United went five consecutive League games without scoring — setting an ignoble club record. The fans gave their verdict by

voting with their feet — average home gates were down by nearly 7000. If Manchester United had been playing across the street from me that season, I would have drawn my curtains.

Sexton inherited a fabulous young side and dismantled it before he should have

At the end of Sexton's last season, when Wilkins and McQueen returned after injury, United achieved some consistency and won their last seven games. Although United finished strongly, the writing was on the wall for Sexton, and Louis Edwards's death had deprived him of an important supporter in the Boardroom. At the end of the season, Martin Edwards announced that the club was terminating Sexton's contract.

When Dave Sexton first arrived at Old Trafford, Tommy Cavanagh had said to him: 'Dave, you've won the pools! All the players here are handpicked.' Sexton had inherited a fabulous young team that was on the brink of great things, and he dismantled it long before he should have done so. And the players Sexton bought as replacements — such as Garry Birtles, Nikola Jovanovic and Mickey Thomas — weren't great successes. Furthermore, in four years of transfer dealings, Sexton made a loss of £1,897,000, and the way the team played — let alone their lack of success — justified a change. The club realised that Sexton would never be able to produce the kind of football that was expected of Manchester United, and that they would be lumbered with dull, unimaginative football.

Dave could not have had a better 'number two' in Tommy Cavanagh

One of my last moves as manager was to set up, through Billy Behan in Dublin, the signing of Kevin Moran. After joining Sporting Gijon of Spain, in 1989, Moran said of his time under Sexton: 'I felt sorry for Dave Sexton. I think if he'd had a different second-in-command he could have done a much better job. Tommy Cavanagh came from the Docherty era and there was a fierce clash of personalities and I thought Dave, sometimes, wasn't strong enough to tell him to go take a jump and say: "This is the way we're doing things!". Had he done that, I think things would have worked out a whole lot better. But the thing about Sexton was that he was as straight and honest with the players as you could get. He was a really nice man.'

I don't agree with Kevin. Dave could not have had a better 'number two', and Sexton actually *appointed* Cav as his assistant. Tommy is a very strong character, but

LEFT: Andy Ritchie, a product of United's youth system, had a superb instinct for goal. He netted 13 times in 22 games for United, but was sold by Dave Sexton in 1979. He went on to score regularly for Brighton, Leeds and Oldham.

Sexton should have been strong enough, if Cav overstepped his authority, to put him in his place. What is closer to the mark, I suspect, is that Cav would make decisions when Dave wouldn't, and people began to believe that Cav was running the team. Even so, Tommy wouldn't have wanted Sexton to flop, because the success of Manchester United was his sole aim.

Dave Sexton is a nice man, but some United players liked him because he was soft and easy-going. Tommy Cavanagh told me that there were times when he would have to drag players away from watching the horse-racing on television just 15 minutes before an important game was due to kick off. Lou Macari said of his manager: 'Sexton's harmless enough. In fact, he's so harmless I can't imagine anyone ever falling out with him.' Even Steve Coppell, who liked and respected Sexton, stated that: 'Dave Sexton was not the right manager for Manchester United.'

Sadly, there was no glory during Dave Sexton's four-year reign

After the FA Cup semi-final win against Liverpool in April 1979, which was the highpoint of Sexton's time at United, he said: 'When you weigh it up, what you are fighting for all the time is to leave a photograph up on the club wall saying: "Cup winners nineteen-so-and-so or League Champions such-and-such-a-year", and that's *all* it amounts to really, isn't it? That's what everybody tries to do, to leave their mark.'

Sadly, there was no glory during Sexton's four-year reign at Old Trafford, and the only trophy Manchester United won was the *Daily Mail* Fair Play League. Sexton is a man of great tactical expertise, but his attempt to impose a playing pattern that was alien to Manchester United was doomed from the start. Sexton's decision to sell extremely talented, entertaining players in favour of ones who could carry out his structured, tactical plans, produced a team which was highly efficient in defence, but which lacked flair and attacking style. United fans simply don't want to watch their team play in a rigid tactical formation. Sexton later went back into coaching, for the Football Association. His epitaph at Manchester United, however, would damn him for transforming a successful and entertaining side into one which failed to win a single important trophy and was painfully boring to watch.

RIGHT: Garry Birtles keeps his eye on the ball. Birtles had looked a useful player at Nottingham Forest, where he had scored 32 goals in 86 games, but when he moved to United, who signed him for £1.25 million, he couldn't cope with the pressure. He went 25 League games without scoring. Jokes about his shoot-to-miss policy were common currency among Manchester United's fans, who were remarkably patient with him. Birtles, who scored 12 times in 64 appearances, was eventually sold back to Nottingham Forest, in 1982, for £1 million less than United had originally paid.

WALKING DOWN THE WARWICK ROAD

Manchester United supporters are the most loyal and passionate in the world, and year after year the club is the best-supported in the Football League. United's fans have thrilled to some of the greatest players in the history of the game, who have performed on a superb stage — Old Trafford — which Bobby Charlton so aptly described as 'the theatre of dreams'.

Manchester United are the best-supported club in Great Britain. The magic of past United teams, and the deep emotions aroused by the Munich tragedy and Sir Matt Busby's European Cup triumph of 1968, earned the club a unique position of honour in world football, which they have never lost.

Since their FA Cup win in 1963, United's average home attendance, in every season, has never fallen below 38,000. There are more than 70 branches of the supporters' association in Great Britain — stretching from Falmouth to Glasgow — 19 in Ireland, and foreign branches in Australia, Cyprus, Germany, Malta and Norway. In the 1990-91 season, more than a million spectators passed through the 93 turnstiles at Old Trafford — into the stadium Bobby Charlton so aptly described as 'the theatre of dreams'.

I've often described Old Trafford as 'the Cathedral'.

I've played in the Bernabeu Stadium in Madrid, the Nou Camp Stadium in Barcelona and the Maracana Stadium in Rio de Janeiro, and none of them can match the thrill and emotion of walking out to a packed Old Trafford.

Old Trafford is still one of the cheapest grounds to get into in the First Division

As manager, there were numerous occasions when, on a Sunday morning (particularly if there were some players reporting in for treatment), Tommy Cavanagh and I would meet at Old Trafford at about 10 in the morning to discuss team matters. We would always stroll out on to the pitch to carry on our conversation, and I can honestly say that it's the only ground in the world where, at that time, the place is buzzing. The stadium is alive, even when there's hardly a soul inside. Sometimes, Cav and I would stand there in silence on a sunny morning, and it's as if you can hear '*bzzzz*'. The electricity is unbelievable, and when you have 50,000 passionate fans inside the atmosphere is just awesome.

Cav and I loved the place so much that we used to joke that if the club would build us apartments at the stadium, then we'd probably never go home. George Best summed up the views of generations of players when he described entering the stadium: 'When you go out on to the pitch, it's like switching on a radio and turning the volume up. One moment there is silence, the next you are swamped in an amphitheatre of noise. I can still recall the way the hairs on my neck stood up when I first went out. It was truly exhilarating.'

United played their first game at Old Trafford in February 1910 — the stadium was designed by architect Archibald Leitch — and since then it has undergone many changes. Its present form emerged in the mid-1960s, when the cantilever stand (built at a cost of £300,000), which now covers three-quarters of the ground, was erected. United had already foreseen the advantages of having the finest stadium in the Football League. During the building work, United constructed the first private boxes in Britain, and the new stand helped United win the right to host three games during the 1966 World Cup Finals (Old Trafford was chosen ahead of Maine Road). It sometimes used to irk our nearby rivals that we had such an impressive stadium, but whenever City's Chairman, Peter Swales, used to mention it, I would say to him: 'If you're not careful, I'll buy Maine Road and use it as our training ground!'

In those remarkable years in the mid-1960s, United became a cult team, with an enormous worldwide following. They possessed the three finest footballers in Britain in George Best, Bobby Charlton and Denis Law,

Old Trafford, seen from the Old Trafford Paddock, before the 'derby' match against Manchester City in May 1991, which United won 1-0. The superb cantilever stand, opposite the Paddock, which covers three-quarters of the stadium, will be extended to cover the Stretford End (far left), at a cost of more than £12 million. When Old Trafford is full, United's wonderful supporters create one of the most pulsating atmospheres to be found in any ground in the world.

On 2 April 1977, United played Norwich City at Carrow Road, and there was a lot of crowd trouble. I had my suspicions about how pre-meditated the violence was, because there were far more pressmen at the game than the occasion warranted. ABOVE: Here I'm telling a young United fan to get back on to the terraces and watch the game in peace.

and people clamoured to see this terrific trio in action: the average home attendance at Old Trafford in 1966-67 was 53,984. A year later, the figure had soared to 57,759 — setting a new League record.

The present stadium has an even more impressive grandeur, and the modernisation of the stadium has meant that the capacity at Old Trafford, which was once over 60,000, has fallen to around 48,600. The capacity will be reduced even further — to take account of the safety recommendations of *The Taylor Report* on the Hillsborough disaster of 1989. Further developments are planned to the stadium. In the summer of 1990, the United Road Paddock was rebuilt to take 3700 plastic moulded seats, and the development of the North Stand Lower brought the number of seats to around 70 per cent of the capacity. In the 1991-92 season, as Manchester United move towards an all-seater stadium, the cantilever roofing will be extended to cover the Stretford End at a cost of more than £12 million, although the Football Trust is expected to provide around 10 per cent of the funding.

Match days at United are a big business. The club employs 150 groundstaff when there is a home game, and the 23 snack bars around the ground sell more

than 8000 hot drinks and 8000 pints of beer and lager on a match day. The club is keen to tap the corporate market, and there are 95 five-seater executive boxes, and eight eight-seater boxes. However, despite the grandeur of the setting, Old Trafford is still one of the cheapest grounds to get into in the First Division.

'The fans can even accept us losing, provided we go down fighting'

Old Trafford may be the most fantastic temple of worship in British football, but it is the followers, Manchester United's superb fans, who are the lifeblood of the club. Without the fans you haven't got a club — and I always enjoy meeting United supporters. During Matt Busby's years in charge, of course, those fans were treated to some of the most exciting and accomplished football ever seen in Britain, and the folklore of the great United players of years past lives on with the young fans today. That is why, nearly 25 years after they won their last League Championship, they are still supporting United in such vast numbers.

However, this heritage of great players has made it hard for successors to the red shirts to live up to the fans' expectations. United fans often turn on a manager who they feel isn't giving them what is required of a United team. The stadium was dubbed Cold Trafford under Sexton, because of the lacklustre approach of some of his teams, yet when his teams *did* really go for it, United's fans responded. Some of the players were astonished to see so many fans turn out to greet them after they had lost the 1979 FA Cup Final to Arsenal. As Sammy McIlroy recalled: 'It was even better than the reception we got in 1977, and it made me realise what United mean to so many people. They can even accept us losing, provided we go down fighting and in style.'

As employers, Manchester United are hiring players to entertain the fans, and if those players aren't doing that, then the paying supporters are being robbed — because they are not getting value for money. As United's manager, I would never allow that from the players. One of the reasons that I still get a good reception from fans at Old Trafford is because the teams I selected were great to watch — successful with it and sporting. Ron Atkinson's devotion to stylish play won him support, and although it has taken Alex Ferguson four years to win over the fans, his acceptance that United should play attacking football has won over most of his critics.

The fans are fiercely proud of United's excellent record against Liverpool

Alex Ferguson did come in for a lot of stick in his first four years, and United fans can be quite vocal about their complaints. In the late 1980s, United supporters found a new channel for their opinions in the burgeoning football fanzine movement. The first United fanzine, *Red News*, started in August 1987, and it has been followed by four others, including *Red Issue*, which has a large readership and is highly controversial. This approach has not found favour with the club, although, ironically, many of the players the fanzines have criticised — such as Viv Anderson, Colin Gibson and Jim Leighton — were subsequently released by the club.

In Matt's time, United fans were always especially pleased when the club beat Manchester City, and there was a keen, yet friendly rivalry, as both teams challenged for honours. Now that United's neighbours are far less successful — City were relegated to Division Two twice in the 1980s, and their League Cup success in 1976 is the only trophy they have won in more than 20 years — Liverpool have emerged as the chief enemy. Sadly, the rivalry between the fans of these two clubs is anything but friendly, and the animosity between Manchester and Merseyside has certainly touched the players of the two clubs — and the managers. The events of 9 February 1986, when Ron Atkinson and his players were attacked by bricks and aerosol as they were entering Anfield, did nothing to improve the image of Liverpool fans at Old Trafford.

Although United fans resent the success that Liverpool have enjoyed, they are fiercely proud of United's excellent record against Liverpool over the past decade, and matches between the two clubs are the most eagerly anticipated fixtures in the season. Liverpool's Ray Houghton summed up his team-mates' dread of visiting Old Trafford, when he described what it was like to enter the stadium before United's 3-1 victory on 1 January 1989: 'The rivalry between the fans for this game is far fiercer and far more intimidating than anything else we experience. There is real hate in the air when we visit Old Trafford.'

'Running at Old Trafford is like running on a beach,' said Gordon Strachan

During the past 25 years, there have been a number of occasions when United fans have tarnished the good name of the club. It was particularly bad in the late 1960s and the early 1970s, and because United's travelling support was so large, the club attracted a bigger section of moronic troublemakers. Thankfully, however, the hooligan element has largely dissipated — and United's fans conducted themselves splendidly on their trips to France, Poland and Holland in 1991.

One of the biggest talking points for United fans in the past decade has been the state of the pitch at Old Trafford. In 1982, an attempt was made to change United's playing surface when undersoil heating was installed. In 1985, this system, which hadn't been perfect, was ripped out and United invested £200,000 in a gas-heated water system. A new drainage system was also put in. By the time Alex Ferguson arrived, the pitch was again in a bad shape and was nicknamed 'the cabbage patch' by United's players. Ferguson said that the pitch was 'terrible', adding that he didn't know how class players were expected to show their best on it. The large quantity of sand on the pitch, he complained, was having a harmful effect on his players' fitness. Further tinkering did not relieve the problem. When United beat West Ham on 26 March 1988, for example, Gordon Strachan scored a dazzling goal. After the game, however, he said: 'I had to score with a long lob because I'd already ran far enough on our pitch. Running at Old Trafford is like running on a beach.'

'The pitch is awful. The surface actually moves under your feet'

Although a new surface was laid for the 1990s, it has run into even deeper problems. The mishaps with the undersoil heating systems have been compounded by the effects of the redevelopment at the stadium. Now that Old Trafford is completely covered on all sides, the air flow to the soil is poor, and this ventilation problem, combined with the strong acid content deep in the soil, has produced a pitch fit only for mud wrestling. When Everton beat United on the quagmire at Old Trafford in February 1991, Everton's manager Howard Kendall said after the game: 'The pitch is awful. The level of concentration you need to control the ball is top-notch. The surface actually moves under your feet.' I've seen it a damn sight better, but I've seen it worse — and during the 1960s, George Best sometimes played on surfaces that were ankle deep in mud. Alex Ferguson even joked after the game against Luton in March 1991 that such was the state of the pitch that the Football League had instructed the club that, like Luton, United must revert to playing on grass for the 1991-92 season. United's pitch, which, at 116 x 76 yards, is one of the biggest in the League, was once one of the most popular among visiting players; with the money available at United, there is no excuse for not getting it put right.

Unfortunately, commercial opportunism has been put ahead of the desire to have a great playing surface. If you are seriously pursuing the League Championship as your absolute goal, then nothing should be allowed to override that aim. At United, however, the pitch has been hired out for Rugby games (six matches were played on the pitch in 1990), and repair work was delayed in June 1991, because Old Trafford had been hired out as a venue for a concert by Rod Stewart!

However, United's lack of Championship success hasn't dampened the enthusiasm of United's fans, who

United's fans are especially enthusiastic about players who have come up from within the club's youth system. Here, homegrown Mark Robins, who joined the club as an apprentice in July 1986, is carried off on the shoulders of joyous fans after he had scored the winning goal in United's 2-1 win in the 1990 FA Cup semi-final replay against Oldham.

have always had their favourites. During the 1960s, Denis Law was 'the King' for Stretford Enders, and during my time at the club, the supporters really loved Big Jim Holton, because he epitomised the club. They admired Holton's commitment and the way he responded to them — when they shouted his name he would give them a heartfelt clenched-fist salute. They loved Martin Buchan for his quiet efficiency, and they relished Gordon Hill for his cockiness and his devil-may-care approach. There were times when Gordon would try outrageous things and then end up on his backside, but the fans made excuses for him.

Hughes, Ince and Sharpe are as popular as Coppell, Hill and Holton ever were

There were very few players 0the Old Trafford crowd didn't take to, but they didn't really accept Tommy Jackson or Colin Waldron, whereas homegrown David McCreery, whom they had nicknamed 'Roadrunner', because he would always charge up and down the touchline when he was substitute, was a firm favourite. Football fans have their own opinions and you can have trouble as a manager because they don't take it too well sometimes if you sell their favourite player. The supporters didn't like it when I sold Ted MacDougall, or

when I gave Denis Law a free transfer, just as they resented Alex's decision to sell Norman Whiteside and Paul McGrath, but, in the end, a manager is paid to do his best for a club and may have to take hard decisions.

Some players have been able to win over the fans after getting off to a bad start — Joe Jordan and Gordon McQueen did so under Dave Sexton — and some players, such as Ralph Milne, Colin Gibson and Jim Leighton (and Danny Wallace and Neil Webb to a certain extent) have always been treated coolly. In Alex Ferguson's team in 1990-91, Steve Bruce, Michael Phelan and Clayton 'Sunbed' Blackmore earned the affection of the supporters after initial qualms, while Hughes, Ince, Pallister and Sharpe are as revered and popular as Coppell, Hill and Holton ever were.

The finest sight in football is a packed Old Trafford celebrating a great goal

Manchester United fans are the best in the world, and you can go anywhere in the world and bump into them. When I was manager of Queen's Park Rangers, for the second time, I signed Gordon Hill and David McCreery. During the summer break in the 1980-81 recess, we went on a pre-season tour of Nigeria, where we played the national team. We also went up to Kanya, in the mountains, for one game, travelling in a dilapidated, windowless bus. We arrived at the ground at about 3 o' clock, and there were people on the roofs of the shacks, and watching from vantage points in nearby

Manchester United's travelling support for the European Cup Winners' Cup Final in Rotterdam (above, banners adorn the Feyenoord Stadium) were a magnificent credit to the club and to the country. Merrily singing *Always Look On The Bright Side Of Life* and *Glory, Glory Man United*, the supporters celebrated United's first European triumph for 23 years — and their first victory in a Final on foreign soil.

trees. As we got off the bus, three local boys approached and they were completely starkers. The only thing they were wearing was a red-and-black United scarf each, and they started to chant: 'Oh Tommy Tommy, Tommy Tommy Tommy Tommy Docherty!' I thought: how the hell do they know me? Then they shouted: 'Hiyah, Gordy!' and 'Chickadee McCreery!' We killed ourselves laughing. It was just remarkable. There must have been 25,000 in the ground and about 5000 outside. Then, suddenly, the police emerged and started cracking their whips and everyone fled. All Hill, McCreery and I could see when the dust settled was the three United scarfs disappearing into the horizon.

Now, whenever I go to see United play — and I cover them regularly as a commentator for Radio Piccadilly in Manchester — the supporters are always very nice to me. United's supporters know that I'm still very interested in what's going on at the club, and they know I want to see United do well. They also know and respect my honesty, and realise that when I'm being critical it's because I like to see the team doing well. For me, there is no finer sight in football than a packed Old Trafford celebrating a great goal.

ATKINSON'S DREAM TEAM

After Dave Sexton's dismissal in 1981, United appointed Ron Atkinson, and his flamboyant approach infused the club. He spent lavishly to bring skilful, entertaining players to United. In his five years at the club, United won the FA Cup twice, yet a coalition of enemies was to bring him down in the end.

Dave Sexton's sacking triggered an increasingly desperate search to find a new manager for United. Ipswich's Bobby Robson and Aston Villa's Ron Saunders turned down the job, and United also tried for Southampton's Lawrie McMenemy. In an interview for this book, McMenemy explained why he never took over at Old Trafford:

'When Dave Sexton was sacked, I was on tour with Southampton in Kuala Lumpur, and I hadn't heard the news. As we waited for our baggage at the airport, a local reporter came up to me and said in pigeon English: "You manager Manchester United!" I thought they'd sent a novice, so I just replied: "No, manager Southampton". When I reached the hotel, however, I was telephoned by a journalist in Manchester, who said: "Dave Sexton's gone, and you're tipped for the job." Press speculation was intense, but when I contacted my Chairman, Alan Woodford, he said: "There's nothing to the stories, just enjoy the tour." However, Martin Edwards *had* made an official approach for me, which the Southampton Board had turned down. I was annoyed that I hadn't been consulted, but Woodford,

Ron Atkinson (far left) brought his own backroom team with him to United, including Mick Brown (centre), who'd been with him at West Bromwich Albion. The third member of the bench, kit manager Norman Davies, has been at United for nearly 20 years, and survived to serve under Alex Ferguson.

who was a solicitor, said that the Southampton Board could hold me to my contract.

'By the time I arrived home, they'd killed off United's interest. Things would probably have turned out differently if I'd been in England. Afterwards, some people suggested that the job had overawed me, but in truth I would have relished it, especially since, as I later learned, that Matt Busby was in favour of me going there. It was a matter of unfortunate timing, really.'

The fourth choice for the job was West Bromwich Albion's ebullient boss Ron Atkinson — who was dubbed 'the tank' in his playing days — and he readily accepted the challenge. He knew that Sexton's team needed major surgery and he said that the seven successive wins at the end of the previous season did not mask a team which was 'coming apart at the seams'.

'I have a dream team in my head. I don't know if I'll be able to get it together'

On 9 June 1981, at a press conference to announce his three-year contract, Atkinson distanced himself from Sexton: 'Manchester United and Ron Atkinson were made for each other,' he exclaimed. 'I will not be just United's manager, I will be an ardent fan. If the team bores me, it will be boring our supporters, who hero-worship the players. I will not allow these people to be betrayed.'

One of Atkinson's first priorities at the club was to get a car that suited his flamboyant image. When Martin Edwards told him that Dave Sexton had been given a Rover, Atkinson said: 'Mr Chairman, I have a dog called Charlie, but we're talking about motorcars, not dogs!' He finished up with a 'champagne-coloured' Mercedes.

Atkinson jettisoned Sexton's backroom team, and he claimed that he had been warned that under Sexton: 'Not all the staff had been pulling in the same direction'. Out went assistant manager Tommy Cavanagh, coach Harry Gregg, physiotherapist Laurie Brown, reserve-team trainer Jack Crompton and youth-team coach Syd Owen. Atkinson was right to have a massive clear out — it's common practice in management now — and there is an old saying that if people aren't working for you, then they are working against you. Ron Atkinson installed people he knew and trusted. When Mick Brown and Brian Whitehouse left West Brom to join Atkinson at Old Trafford, United had to pay West Brom £70,000 in compensation.

Atkinson's ambition was to buy, rather than build, a winning team. In July 1981, he told the *Daily Express*: 'I have a dream team in my head. I don't know if I will be able to get it together completely, but I intend to have a damned good try. If I can get all of the men I would like, then only one or two players from the existing team will remain. To my mind, this job is bigger and tougher than managing England.' Fortunately for Atkinson, Martin Edwards was willing to back his vision.

Atkinson had trouble assembling his dream team. He failed to sign Tottenham's Glenn Hoddle, and missed out on Brighton's Mark Lawrenson, who opted for Liverpool instead of United, and he was even linked with an attempt to get France's Michel Platini. However, Atkinson did start clearing out players. Mickey Thomas laid down his conditions for staying: 'I need more money. I just seem to spend more money than I earn,' he said, but he was on a lot of money as it was, and it was hardly a surprise that he was earmarked for a speedy exit. Another player soon on his way was Jimmy Nicholl. 'He'd never really impressed me at all,' Atkinson commented, a result, perhaps, of the way that Nicholl had been given a torrid time by West Brom's winger Willie Johnston in the clubs' recent encounters.

One of the real problem areas was the attack (United had scored 51 League goals in 1980-81, 21 fewer than Champions Aston Villa), and the leading scorer of the past two seasons, Joe Jordan, had already announced that he was leaving for AC Milan.

Atkinson toyed with the idea of bringing Nottingham Forest's Trevor Francis to United, but the move collapsed because Atkinson (rightly) judged that Francis was 'too injury prone' to justify the £1 million fee Brian Clough was demanding. Instead, Atkinson signed Frank Stapleton from Arsenal for a fee, decided by tribunal, of £900,000. Stapleton was a very good buy. He has always been a magnificent professional, and although his pace was starting to fade, his ability in the air, his skill at shielding the ball and experience at leading a forward line, were superb compensatory factors.

'Bryan Robson is one player who is not available at *any* price'

Atkinson's team started poorly — they failed to win in their opening five League games — and the first League win under Atkinson was memorable, because the scorer of the goal, in United's 1-0 victory over Swansea, was Garry Birtles. The goal was his first in 25 League appearances for United.

In October, United made their most important signing of the decade. After Atkinson had left the Hawthorns, West Brom's Chairman, Bert Millichip, said that Bryan Robson: 'Is one player who is not available at *any* price'. Ron, however, knew that Robson had not signed a new contract, and he was convinced of Robson's ability — 'Robson leads by example, he's a brilliant tackler and he then has the art and the vision to use the ball constructively once he has won it,' said Atkinson. When Atkinson asked Bill Shankly how much he should venture to secure Robson, Shanks told him: 'Every penny that it takes Ron, every penny!' Robson has been a glorious player for United. Bryan is a dynamic and dominating player, immensely hard to beat and occasionally downright hard. Robbo is good at going forward, and in his prime he would get through the work of two men.

On 3 October, Robson signed in front of 46,837 fans at Old Trafford, and then watched his new team-mates

hammer Wolves 5-0. In the end, United paid £2 million for Robson and Moses. At the time, I said: 'Half a million for Remi Moses? You could get the original Moses and the tablets for that price!', because I thought he had paid too much for Moses. However, Atkinson knew his worth better than anyone else, and Moses proved to be an extremely valuable player for United.

Most of Dave Sexton's former players welcomed the change in atmosphere at the club, and the new approach to training sessions. Atkinson's emphasis was on basic skills, particularly passing and crossing and five-a-side games, which Atkinson really enjoyed, became a key part of training. Liverpool have always relied on five-a-side games as part of their training — they teach the essentials of short passing and support work — and if players enjoy training then they improve. The trouble starts when they find training boring.

Atkinson admitted to having 'strong reservations' about certain players he inherited, but one of them, Arthur Albiston, proved Atkinson wrong, and two months into the season, Albiston scored the winner in a memorable 2-1 win at Anfield (under Atkinson, United lost only two out of 13 games against Liverpool, the best record of any of Matt Busby's successors).

Norman Whiteside was the youngest player to appear in the World Cup Finals

By November, United were top of Division One, but they failed to maintain their momentum in the League and finished in third place. Although it had been an unsuccessful year in the cup competitions, there were good omens for the future. United had signed Paul McGrath from Dublin-based club St. Patrick's Athletic for a bargain £25,000, and he was one of their best buys of the decade. McGrath had been repeatedly recommended to the club by Billy Behan in Dublin, and after about the seventh reminder — I was trying to buy him for Derby County — United finally signed him. I went to see him a week later playing for United's reserves, and even then it was obvious that he was a world-class player.

A month after signing McGrath, in April 1982, United signed Norman Whiteside, who made his League debut against Brighton at the age of 16. His stunning promise was confirmed at the end of the season, when he was selected for the Northern Ireland squad and became the youngest player ever to appear in the World Cup finals — breaking the 24-year record held by Pele.

As the 1982-83 season neared, there still seemed to be a problem with the midfield. Kevin Keegan was too expensive to sign, and Sammy McIlroy, who had been

In 1982, Ron Atkinson signed Peter Beardsley (right, with wife Sandra) from Vancouver Whitecaps, but he played only once for United. Two of Atkinson's best signings were Frank Stapleton (opposite top, going past Liverpool's Mark Lawrenson, who rejected United) and Bryan Robson (left), who is one of United's all-time greats.

sold to Stoke City for £350,000, said: 'It's a bit ironic, because I was the one player in the United dressing room plugging for Ron Atkinson when Dave Sexton was sacked.' In the event, Atkinson greatly strengthened the midfield when he bought Holland's Arnold Muhren from Ipswich Town, who was one of the finest foreign players to grace the Football League.

Atkinson's squad took the domestic cup competitions by storm

Ray Wilkins had been Sexton's key midfield player, but Atkinson believed Wilkins was not living up to his potential: 'I deliberately attempted to rile him by nicknaming him "the crab",' he said. I also criticised Wilkins, when I said: 'He can't run, he can't tackle and he can't head a ball. How can people call him a world-class player? The only time he goes forward is to toss the coin.' Wilkins always lacked the ability to win the ball, but once he had Moses and Robson with him in midfield he blossomed and he was able to show some of his brilliant tactical skills — he had the passing vision of Paddy Crerand — and Atkinson brought out the best in him.

After winning five of their opening seven League games, United's form in the League melted away and they never reproduced these successful performances regularly. However, Atkinson's forays into the transfer market — in his first season he'd spent £4.3 million on John Gidman, Frank Stapleton, Remi Moses, Bryan Robson and Paul McGrath — had helped amass a formidable squad, who took the domestic cup competitions by storm. Indeed, the squad was so strong, that Atkinson overlooked one of the best players in Britain.

In August 1982, Ron Atkinson had bought 21-year-old striker Peter Beardsley for £300,000 from Vancouver Whitecaps, but during a six-month stay at the club

Beardsley played in the first team for only 45 minutes, in a first-round Milk Cup match against Bournemouth. At the end of the season, Beardsley said: 'It's going to take a lot of hard work for me to get into the first team, but I am prepared to work and I have youth on my side.'

United weren't prepared to give Beardsley time — Martin Edwards had arranged a money-back guarantee with Vancouver Whitecaps, whereby the Canadian club would pay back the transfer fee — and the interest earned on the money — if Beardsley was rejected. I'd seen him play as an inside-left for Carlisle United, and I couldn't understand why, at the price Vancouver wanted, United didn't sign him. At the time, however, Mark Hughes and Norman Whiteside were coming through the ranks, and Beardsley was allowed to slip away.

'Alan Brazil is to goalscoring what Bryan Robson is to midfield play'

United's run in to the Milk Cup Final included a brilliant 4-0 win against Nottingham Forest, and a superb two-legged semi-final win over Arsenal. Unfortunately, Robson — who had emerged as United's captain and their dominant player in the absence of the injured Wilkins — himself sustained an injury and was missing for the Milk Cup Final against Liverpool, which United were unlucky to lose 1-2.

Atkinson, in an attempt to bolster the front line, tried to sign Alan Brazil. Atkinson said: 'Brazil is to goalscoring what Bryan Robson is to midfield play. I was completely and utterly convinced that he was the player I

must acquire for United: his skills looked made to measure for our set-up.' At that stage, however, Brazil went to Tottenham Hotspur and Atkinson later said: 'Missing out on signing Brazil was in all probability the biggest mistake I made at Manchester United in those first two years.' When Brazil did eventually arrive, his injury problems had taken a grip, and his impact was limited — he played just 41 games in two seasons, scoring 12 goals.

United knocked out Everton in the quarter-final of the FA Cup, and then disposed of Arsenal in a thrilling semi-final at Villa Park. Although Atkinson possessed a squad which had won through to two major Finals in a season, he continued his relentless hunt for new players. Before the FA Cup Final, United signed Laurie Cunningham on loan from Real Madrid, and pencilled him in to replace Coppell in the FA Cup Final against Brighton, but Cunningham declared himself unfit, and Atkinson selected Alan Davies in his place.

It never seemed likely that Brighton could stop United winning the FA Cup, and it seemed impossible after Ray Wilkins's brilliant goal had put United 2-1 ahead. After Brighton equalised, however, it was United who held on

ABOVE: In the dying seconds of the 1983 FA Cup Final, with the score at 2-2, Brighton's Gordon Smith was put through with just Gary Bailey to beat. Gordon McQueen looked on as Bailey made a fantastic save, earning United a replay, which they won 4-0. In that replay, Arnold Muhren, a member of the great Ajax side of the early 1970s, scored a penalty (right, raising the Cup). Muhren was an impeccable passer, and Martin Buchan said: 'Arnold is the only player in English football I would actually pay to see. He's a joy to watch.'

to avoid defeat; and only a brilliant last-minute save by Gary Bailey, from a Gordon Smith shot, prevented the Seagulls from taking the Cup. In the replay, United's class told and Atkinson's team walked the game 4-0. Ron had thus brought a trophy to Old Trafford for the first time since my 1977 FA Cup win, and his signings had proved their worth.

After the game, Atkinson moved to sign Celtic's Charlie Nicholas, but after their meeting Nicholas complained that: 'Atkinson talked more about himself than he did about Manchester United and me. Atkinson came on far too strong and by the time the meeting was half-way through I knew my dreams of playing for United had ended. Ron and I would not have got on.' In those early years at United, Ron was very confident — his ex-wife Margaret once said that: 'As far as Ron's concerned, he is God. There's nobody big enough to tell him what to do' — but as it happens things probably turned out for the best, because Nicholas wasn't very successful when he played in England.

Atkinson's success earned him a two-year extension to his contract, and he approached the future with confidence. The 1983-84 season started well, with a 2-0 victory over Liverpool in the Charity Shield, but United and England were dealt a severe blow a month later when Steve Coppell had to quit the game at the age of 28, because of a knee injury. Steve had been an outstanding player. He was unfailingly cool — an impeccable positional player and a consummate professional.

He was the linchpin of United's right-hand play for more than eight years — and they haven't ever replaced him.

United tried out a new player that season, but it ended unhappily for both player and club. United took Garth Crooks on loan from Tottenham for seven weeks, but Crooks, who was kept in the dark about his progress at the club, was summarily rejected. The 'final humiliation' was, said Crooks: 'When I went into my hotel on a Thursday night, and the hotel porter said he'd heard I was finished and would be checking out that evening. Yet I hadn't heard a word about it from Ron Atkinson.' Atkinson said: 'I wanted the Crooks of two years ago. I didn't get it. All I saw was a shadow, who couldn't live up to United's demanding standards. The future was in his hands, but missing most was the determination to succeed. It's as simple as that.'

United's win over Barcelona was one of the greatest nights ever at Old Trafford

United's Milk Cup campaign ended after a marathon battle with Oxford United, and their FA Cup defence ended in ignominious defeat at Bournemouth in the third round. The highlight of the season was the great run in the European Cup Winners' Cup, which was capped by a marvellous 3-0 win (overcoming a 0-2 deficit from the away leg) in the quarter-final against Diego Maradona's Barcelona. It was one of the great-

est nights ever seen at Old Trafford.

With 10 League matches left, United were ahead of Liverpool, but United claimed only 10 points out of the next 30 available and finished in fourth place — and lost in the semi-final of the European Cup Winners' Cup to Juventus. Atkinson said at the end of the season: 'We've squandered the greatest chance to date to establish ourselves as the top team in English soccer.'

Atkinson still appeared confident about the future, and when news of his affair and the break-up of his marriage hit the headlines, Martin Edwards immediately scotched any rumours that this would end Atkinson's career at Old Trafford. Atkinson had good reason to be confident about some of the new faces at the club, especially the young Welsh forward, Mark Hughes, whose 25 goals in the 1984-85 season was the best individual scoring performance at United for 13 years.

'Jesper Olsen will become the biggest playing sensation since George Best'

In that 1984-85 season, United's best efforts were, once again, reserved for cup matches. United were playing some of their best football for years and the team were given width by Jesper Olsen, the £200,000 signing from Ajax. Although Olsen didn't live up to his promise — Atkinson had said: 'Olsen will, I feel certain, become the biggest playing sensation at Old Trafford since George Best' — he was a stylish player and his jinking runs brought back memories of Gordon Hill. With Olsen and Gordon Strachan — a similarly shrewd buy from Aberdeen for £600,000 — United reached the quarter-final of the UEFA Cup, and avenged a Littlewoods Cup defeat by Everton some seven months later when they beat them in the FA Cup Final. That win, in an explosive game in which Kevin Moran was unjustly sent-off and Norman Whiteside scored a fantastic winning goal, made Atkinson the most successful manager since Busby.

The ban on English clubs going into Europe, imposed after the murderous riot by Liverpool fans at the 1985 European Cup Final, helped United concentrate more than ever on the League campaign, and in the 1985-86 season, Atkinson's final full season in charge, United got off to a dream start, winning their first 10 League games (they drew two and won 13 of their first 15 games and opened up a 10-point gap in the League).

Before their 11th match, at Luton, Matt Busby — who was celebrating 40 years at Old Trafford — said: 'It is all coming together again. You could say we're United again!' Bryan Robson said that their manager was a

Paul McGrath (left, during the 1985 FA Cup Final) — a bargain buy from Dublin club St. Patrick's Athletic — was superb for United; unfailingly cool, creative and a great last-ditch tackler. Mark Hughes said: 'Ron Atkinson called him "Dolly Daydream", because of his laid-back style, but when Paul flicked on the power, no one could live with him.'

changed man: 'It is good to see Ron has changed. When I first joined United, only a few months after Ron had got the job, he seemed different. I think he felt the strain. But he is his own man now, he is doing things his way and I think he is better for it. In fact, I think the whole club is benefitting.'

The day United sold Mark Hughes was the day the title went out of the window

United's defence — Mike Duxbury, Arthur Albiston, Paul McGrath and Graeme Hogg — was rock solid, and 'keeper Gary Bailey conceded just three goals in the first nine games. In that stunning start to the season, United had been winning with the same team, but a series of injuries broke up the team. Bryan Robson was plagued by injuries — including a dislocated shoulder — and he made only 21 appearances that season. One of the main forces behind their brilliant play was Mark Hughes, who had a glorious start to the season, scoring 10 goals in the first 15 games. In December 1985, he signed a new five-year contract, but on 11 January 1986, when United were playing at Oxford United's Manor Ground, news broke that Hughes would be a Barcelona player before the end of the season.

Finally, in March, the club confessed that a deal had been struck — and numerous stories were appearing that Hughes, in his own words, 'was reluctant to leave'. There was disbelief among United's fans that the club had made such a shortsighted move, but the Board were concerned about raising money in the wake of the ban, imposed after the Heysel disaster, on English clubs playing in Europe. Hughes, with his concentration floundering, had gone off the boil, and after that game against Oxford, he scored just one goal in 17 games.

Ron Atkinson (far left) with his second batch of signings, in 1984 (from left): Jesper Olsen, Alan Brazil and Gordon Strachan. This trio never really gelled, because Brazil wasn't the type of centre-forward who could thrive on the floated crosses that Strachan and Olsen specialised in.

The day Manchester United sold Mark Hughes was the day the Championship went out of the window. In the end, Liverpool took the title and United — who had been widely predicted to run away with the title — finished fourth, 12 points behind their Anfield rivals.

The Hughes affair undoubtedly sharpened the knives for Atkinson, because many people felt that he should have made a stand against the sale. There was also bitterness that the money the club had received from the sale of Hughes was not used for better effect.

There was a feeling that United were 'coming apart at the seams'

In March 1986, Atkinson bought Peter Davenport from Nottingham Forest for £570,000, and he was unsuccessful — it was as if they had bought Garry Birtles with a shave. His transfer was rivalled by the signing of little Terry Gibson. I think they would have been better off buying Ronnie Corbett, and he might have got more goals, as Gibson scored only once in 23 games.

Atkinson lasted only four months of the 1986-87 season, and they had been bad months. The club had been plagued by reports of ill-discipline — including seven players being fined for after-hours drinking on a pre-season tour of Holland — and there was a feeling that United were 'coming apart at the seams'. Certain players were drinking to excess — Arnold Muhren's autobiography *Alles Over Links*, published in 1987, refers to frequent heavy drinking bouts at lunchtime, from which players would 'stagger home' — and player-power seemed to be rearing its head again. Atkinson may not have been the best man to deal with these problems, as Bryan Robson said: 'Ron loves being with his players. He enjoys the camaraderie of the dressing room, and I wonder at times whether he is in danger of getting too close to us.' It's a difficult area for a manager; while you shouldn't be aloof, you have to be approachable without being one of the boys.

When United lost 1-4 at Southampton, Atkinson's time was deemed to be up

Atkinson's bravura image was not accepted by all the players, as Kevin Moran explained: 'Ron had his fail-

BELOW: United's players celebrate their 1-0 victory against Everton in the 1985 FA Cup Final (from left: Jesper Olsen, Gary Bailey, Kevin Moran and Norman 'Rambo' Whiteside). Whiteside's winner was his third goal in a Wembley final.

ings. For all of his big image, I thought he was a shy sort of person, who found it almost difficult at times to relate to people. Away from the dressing room, it could be difficult coming into a room and going up and having a conversation with him.'

These problems off the pitch were compounded by United's poor form on the field. United were fourth from bottom and had won only three of 13 League games that season. The final straw for the Old Trafford hierarchy came on 4 November 1986. When United were beaten 1-4 in the Littlewoods Cup at Southampton, Atkinson's time was deemed to be up.

The dissatisfied element within the Boardroom was quite vocal. In 1985, James Gulliver quit the Board claiming that he had grave 'misgivings' about Martin Edwards' ability to control Atkinson — in particular his spending policy: 'I think Martin Edwards has got some toughness, but he's just not able, for various reasons, to handle Ron Atkinson.' Gulliver added, in an interview with *Business Magazine*, that: 'I think Ron Atkinson's been a good buyer, but he's a man with no knowledge of the use of money. He's got a blinkered approach...he

needs controlling.' There were rumours that Bobby Charlton, a director since 1984, had been a vociferous critic of Atkinson, but he confined himself to saying that the sacking was: 'A horrible thing to have to do'.

After the defeat by Southampton, the Board moved speedily. Atkinson, however, said: 'I'd no indication it was going to happen until I got the call to see the Chairman. I was just getting ready for a nice five-a-side game.' Atkinson, who was summoned at 10.30 in the morning, said: 'I should have gone in the summer when my instincts told me to quit.' As Atkinson drove to see the Board, he managed a jocular aside to Mick Brown: 'I don't think we're going to get a rise, pal,' he said. They didn't leave empty-handed, though. Atkinson was paid £115,000 compensation, and Brown £45,000.

Atkinson's teams at United had style, and were attractive to watch

A combination of factors had led to Ron Atkinson's dismissal. Falling gates, poor results and anger at his transfer policy had combined to create a coalition of enemies. Although Atkinson appeared over-bearing and egotistical to some players, to others he inspired great loyalty, as Bryan Robson put it: 'He may not be the greatest manager in the game, but I haven't met a finer bloke. He is the tops for me, and not even the sad events of his sacking will change that.'

For many players, his greatest gift was his motivational powers. Steve Coppell described how: 'Ron always made talks interesting with his off-the-cuff chat, which helped put everyone in the right frame of mind. His main failing was that he was inflexible,' and Ray Wilkins said: 'Ron is an aggressive manager and that's how he wants his teams to play. Motivation is his key strength.'

Atkinson had a wholehearted approach to the job, and on the whole he was a good manager. He gave youngsters a chance and he encouraged attacking football. Chris Turner, who played under Atkinson at United, and kept goal for Atkinson's Sheffield Wednesday team when they beat United in the 1991 Rumbelows League Cup Final, said: 'The good thing about Ron is that you know one of his firmest beliefs is that players should go out and play entertaining football. He loves flair players, but he is also a knowledgeable manager, and his preparation for matches is very thorough.'

Atkinson was true to his philosophy at Old Trafford and he bought and encouraged flair players. His teams had style and were attractive to watch, and two FA Cup wins in five seasons is success by any standards. Dave Sexton's sacking came not a moment too soon, but Ron Atkinson should have been given more time.

Mark Hughes (right), an awesomely powerful player, was given his first-team debut by Ron Atkinson in 1983, when he was 19 years old. In 1985, 'Sparky' Hughes was the club's leading scorer, won an FA Cup winners' medal and was chosen as the PFA 'Young Player of the Year'.

FROM BABES TO FLEDGLINGS

In the 1950s, Old Trafford's youth system spawned the 'Busby Babes' — the most dynamic team of youngsters ever seen. In the three decades since, a host of great players — including George Best, Sammy McIlroy, Norman Whiteside and Mark Hughes — have come through United's juniors.

Manchester United's golden era of success was built on their youth system, and its chief architect, Matt Busby, had a simple, but wonderful, adage about young players which he always adhered to: 'If they are good enough, they are old enough,' he said. In 1967, Manchester City manager Joe Mercer said: 'Matt Busby

BELOW: Bobby Charlton in 1956. In that year, this famous 'Busby Babe' won an FA Youth Cup winners' medal, and made his League debut, against Charlton, scoring twice.

The winners of the 1964 FA Youth Cup. Left to right: (back row) Fitzpatrick, McBride, Farrar, Rimmer, Duff, Noble ; (front row) Anderson, Best, Sadler, Kinsey and Aston.

was one of the first managers in the game to realise the importance of a thriving youth policy. With conveyor belt precision, he has produced a host of stars who have admirably graced the flaming red shirts.'

United's youth policy was run by four of the sharpest men in British football. Busby was the key man, but he was ably supported by his assistant manager Jimmy Murphy and chief scout Louis Rocca — who wrote a letter to me in 1948, when I was serving with the British Army in Palestine, asking me to come for trials with Manchester United. The final member of this quartet of visionaries was scout Joe Armstrong — who was United's scouting secret agent for more than 20 years up to his retirement in August 1970 at the age of 76.

Bob Bishop sent a telegram to Old Trafford: 'I have found a genius!'

In October 1952, Manchester United — then reigning League Champions — were bottom of the First Division, and numerous players were past their best. At the club's annual general meeting that month, Busby said: 'Don't worry, we have £200,000 worth of talent in the youth and reserve teams.' This sparkling new crop of United youngsters — including Eddie Colman, Duncan Edwards, David Pegg and Jeff Whitefoot — won the Youth Cup five years in succession and they were nicknamed the 'Busby Babes'. Bill Foulkes, a first-team regular, said of this time: 'You couldn't step out of line or have a bad game. There were two others waiting to step into your shoes.' The Busby Babes were an integral part of the Championship winning side of 1955-56 (the

average age of the team was 22) and Roger Byrne, who captained United to the title, said: 'One of the secrets of Manchester United's success is that nearly all of us grew up together as boy footballers. We were knitted into a football family.'

Tragically, this superb football family was cut down in its prime by the Munich air crash of February 1958, and it is to Busby's eternal credit that he managed to rebuild a youth policy. By 1963, United again had a superb outfit — and a new young genius had been unearthed, a player who would have shone even among the glorious Babes.

One of United's best hunting grounds for young players has been Ireland, and Ireland provided United with its most skilful player. George Best was often told he was too small to make it as a professional, but United's scout in Belfast, Bob Bishop, was certain Best was a born star. As Best later recalled: 'By the time Bob Bishop came to look at me I had given up all hope of ever becoming a professional football player.' After seeing Best in action, Bishop, who ran Boyland (the top youth club for soccer in Ulster) immediately sent a telegram to Old Trafford: 'I have found a genius!' it said. For unearthing this genius, Bishop was paid £100.

Bishop was still working for United when I arrived in December 1972, and we called him the Pied Piper, because whenever he came to Old Trafford he always had about a dozen boys in tow. As well as Best, Bob found United Sammy McIlroy, David McCreery, Jimmy

Nicholl and Norman Whiteside. He knew the game inside out and he was a great judge of schoolboy talent. There are always plenty of people at a football club who can assess professional talent, but it takes a rare talent to be able to spot a 10-year-old kid and say for certain that he will be a great player. Bob was so devoted to United that he always carried with him the name and address of his handpicked successor — and that man, Eddie Coulter, succeeded Bob Bishop in June 1990, when the Pied Piper died at the age of 90.

George Best was an inspirational member of United's FA Youth Cup winning team of 1964 — the last in the club's history to win the trophy. Eight players from that team became first-team players — saving United a fortune in transfer fees, and bringing them players who possessed an in-bred desire to help United triumph. The team that Busby fielded against Liverpool at Old Trafford in December 1966 included only three players who had been bought — Alex Stepney, Pat Crerand and David Herd — proof that a title winning team can be built rather than bought.

Busby *did* sign players, but this huge pool of talented homegrown players allowed him the time and confidence to buy only the players he really wanted. As a result, his blend of buying and nurturing was superb, as Denis Law explained: 'Matt Busby had the perfect formula — to bring young players into a successful side, as, for instance, Liverpool do. Too many clubs bring youngsters in when the side is struggling and it is really hard for them to do well. Bobby Noble came into our side in 1966, and was immediately at home.'

If the 1950s was the golden age of the youth system at United, and the 1960s a triumphant sequel, then the 1970s and 1980s have been a rather flat encore. Sammy McIlroy, who joined United in September 1969 and made his debut against Manchester City — scoring in a 3-3 draw — in November 1971 at the age of 17, was the last of the Busby Babes. He was the one striking success of the youth policy in the latter 1960s. In the first years of the 1970s, United's youth policy went into a slump that mirrored the decline of the first team.

When I was appointed manager, the youth system was a pale shadow of its former glory. Jimmy Murphy, who had overseen the 'conveyor belt' of youth talent for more than 25 years, had been let go during Frank O'Farrell's reign, and Paddy Crerand had been put in charge of the youth team. On my first Saturday at the club, 23 December 1972, before the home game against Leeds United, Paddy took me to see the youth team play Oldham Athletic's youngsters. Our team included recent signings Jimmy Nicholl, Arthur Albiston and David McCreery, and this trio possessed great potential. At the time, however, there were about 40 professionals at the club, and they were blocking the progress of the youngsters. A clear-out of the senior players was vital to prevent the club's youth level from

stagnating. The sight of these youngsters was a cause for optimism, but the youth system had greatly deteriorated in the previous four years, and great talent had been allowed to escape from Old Trafford.

Bob Bishop's counterpart in Dublin was Billy Behan, who sent his first player to Old Trafford in 1937, and finally retired 50 years later at the age of 82. Along the way, he discovered Johnny Carey, Johnny Giles, Tony Dunne, Gerry Daly, Mick Martin, Ashley Grimes, Paddy Roche, Kevin Moran and Paul McGrath. To that illustrious list should have been added the three teenagers he sent over during Frank O'Farrell's reign. Incredibly, however, when Liam Brady, David O'Leary and Frank Stapleton came for trials at United's training ground, the Cliff, all three were rejected. United's loss was most certainly Arsenal's gain. United's Irish connection has played a major part in the success of the club — indeed, during the 1978-79 season, nine Irishmen, at various times, played in the first team.

A youth policy is like planting a batch of seeds — only a few will bear fruit

Finding young players is a vital task at a club the size of Manchester United, and when I arrived we weren't getting the best kids. Chief scout John Aston had been sacked along with O'Farrell, so I appointed Norman Scholes as chief scout, and Gordon Clayton — a former youth-team goalkeeper — as his assistant, as well as recalling Jimmy Murphy to the scouting staff.

Norman Scholes, who had worked part-time for the club for more than 20 years, was a sharp judge of talent and a good judge of character, and he managed to see about 3000 boys in action during a season. Scholes was a retired headmaster, had good contacts and knew how to go about getting boys without upsetting their schools, and he made sure that youth players attended night school. Under Scholes and Clayton, the place began to buzz again with talented youngsters.

I also brought back Johnny Carey, who had won an FA Cup winners' medal under Busby in 1948, to join the scouting staff, and I hired the former Brentford manager Frank Blunstone to run the youth team. Blunstone's work with the youth team soon paid handsome dividends, and he helped promising youngsters develop into first-team certainties. The first to come right through the ranks was 18-year-old Jimmy Nicholl, captain of the youth team, who made his debut against Southampton in April 1975. Under Blunstone, United won the Lancashire FA Youth Cup and, watched by Matt Busby, the Blue Star International Youth tournament in

Switzerland, 21 years to the day they'd first won it.

Running a youth policy is fraught with disappointment, because it's like planting a batch of seeds knowing that only a few will bear fruit. When I was manager, for example, I signed a youngster from Swansea called Jonathon Clarke. Scouts still talk about him as the best Welsh schoolboy player they have ever seen, and at 15 you would have staked your mortgage on his future as a top-class player. On 27 November 1976, he made his first-team debut at Old Trafford, as a substitute against West Ham United, but it was his only appearance. He didn't make the grade and his career fizzled out. There was a host of youngsters just like him.

In the years following my departure from United, a lot of good players continued to rise through the ranks. While I was there, Norman Whiteside had started to come over with Bob Bishop during school holidays, and he liked the spirit the backroom team had created: 'The great thing was the friendship and the family atmosphere at the club, and as a youngster it's the sort of atmosphere that makes you committed to a club.'

One of the best players to come through in the late 1970s was Andy Ritchie, whom we signed just ahead of Manchester City. Gordon Clayton said of Ritchie: 'We were as certain about Andy's future at the age of 14 as it is ever possible to be sure about a kid making the grade. I don't think he has disappointed anyone with his progress.' Unfortunately, Ritchie never found favour with Dave Sexton, and was sold before he had the chance to establish himself, but — and this happens frequently — it was the money United made from selling him that financed the signing of a big-name player.

Hughes, who signed for United at 15, is the best homegrown player since Best

After Sexton's sacking in 1981, the youth policy again went through some swings in fortune. During Ron Atkinson's reign some remarkably talented players came through the junior ranks and, to Ron's credit, he gave them their chance. The pick of them were Norman Whiteside, who physically was a grown man at 15, and Mark Hughes — who had been receiving Christmas cards from the club ever since he had turned 12.

United's youth coaches helped Hughes enormously. 'As a youth', said Hughes, 'games were passing me by'. Then Syd Owen, youth-team manager, moved him from midfield to striker, and Hughes scored three goals in his second game in his new role. Owen said: 'Mark found midfield too congested. He needed the scope to move across the width of the field. He had all the necessary qualities of a top-class forward: tenacity, mobility and control, not least the ability to screen the ball. You don't have to be big, but sometimes you need guidance.' Hughes, who signed as an apprentice at 15, is United's best homegrown player since George Best. It was a strike force of Hughes and Whiteside that took United to the Final of the FA Youth Cup in 1982 — their

first appearance for 18 years. Although the team lost that Final to Watford, the side included three other players — Clayton Blackmore, Graeme Hogg and Mark Dempsey — who would make it into the first team.

Although Atkinson did encourage young players, his policy as a whole lacked coherence and during his reign a number of great players slipped through United's net. Every club has suffered its share of mistakes in letting players go, but during Atkinson's time there were some spectacular gaffs. Leeds United's Gary McAllister Crystal Palace's John Pemberton, Southampton's Alan McLoughlin and Queen's Park Rangers's Roy Wegerle were rejected as trialists. These mistakes paled beside the decisions to release Peter Beardsley and to reject England and Aston Villa star David Platt, who had four years of close association with United.

Platt was a United fanatic — his Teddy Bear was called Nobby Stiles — and he so impressed United's scouts when he played for Chadderton United that he was given a full-time YTS traineeship. In 1984, aged 18, he signed professional forms with United. At that time, however, Alan Brazil, Mark Hughes, Frank Stapleton and Norman Whiteside were all jockeying for places in the first team and, said Platt: 'I was relying on injuries to other players to get me into the reserve team.' Ron Atkinson let him leave on a free transfer to Crewe, which Platt regarded as a positive move, as he put it: 'You need to have football taxing you. It was a step down clubwise, but it was a step up in the level of football. When I was at United I wasn't good enough to get into the first team. Crewe were offering League football, and I wasn't developing at United.'

When Alex Ferguson succeeded Ron Atkinson in November 1986, United's youth system was being compared unfavourably to the one at Maine Road. Manchester City's youth team — who were mainly local lads — had just won the FA Youth Cup, and many were progressing right through to the first team. Ferguson pledged to overhaul Manchester United's youth programme, and he said: 'The production of our own players is now at the core of this club's policy. One of the great things about having a number of homegrown youngsters in a team is that they can nearly always be relied on to have a fierce sense of loyalty towards the club and a strong sense of unity.'

In special need of renovation was United's scouting system. Losing out to Newcastle United in the hunt to sign talented Coleraine striker Michael O'Neill, was just one example of United's poor state: 'Newcastle moved faster than we did,' admitted Ferguson. 'Now there are schools of excellence all over the northeast and north-

west. The scouting system was flagging when I arrived. Local people had become apathetic because the club wasn't doing much about kids. They were expecting boys to appear from nowhere without doing the work to find them. We had four scouts covering Manchester, a city of 500,000 people. Now, at least people know we *are* looking.' By 1991, United had 12 local scouts.

In 1987, Ferguson appointed Les Kershaw — a former senior lecturer in chemistry at Manchester Polytechnic — as his new chief scout, but in a re-organisation in December 1990, he stepped down to work on a part-time basis for the club, and Brian Kidd was appointed as the new scouting supremo of Old Trafford. Kidd was given the titles of Youth Development Officer, and Director of the School of Excellence, and Nobby Stiles was made his assistant. Ferguson helped establish new centres of excellence for the club, including one in Ireland, and one in Durham, which is run by Bryan 'Pop' Robson, the former Sunderland striker.

The acid test of a policy is the quality and quantity of players who make it

Alex Ferguson obviously had the will to resurrect the youth policy, but the lower levels at United went through some difficult times in 1989, when United faced relegation from the Central League. Needing to win their last game, they packed the reserve team with nine first-team players and stayed up by winning 4-0 at Coventry City. That season, and in 1991, the League title went to George Graham's Arsenal, a club which possesses the finest youth set-up in Britain — a salutary reminder that United's glory days still rest in the past.

Despite these problems, Ferguson has made some progress, as Bobby Charlton, himself one of the greatest products of the Busby youth system, put it: 'Like Sir Matt, Alex has the ability to get through to the kids. Matt wasn't as active as Alex and never did his own coaching. Alex gets a lot more involved personally.' One of the best discoveries of Ferguson's reign has been Mark Robins, whose potential was immediately obvious: when United won the Lancashire League Division One in 1987-88, Robins scored 34 goals in 24 games.

The acid test of a youth policy, however, is the quantity and quality of players who make it through to the first team. For a spell at the start of 1989, a host of youngsters were brought into the first team to replace injured players. These talented youngsters were nicknamed 'Fergie's Fledglings', and it seemed, for a brief time, as if youth players were once again going to triumph for United. However, these fledglings — Lee Martin, Russell Beardsmore, David Wilson, Mark Robins, Deiniol Graham and Tony Gill — who had been called in to shore up the depleted first team were relegated to the juniors, and when the established stars returned United again floundered. Ferguson defended his decision: 'Young talent must be introduced slowly, in stages, not sucked dry prematurely by over-exposure.'

OPPOSITE: Norman Whiteside goes past Millwall's Terry Hurlock at the Den in April 1989. Whiteside, who was discovered by United's Belfast scout, Bob Bishop, was promoted to the first team at 16. His very physical style — David O'Leary once said: 'Whiteside came at me like the karate kid' — took its toll, and he suffered a series of injuries in his 20s that restricted his subsequent career with Everton.

In that 1988-89 season, Mark Robins again showed his readiness to play at the top level — he was the top scorer, with 22 goals in 29 games, for the Central League team and netted a further 7 goals in 12 matches in the Lancashire League. In the following season, Robins was Ferguson's saviour in the victorious 1990 FA Cup run — scoring the winner in the semi-final replay against Oldham — and there is no doubt that he has proved himself as a superb First Division player.

Another fledgling who has proved himself worthy of a first-team place is Russell Beardsmore, who made his debut in September 1988 at the age of 20. He has struggled in the years since then to command a regular place. Robins and Beardsmore are at the stage where they need First Division football — they are both excellent prospects, but they are not going to improve by playing in the reserves or sitting on the substitute's bench. Beardsmore was superb in the famous 3-1 victory against Liverpool at Old Trafford on 1 January 1989, but he needs a chance to realise his full potential. If youngsters don't get that chance then they become disillusioned and they go backwards, and that has happened to Beardsmore. If United had persevered with him — and United supporters love to see players come through the ranks — they would have saved the £1.2 million they spent on Danny Wallace. Personally, I would relish seeing United playing a 4-2-4

Alex Ferguson described Ryan Giggs (right, in action for the Lancashire League team in January 1991) as: 'The best prospect I've ever had as a manager'. Giggs, who scored on his full League debut against Manchester City in May 1991, was given a five-year contract on his 17th birthday, in 1990.

formation again, with Hughes and Robins in the middle and Sharpe and Beardsmore on the flanks.

Although Alex Ferguson hasn't given the youngsters enough of a chance in the first team — Giuliano Maiorana, who made his debut against Millwall on 14 January 1989 and was given a four-year contract, has appeared only five times for United in the subsequent 28 months; and David Wilson, one of the fledglings, was released on loan to Charlton in March 1991 — the youth policy at Old Trafford is in the best shape it's been in for more than 15 years. Unfortunately for Alex, his massive spending policy has obscured the work he's done at youth level, and he is known for players he has purchased rather than nurtured.

Success, however, is starting to come. In 1990 and

**BELOW: Wigan-born Russell Beardsmore, one of the 'Fergie Fledglings', wrongfoots the Nottingham Forest defence.
OPPOSITE BELOW: Mark Robins, who graduated from an FA School of Excellence. is about to shoot past Forest's Brian Laws in the 1990 FA Cup third-round tie at the City Ground.**

1991, United reached the semi-finals of the FA Youth Cup, and there are a host of young players who could well become international stars. Perhaps the most promising is 17-year-old Ryan Giggs, who made his League debut in March 1991. In the 1990-91 season, there were also debuts for Alex's own son Darren Ferguson, and Neil Whitworth. Also coming through are Brian Carey, Adrian Doherty and Paul McGuinness. However, Ferguson is mindful of his experiences at Aberdeen. Five teenagers were in his European Cup Winners' Cup winning team of 1983, and not one of them was playing regular first-team football in 1991. Alex is determined not to burn out his young stars.

If United are to win the Championship again, however, they will need a thriving youth policy from which they can draw players to supplement their costly signings, as Matt Busby explained: 'Big signings are sometimes invaluable, but for depth, for immediate replacement in emergency, only a piece that fits the pattern will do. The pieces that usually fit best are those you have carved yourself, to your own design. Unluckily, the production line from a nursery cannot be constant or consistent, because these are human, not inanimate pieces. There are boom years and there are lean years, but that does not mean that the search for youth can be given up. It must never be given up.' United's search for youth does, at last, appear to be on again, even if it is going hand-in-hand with a passion for writing large cheques.

THE EDWARDS' ERA

In 1965, a new era in United's history began when Louis Edwards was appointed as Chairman. In 1980, he was succeeded by his son Martin, who has negotiated to sell the club several times. In 1989, this resulted in one of the most traumatic episodes in the club's history.

Manchester United Football Club plc is a major business with a turnover of more than £10 million per year, a staff of more than 150 people and it employs some of the highest-paid sportsmen in Britain. The running of this mighty empire has, for the past 26 years, been in the hands of the Edwards family.

While Matt Busby built a brilliant football team, Louis Edwards — who joined the United Board on 7 February 1958, the day after the Munich tragedy, and became Chairman in June 1965 — supported by long-serving club secretary Les Olive (who was in the job for more than three decades), helped build Manchester United into a massive business concern. Louis Edwards, who was Chairman for 15 years, was a shrewd businessman and I always found him a tremendously likeable person. He wasn't a football fanatic, and he didn't pretend to be an expert, but he was very proud of being Chairman, and he loved sharing in the success of the team. Steve Coppell's tribute to 'Champagne Louis': 'A large, genial character, who loved Manchester United. He was the soul of the club. His infectious laughter could often be heard as you walked into the club' — was shared by most players.

However, Louis Edwards came in for a lot of adverse publicity — and in January 1980, a World In Action programme, entitled *The Man Who Bought United*, alleged that Edwards had used corrupt means to gain control of the club, and claimed that he had established a slush fund to bribe the parents of prospective schoolboy players. In response, Edwards said: 'I haven't got a guilty

Under Matt Busby and Chairman Louis Edwards (left, with a cigar in hand, as usual) Manchester United developed into one of the greatest clubs, with the finest teams, in the world. Busby and Edwards became friends in the 1950s, and in February 1958 Louis became a director of the club.

conscience in any way about the business. I am very proud of what I have done for Manchester United.' Louis died within a month of the screening of the programme, and many people who knew Louis believed that the thought of going into the witness box — the police had started investigating the allegations — worried him to death.

United's players are on a promised reward of £100,000 for winning the title

There is no doubting, however, the contribution he made to United, and he was especially proud of the way he had helped transform Old Trafford into a marvellous stadium. He had also overseen the growth of highly profitable ventures such as the building of the Grill Room and Executive Suite, and the formation of the Manchester United Development Association, which, through enterprises such as lottery tickets, had raised millions of pounds for redevelopment.

As a Chairman, he was ideal. He never interfered in the running of the team and he was generous to a fault about buying players. During my managerial stint, however, the Board were slow to see that in order to get the best players United would have to provide a competitive wage structure. We lost out on buying Peter Shilton, because they wouldn't sanction wages of £400 a week, and I sometimes felt that they believed it was such a privilege to work for United, it was as if to say: 'You're working for us and, by-the-way, we'll pay you as well.'

Now, with the shadow of agents looming ever larger, United players receive extremely good basic salaries — eight players earn more than £100,000 a year — and first-team players receive a crowd bonus, a win bonus, £100 per point and are given a company car. They are also on a promised reward of £100,000 each for winning the Championship, but whether these cheques will ever have to be signed is a moot point. United's players may also get huge signing-on fees — Brian McClair, for example, reputedly received £100,000. United's wage bill — and the club started the 1990-91 season with 41 professionals and 19 trainees — was over £3 million for 1990-91, the club's biggest single outgoing.

I would like to have seen Matt Busby succeed Louis Edwards as Chairman

When I was the manager at Old Trafford, Martin Edwards was a junior director, serving his apprenticeship with the reserves. He liked to hobnob with certain influential players, and I was always a little wary of him. He often gave an opinion on a player's ability, even when he didn't have a full grasp of the subject. I would actually have liked to have seen Matt Busby succeed Louis as Chairman. I think the club owed him that for the service he had given them. Martin's brother, Roger, joined the Board soon after Martin Edwards became

Chairman, but he resigned in February 1985, after serving for only four years as a director.

During the 11 years of his Chairmanship, Martin has been a supportive Chairman in terms of finance — nearly £25 million was spent on players between 1980 and 1991, and he was prepared to push United into the red to the tune of nearly £3 million in 1989.

In the 1980s, United devised numerous schemes to make money, some of which succeeded and some of which backfired. The attempt to run a Sunday market in the Old Trafford carpark, for example, was a dismal failure, as was United's tie-up with Glasgow Rangers, in February 1983, to run a competition called 'Spaceshot' — a sort of spot-the-ball contest — which lost United more than £70,000. United's venture into the world of basketball lost them more than £250,000 in two years, and in March 1988, United sold their basketball team, and the new owners changed its name from Manchester United to Manchester Eagles. United also had problems with the launch of their own newspaper, *Man U News*, in September 1987. In the first issue, Martin Edwards declared in a front-page editorial: 'Like some of the soap operas on TV, I hope this is the first of a series that will run and run.' Unfortunately, *Man U News* folded after only three issues.

Old Trafford has 103 executive boxes — more than any other ground in Britain

Despite these set-backs, the name of Manchester United is still a major attraction, and when the club is successful, the income from television rights — United earned nearly £3 million from ITV, BBC and BSkyB during the 1990-91 season, when they were featured in 'live' matches on television and satellite television on 15 different occasions — and ticket revenue boosts the club's earnings tremendously, and the crowds are still flowing in: more than a million people passed through the Old Trafford turnstiles in 1990-91.

The commercial department, headed by Danny McGregor — who was a striker, during the 1950s, for United's junior sides — is expanding rapidly, and the sponsorship deal with Sharp (first signed in 1981, it has been renewed four times and will continue at least until the end of the 1993-94 season) is reputedly worth more than a million pounds a year, although both United and Sharp withhold the exact fee. Sales of the *United Review* bring in more than £100,000 per year — and United is gearing itself more and more towards the earning potential from its executive customers: Old Trafford has 103 executive boxes, more than any other ground in Britain. A host of new marketing enterprises are also bringing lucrative returns.

The club has enjoyed great success with its video launches, and the Manchester United Club Line, a telephone information line, brings in substantial revenue (a rival, unofficial, 'United Club Call' also operates), the leisure-wear market has expanded enormously, and in

Martin Edwards (above) joined the United Board in 1970 and succeeded his father as Chairman 10 years later. He has overseen a great expansion in the club's financial ventures, although the club's own newspaper, *Man U News* (left, a copy of the first issue) folded after only three editions.

1988 the club began direct management of the Red Devils Souvenir Shop (previously owned by the Busby family and run by Matt's son Sandy). The club is also rightly proud of its own museum, the first purpose-built museum in British football, which was opened in May 1986 by Duncan Edwards's mother.

'United is a club where even the hangers-on have a pecking order!'

Another venture which has aroused great debate is United's membership scheme. To become a member in the 1991-92 season will cost £8 for an adult and £4 for a junior. In 1991, with 51,000 members, the club closed the list for the season. Membership entitles the holder to priority in ticket applications, free admission to Pontins League games, a free booklet and reductions in the souvenir shop and in entrance fees to the Manchester United Museum. Several sections of Old Trafford are now for members only.

United's expansion in the past 25 years into such a powerful and prestigious club, has attracted to the club people who want to be associated with, and have influence over, members of the Board. These are the group Tommy Cavanagh christened the 'junior board', and Louis Edwards, Cav and I would toast them, in jest, when we drank champagne. Alex Stepney once said: 'Manchester United is a club where even the hangers-on have a pecking order!' You have to play the politics game at United, and that's what I was referring to when I said: 'There's so much politics at United, Henry Kissinger wouldn't have lasted 48 hours at the club.'

Over the years, there have been several attempts to wrest control of United from the Edwards family. Louis Edwards would never have considered selling the club. When, in 1972, a group of businessmen from Wales, headed by John Thomson, made a takeover bid, Louis dismissed it out of hand: 'I just don't believe that this consortium even exists. This man Thomson talks about people behind him, but who are they? The whole thing is a standing joke at the club. I'm told there is a letter on the way inviting me to resign. Why should I? I read they even want to invite Frank O'Farrell back as manager. It's laughable.'

Robert Maxwell: 'The Man Who Wants To Be Mr United'

Martin Edwards, however, has negotiated to sell United a number of times. On 8 February 1984, Robert Maxwell, the Czechoslovakian proprietor of Mirror Group Newspapers, emerged as a prospective buyer, when he published an article in the *Daily Mirror* headlined: 'Robert Maxwell (Born Jan Ludwig Hoch): The Man Who Wants To Be Mr United.' Maxwell's bid for United — reported to be near £10 million — was, however, unsuccessful.

On Friday 19 August 1989, news broke of a new buyer. Michael Knighton had been negotiating secretly with Edwards for two months, and the deal they signed allowed Edwards to remain for three years as vice-chairman and chief executive. Announcing the deal, Edwards said: 'This has been a pressure job, and after 10 years I felt it was time for a change. I feel this club can go even further under Michael.' The deal was worth £30 million (a third for Edwards's shares, a third to buy other shares and the last £10 million pledged to go towards redeveloping the Stretford End). At this press conference, Knighton handed out a 14-page press release about himself. When asked about the source of his money, he said: 'You could say the secret is location, location, location.' During the next two months, that one question mark about the source of his money fuelled constant speculation.

On the next day, before the home game against Arsenal, Knighton again grabbed the headlines. Brian Marwood, who played for Arsenal that day, later described Knighton in the players' tunnel: 'He was like a kid of 16 about to take his 'O' levels. He was shaking with nerves, and the sweat was pouring off him. I wasn't impressed. I have always believed that the pitch is the preserve of the players. The directors belong upstairs.' Knighton then went out before the Stretford End and ostentatiously played with a football.

It is remarkable that Edwards and Knighton didn't just put the deal in the hands of brokers and let them conclude matters. The wheels were obviously in motion, as Knighton was using letterheaded paper and signing himself 'Chairman Elect'. As it was, 56 days of confusion ensued, during which time there were regular press reports about Michael Knighton's difficulties in concluding the deal.

'The speculation and the ugly rumours have been damaging to the club'

The club's embarrassment prompted them to cancel the launch of their new video, *United: The Inside Story*, because the final sequence showed a 'new era' beginning with Knighton's parade before the Stretford End. Bobby Charlton complained about the situation: 'I hate what has been going on. As a Board, we felt impotent. The headlines, the speculation and the ugly rumours have been damaging to the club. Perhaps Mr Edwards will admit he has made a mistake selling to the person he has done and in the manner in which he has sold it.'

The saga eventually ended on 11 October, when Edwards and Knighton finally tore up their contracts. However, Knighton was given the chance to buy the 1000 shares necessary to become a director. In a television interview, Paddy Crerand asked Edwards to explain why Knighton had been given a place on the Board: 'The fear was', admitted Edwards, 'that Michael Knighton would not tear up his contract unless he was offered a seat on the Board. We offered it.'

The sale was a shambles from the start — and made the club a laughing stock

A month after the deal collapsed, Edwards was severely criticised by shareholders at the club's Annual General Meeting, and on 19 December, United's President, Sir Matt Busby, expressed his concern to the *Manchester Evening News*: 'Recent events have demonstrated only too clearly the problems that can arise from private ownership when the time comes for the club to be sold. I agree with people who believe we would get more stability and a better guarantee for future well-being of Manchester United if it were to pass into the control of a number of responsible shareholders.'

While United's supporters are grateful that Martin Edwards has invested a lot of money to help build a successful team, and have no doubt that the club should be profitable, there is also a feeling that he has done too well personally. While Everton's Chairman, Philip Carter, and Liverpool's Noel White — and his predecessor John Smith — have overseen successful clubs, none of them rewarded themselves (as Edwards

does) with annual bonus awards, large dividend payments and a huge salary. Edwards, who confessed that his 'first love' is rugby, is unpopular with the fans, and if Knighton had gone about the deal in a different way, he might have become Chairman. The fans certainly wanted Edwards out, but the result was a shambles from start to finish — it cost Edwards over £650,000 in legal fees, and made the club a laughing stock.

United will need a lot of finance if they are to triumph in the 1990s

In the 18 months that followed the Knighton saga, there were a number of reports of takeover plans for United, including ones by ICI, and Rupert Murdoch. But in May 1991, the club was fundamentally restructured. A public company was created, under the Chairmanship of Sir Roland Smith, Chairman of British Aerospace, who has been an advisor to the Edwards family since the early 1970s. Martin Edwards, meanwhile, continues as Chairman of the football club, and drew a salary of £106,000 in 1991 as Chief Executive, on top of his personal share profits of more than £6 million.

With the tremendous success United enjoyed in 1990-91, and in particular the boost of the club winning its first European Final since the days of Matt Busby, Manchester United are as bankable an investment as they have been in their history. However, United will need a lot of finance if they are to triumph in the 1990s. The best players now cost at least a million pounds — and top-class players will be necessary if United are to succeed in the proposed Premier League — and the cost of making Old Trafford an all-seater stadium is likely to run to at least £12 million, but it's an expenditure that is absolutely critical if United are to possess a stadium to take them into the 21st century.

I think that now is the time for Martin Edwards to sell his controlling interest in the club and let new men take over Manchester United. The dream ticket would be directors Amer Midani, Nigel Burrows and Bobby Charlton. Midani — who joined the Board in February 1987 — could say to his father, one of the world's richest men: 'I want a Subbuteo game for Christmas!' and his dad could buy him Manchester United. The ideal choice for Chairman is Bobby Charlton — what better ambassador could a club have? Martin Edwards will never be a Chairman like his father if he lives to be a thousand years of age.

OPPOSITE: Michael Knighton displaying his ball skills in front of the Old Trafford crowd on 19 August 1989 — before the 4-1 victory against champions Arsenal — after announcing his decision to buy Manchester United. Although Knighton was in a position to conclude the purchase, the deal was cancelled at the last minute. Sir Matt Busby (right), who was knighted in the wake of United's 1968 European Cup triumph, was appointed President of the club in 1980, and was later made a life member of the Football League.

FERGUSON GOES FOR BROKE

Alex Ferguson's first four years as United's boss were dramatic. By 1990 — after he'd spent nearly £13 million on players — his position was under threat. Yet he weathered the storm, and was rewarded in May 1990 when United beat Crystal Palace 1-0 in the FA Cup Final replay.

When Manchester United sacked Ron Atkinson in November 1986, the Board had already earmarked Aberdeen's boss, Alex Ferguson, to replace him. During Ferguson's eight-year reign at Aberdeen, he led them to 10 major honours, including the European Cup Winners' Cup, in 1983, when they beat Real Madrid.

Ferguson had previously been a player with Queen's Park, Dunfermline Athletic, Ayr and Rangers, and had managed East Stirling and then St. Mirren — where he was sacked, the club said, 'for unpardonable swearing at a lady on the club's premises' — before taking over at Aberdeen in 1978. It was his achievements there, in breaking the Celtic/Rangers stranglehold on Scottish football, that earned him wide recognition — Arsenal, Aston Villa, Rangers, Tottenham and Wolves had all tried to lure him from Pittodrie before he joined United.

I knew Alex when he was at St. Mirren. He was a great motivator, passionate and autocratic — he once made four players sing nursery rhymes after they had misbehaved: 'If they act like children, I treat them like children,' he said, but he was a class manager and a good

BELOW: Alex Ferguson (left, with Archie Knox to his side) urges on United. Ferguson and Knox were a very successful managerial partnership for Aberdeen and Manchester United, but the duo split in May 1991, when Knox left to become Walter Smith's assistant at Glasgow Rangers.

choice to succeed Atkinson. Ferguson said: 'United are the only club I would have left Aberdeen to join. I recall the late Jock Stein once telling me that the biggest mistake he made was to turn down United, and I made sure that I wouldn't do the same.' Ferguson took his assistant, Archie Knox, with him to Old Trafford.

Ferguson said after taking over: 'It's unfortunate that almost 20 years have gone by since United last won the Championship, but for me that adds up to a great challenge. I won't be satisfied until the European Cup is back at Old Trafford.' His ambition was obvious, but I don't think Alex realised the scale of the task ahead — or of the pressure that is generated by the tremendous expectations of United fans.

At United, Alex Ferguson was re-united with Gordon Strachan, who'd played in that Cup Winners' Cup Final against Real Madrid in 1983, who described his boss as: 'The greatest tactician in the game today'. Strachan had also witnessed some of Ferguson's tantrums: 'Nobody escapes the wrath of Fergie,' said Strachan. 'His half-time crack-ups have really to be seen to be believed. Put together, they could be made into a best-selling video programme.' Mark Hughes later confirmed that: 'When Fergie has a verbal blast, it can be measured on the Richter scale.' Alex *is* a short-fused man, but it has probably done him good to have these outbursts. It gets the tension out of his system — and he has been under the sort of strain at Old Trafford that would be enough to send anyone round the bend. If Kenny Dalglish had found a way to release his tension, he might not have quit as Liverpool's boss in 1991.

Ferguson inherited a somewhat demoralised and slightly wayward squad from Ron Atkinson, but speculation that Ferguson immediately cracked down isn't accurate, as Kevin Moran explained: 'All the press jumped on the bandwagon categorising Ferguson as a strict disciplinarian and fitness fanatic. Within three months we were supposed to have been fitter than we had ever been in our lives — which was totally untrue. We did nothing extra in training and he never came in and laid down any new rigid, disciplinary structures that weren't in existence before.'

The team Ferguson inherited was struggling in the League, but he managed to pull them round and, in his seventh game in charge, he had the satisfaction of seeing them beat Liverpool 1-0 at Anfield. United went out of the FA Cup in the fourth round, at home to Coventry, and although they pulled out of danger and finished 11th in the League, their form was very poor, and Ferguson himself admitted in May 1987: 'You have to be something of a masochist to watch United away from home.'

Ferguson started the 1987-88 season with a positive approach. It was his first full season in charge, and he was beginning to shape the team to his own design. He sold Terry Gibson to Wimbledon, Frank Stapleton left for Ajax on a free transfer and he bought Celtic's leading striker, Brian McClair, for £850,000. McClair has proved a useful buy for Alex. Although he doesn't con-

tribute much to the team's passing movements, he runs well with the ball, can send over dangerous crosses and always gets in among the goals. In his first season, 'Choccy' McClair became the first player to score more than 20 League goals in a season since George Best had done so exactly 20 years before.

In August, he also bought Arsenal's Viv Anderson to replace John Sivebaek, who had joined St. Etienne for £227,000. United hadn't possessed a really tough-tackling, consistent right-back since Jimmy Nicholl. The position is a critical one, and I don't think that Anderson was a good, long-term solution. He sometimes looked impressive when going forward, but he was a liability at the back, because he was easy to turn and gave away numerous free kicks and penalties. In nearly four years at the club, he played only 54 times, and he left the club as a free transfer in January 1991 to join Ron Atkinson's Sheffield Wednesday.

Gordon Strachan went to the Kop and pretended to smoke a cigar

In that 1987-88 close season, United also tried to sign Glenn Hysen, but he opted for Fiorentina, who bettered United's financial package. Two years later, the same thing happened with Liverpool. I think United were doubly lucky, because Hysen hasn't been able to cope with the pace of First Division football, and the weaknesses in his aerial play have been badly exposed at numerous set pieces. Instead, in December 1987, United paid £850,000 for Norwich City's Steve Bruce. He's proved an excellent buy. He's great in the air, is totally dedicated to United and is one of the best competitors at the club; and in 1990-91, his 19 goals were a critical part of the team's success.

United started well in the League in August 1987, but their season didn't run completely smoothly. At Coventry, in September, Ferguson was booked for swearing at an official — and subsequently fined — and the behaviour of Whiteside and McGrath, who both put in transfer requests, was a worrying factor. Although United went out of the FA Cup in the fifth round at Arsenal, losing 1-2 (when, ironically, top scorer McClair missed a last-minute penalty), United battled in the League to keep pace with leaders Liverpool.

On 4 April 1988, United met their deadly rivals at Anfield, and the match was a classic. United, down to 10 men after Colin Gibson had been sent off, fought back from 1-3 down, and substitute Norman Whiteside scythed through the Liverpool midfield in the second half. When they were trailing 2-3, Strachan coolly beat Bruce Grobbelaar in a one-on-one situation and stroked the ball home to make it 3-3. Then, to the delight of United's fans, and the chagrin of the Merseysiders, he went to the Kop and pretended to smoke a cigar, cupping his ear in mockery at a barrage of abuse.

The animosity on the pitch overflowed into the back-room. After the game, there was a stormy bust-up

between Alex Ferguson and Kenny Dalglish. They had fallen out while Alex was in charge of the Scotland team in the summer of 1986 — and Alex is ex-Rangers, Kenny ex-Celtic, of course — and both were fired up by the game. I was waiting to go into Kenny's office for a chat when we passed Ferguson, who was doing a radio interview. Kenny, who was carrying his six-week-old baby, said: 'What's he saying?' Ferguson snapped back at him: 'You behave yourself! You'll get your turn in a minute.' 'I don't know why you're talking to him, you'd get more sense out of her,' said Dalglish, pointing to his baby. I said to them both: 'Well, with the accents you two have got, we'll probably understand her better than either of you!' It was all a storm in a teacup, really, but it shows the depth of feeling between the two clubs.

'There was a lot of speculation among players about who would be booted out'

Although United were beaten only five times in the League that season — the fewest amount of defeats in a season since 1909 — they finished second, nine points behind Liverpool. Ferguson said: 'We must build a side who can be as exceptional as Liverpool. This is the gap we must bridge. Some may be happy if we finish as runners-up, but the truth is that second in the League means second best. I expect more than that.' It was only their third runners-up position since winning the title in 1967, but it helped convince Ferguson that if United were to become Britain's top team, it would have to be with new players.

In that 1987-88 season, Chris Turner played 30 games, keeping nine clean sheets. Yet Turner, along with a number of other players, were not part of Alex Ferguson's long-term plans, as Turner said: 'I joined United in 1985, and when Alex took over a year or so later, there were a few players who were concerned that he'd make big changes. Because of his fantastic record at Aberdeen, great things were expected of him straight away. We knew he had players that he wanted to bring to Old Trafford, but hadn't been able to, and there was a lot of speculation among players about who was going to be booted out. What perplexed the players involved, was that the decisions were taken after we had done so well. United lost only five games that season and we won our last eight matches at home on the trot — *with* the players he was about to discard.'

Ferguson had wanted to make changes for some time, but he was slightly hamstrung by the fact that many of the existing players were on lengthy contracts. In 1988, however, many established players finally left

In July 1989, United signed Neil Webb (top left). In September, while playing for England, he tore his achilles tendon and was out for six months. Michael Phelan, signed from Norwich (left, shielding the ball from Oldham's Andy Ritchie), is, said Brian McClair, 'a players' player, reliable and always working hard for the team. If he makes a mistake, he never hides.'

the club. Arthur Albiston and Kevin Moran, two wonderful servants of the club, were granted free transfers. They were followed by a flood of departures: Graeme Hogg, in August, to Portsmouth; Chris Turner, in September, who left for Sheffield Wednesday; Peter Davenport, in October, to Middlesbrough; and Liam O'Brien, in November, to Newcastle United. In that same month, Jesper Olsen, who claimed Ferguson had made him a 'laughing stock' by leaving him on the bench, joined Bordeaux. United received £1.7 million for these five players — and it signalled Ferguson's desire to raise the quality level of United's squad.

Ferguson had started to complain that he wasn't receiving sufficient financial backing. At the time, Ferguson realised that Liverpool had invested wisely in excellent players — spending, in 1987, £4 million on a new forward line of John Aldridge, John Barnes and Peter Beardsley — and he was quite straightforward in his approach: If United wanted the glory days back, he said, then the Board would have to dig deep. To match Liverpool, United had to spend, he said, and the choice for Martin Edwards was simple: a very good team or balanced books. Yet Ferguson wasn't solely interested in buying a good squad. He was also working very hard to rebuild the youth system.

Gazza would have been tailor-made as a Manchester United star

One of his central concerns was the goalkeeping position. Gary Bailey had been forced to quit in 1987, and in July of that year, Ferguson tried to sign the Soviet international goalkeeper Rinat Daseyev from Moscow Spartak. Unfortunately, financial red tape prevented the deal from going ahead, and in his place Ferguson eventually signed, in the summer of 1988, his former goalkeeper, Aberdeen's Jim Leighton. There is a saying in football that it rarely works when you go back for former players, and this was definitely the case with poor Jim Leighton. Unlucky Jim was never popular with the fans, and every time he fumbled and flapped at the ball, the TV cameras were there to record his mishaps.

In 1988, United also tried to sign Newcastle's Paul Gascoigne (whom Bobby Charlton was lobbying for). Gazza had a meeting at Old Trafford, but after he stated his terms — reported to be a £100,000 signing-on fee, a basic salary of £125,000 per year; £5000 for every England cap he won; a £15,000 club car; a £200,000 house; and a substantial slice of the transfer fee if he left United — Edwards refused to meet his demands. Gascoigne was bought by Tottenham for £2 million and by 1991, he was rated at £8.5 million. The Board should have backed Ferguson's judgment, because Gazza would have been tailor-made as a United star.

In the event, Ferguson made an excellent signing when, for £1.6 million, he brought Mark Hughes back to Old Trafford. Hughes, who had been at Barcelona and then Bayern Munich, became the first United player in postwar years to leave and return to United. Hughes is one of the best strikers in the world, and his experiences in Spain and Germany, had taught him to channel his strength and power. Hughes had always been a master at receiving the ball, killing it, swivelling and pushing off in one movement, but he was starting to combine this personal awareness with a sharper sense of space and improved timing at getting into the box. His talent at scoring spectacular goals, especially volleys, makes him a readymade TV highlight, and since his return, Mark has been the linchpin of the team. His brilliant form has twice earned him selection (in 1989 and 1991) as the PFA 'Player of the Year'. Hughes, who was 24 when he returned, signed a five-year contract, and said: 'I want to stay at Manchester United for the rest of my career.'

The finest moments of a dismal season were provided by United's youngsters

In October, United signed Luton's 31-year-old Northern Ireland defender Mal Donaghy, for £750,000, on a four-year contract. Some people were puzzled at the decision to invest so much in Donaghy, but he has been a useful utility player, and because of his experience he has been the perfect defensive cover in important matches. A less impressive buy was Ralph Milne, signed from Bristol City for £175,000. Milne is simply not a player who will help you win the Championship. The fans didn't take to him, and I've seen milk turn quicker than Ralph Milne. He made only one appearance in the 1989-90 season (as a sub), and in 1990-91, he spent the season languishing in the 'A' team.

United started the 1988-89 season with high hopes, but they were once again dashed. In February, there was the sad news that both Nicky Wood (a talented youth player) and Remi Moses (whom Ferguson rated highly) would both have to retire prematurely. The finest moments of a dismal season were provided by United's youngsters, who were dubbed 'Fergie's Fledglings'. Russell Beardsmore (20), Tony Gill (20) Deiniol Graham (19) Lee Martin (20) Mark Robins (19) Lee Sharpe (17) and David Wilson (19), all made brilliant contributions when they came in for injured regulars. Bobby Charlton said: 'Most of these lads have been thrown right in because of injuries to senior players. They've done brilliantly for the club under a lot of pressure.' However, their period in the team was shortlived.

In March 1989, Ferguson signalled his determination to rebuild when he sold Gordon Strachan to Leeds United. Ferguson may have felt that Strachan, who was then 32, was past his best, but Gordon went on to have three fantastic years at Leeds United, and was selected as 'Footballer of the Year' by the Football Writers' Association in 1991. Many United fans were dismayed to see such a great playmaker leave the club, when the team was so bereft of subtlety and imagination — both qualities that Strachan had in abundance.

United stuttered and slipped that season, and were knocked out of the FA Cup quarter-final by Nottingham Forest: 'The season did not just slip away, it collapsed,' said Ferguson, and when United played Wimbledon at home in May, they were watched by only 23,000 fans. Ferguson got the message, as he explained: 'The other night against Wimbledon was a great lesson. If we don't perform, people these days will simply stay away — even from Manchester United.'

Ferguson was still having trouble with Whiteside and McGrath, who'd had a fifth knee operation, and Fergie admitted he wanted to get rid of: 'Old Trafford's super-star syndrome of swaggering, socialite free spirits.' In July 1989, McGrath signed for Aston Villa.

'Of all the players I've had at Old Trafford, McGrath is the most talented

It was public knowledge that McGrath and Ferguson did not see eye-to-eye (McGrath was fined £8500 in November 1989, for criticising Ferguson in a Sunday newspaper article), but I was against his transfer. Alex should have persevered with McGrath. Their personality clash shouldn't have been an insurmountable problem. You're paid to solve problems as a manager, and keeping Paul at United should have been a priority. He is a world-class player, who possesses tremendous acceleration, great balance, superb passing ability and he tackles with the strength of a lion. Ironically, Alex said: 'Of all the players I've had at Old Trafford, Paul McGrath is the most talented.' Since leaving United, he has shone for Aston Villa and was absolutely dynamic for the Republic of Ireland in the 1990 World Cup in Italy.

During the three long months between the finish of that dismal season and the start of the 1989-90 season, Ferguson decided that he would have to go for broke and build a new team. Spurred by the belief that Michael Knighton would be injecting a vast amount of capital into the club, Ferguson launched the biggest financial assault on honours in the history of the British game. He knew it was make-or-break: 'My future is at stake, because to continue as manager of Manchester United involves being successful.' Within three months, he had spent more than £6 million, on Norwich City's Michael Phelan, Nottingham Forest's Neil Webb, Middlesbrough's Gary Pallister, Southampton's Danny Wallace and West Ham United's Paul Ince.

Ferguson knew that nothing short of major surgery would suffice: 'The midfield cracked up last season, and it was necessary to do something drastic,' he said. To that end, he signed Phelan and Webb. Phelan has been a decent investment. Although he is not an exceptional player, he is committed, dependable and hard-working. He's a good professional and he can make a squad look solid, because he can play well in so many different positions, and his running capacity allows him to cover his team-mates throughout 90 minutes.

Neil Webb had a dreadfully unlucky start to his career

at United when, a month after signing, he tore his achilles tendon playing for England, an injury which put him out for six months. Webb is a good attacking player — he scored 47 goals in 146 appearances for Forest — but his overall performance at United hasn't been impressive. He's the type of player who'll be the best on the park when you are 2-0 up and the sun is shining, but his defensive game is weak and he simply doesn't get stuck in. There are too many games when you could put his kit back in the plastic bag and use it for the next match it's so clean.

In August, Manchester United broke the British record transfer fee when they paid £2.3 million for Middlesbrough's Gary Pallister. If he's worth that, then Paul McGrath is worth £10 million. Pallister is a good defender, but I have my doubts about him. He's quick, but he can look a bit casual on the ball. His great strength, which you'd expect from someone who is 6'4", is his ability in the air, but he can sometimes be turned with ease, and because he's so tall, once he is turned he's left for dead.

Because of a medical problem, Paul Ince's transfer ran into a hitch, which was eventually settled when West Ham accepted United's offer of a down payment of £800,000, followed by £5000 per game up to a total of £1.8 million. Ince is a highly talented player, but there have been numerous matches in his first 18 months at the club where he has talked a better game than he has played.

Of this quintet of new arrivals, the least effective has been Danny Wallace. Southampton actually tried to get £2.5 million for him, but in the event, Jock Wallace might have been a better bargain than Danny Wallace. Danny has been plagued with different injuries (he's missed more than 50 games in two seasons at the club), and when he's been in the team he hasn't really proved his worth.

Ferguson's buying policy has not been a complete success, yet the strategy behind it was sound. United needed a new midfield, and they needed different types of player. Firstly, they needed a grafter, someone who would tackle back and cover his colleagues, and Michael Phelan fitted this role. Paul Ince had just had a marvellous season at Upton Park, and he seemed tailor-made as a skilful, ball-winning competitor, while Neil Webb, one of the best distributors in the country, was chosen for his ability to set moves in motion and deliver the ball to Hughes and McClair in dangerous positions. Danny Wallace, meanwhile, had done quite well for Southampton, and looked a useful player, who could

OPPOSITE: Gary Pallister, United's £2.3 million signing from Middlesbrough in August 1989, challenges the Manchester City defence at a corner. Pallister's ability in the air — he is 6'4" — is valuable at set-pieces both in defence and attack. He made his debut against Norwich City in August 1989, and his enthusiastic performances in his first season at Old Trafford earned him the award of 'Player of the Year' from the Manchester United Supporters' Association.

give United width on the right wing. The theory behind these signings was fine, it was just unfortunate that not all of his acquisitions were able to fulfil their promise.

This new batch of players took time to settle in, and as a result United had trouble establishing a pattern of play. They were capable of good performances — they beat the eventual champions Arsenal 4-1 and crushed Millwall 5-1 — but they began to slide down the table. A poor run culminated, in September 1989, in a 1-5 defeat at Maine Road. It was Manchester City's biggest win over United for 64 years, and even the memory of Hughes's splendid acrobatic volleyed goal did not lessen the sting of humiliation. Ferguson later said: 'After such a result, you feel as if you have to sneak round corners, like a criminal. It has been the longest 10 days of my life since that game. We must use this bitter lesson as a driving force to do better.'

The FA Cup had been Alex's lifeline, and he grabbed it with both hands

On and off the field, United were a mess. The Knighton fiasco was dominating the sports headlines, and the knives were coming out, among the fans and the media, for Ferguson, who was resolute: 'I don't think the speculation about my future is personal. It's just because I'm manager of Manchester United, and people in this job have always been the whipping boys for the press. There is no manager in the country who could do this job better than me,' he stated. 'I know that and the directors know that, and that's why they have given me a new three-year contract.'

Despite this vote of confidence, United had a miserable October. They had two scoreless draws in the League and were knocked out of the Littlewoods Cup by Tottenham, losing 0-3 at Old Trafford. The frustrated fans booed the team off the pitch and called for the sacking of Ferguson and the resignation of Martin Edwards. This defeat, however, was to prove a watershed — after that game United went until February 1991, playing 21 matches, without suffering a single defeat in any cup competition.

The last two months of 1989 brought scant relief for Alex. United won only two matches, and the fans were incensed by his decision to drop Mark Hughes. Ferguson was finding it almost impossible to assimilate the contrasting styles of his new players, and the team lacked any cohesion or strategy. Too often, the sole attacking tactic was to hoof a high ball up the middle of the park, even when Danny Wallace was up front — and he has to jump to reach a low ball. United added up to

OPPOSITE: Paul Ince, who supported United when I was the manager, signed for his boyhood dream team in September 1989, on a staggered payment deal. Ince is fast, strong and has great vision. He has everything necessary to develop into a world-class player, and will do if he's resolute enough, but his lack of concentration sometimes lets him down.

distinctly less than the sum of their parts, and the team who'd started the season claiming that they were going to win Division One, were having to fight to stay in it.

The New Year opened with another goalless draw, and Ferguson — facing mounting pressure — wasn't handed any favours in the FA Cup draw, when United were chosen to play away against Nottingham Forest, and the BBC chose the game as their 'live' presentation. In the *Sunday Times*, on the morning of the game, Brian Glanville wrote: 'Ferguson's transfer policy has been a disaster, his team selection has often made little sense and results, given the greatness of the club, have been abysmal. Today his job literally hangs in the balance.' The media were certain he was finished, and I thought Alex had a new name, because every time anyone mentioned him, they called him beleaguered.

Martin Edwards said that Ferguson's job wasn't on the line, but at that stage, I think it was a game-by-game existence. Alex pulled United through the hard way. They were drawn away in every round of the FA Cup, and the teams they beat: Forest, Hereford United, Newcastle United, Sheffield United and Oldham Athletic — were all really tough opponents. The players showed great resilience and young Mark Robins was the perfect 'supersub'. He scored four precious goals during the run — including the semi-final winner — as though his story was scripted for *Roy of the Rovers*.

The cup run enabled United to regain their confidence. Bryan Robson returned from a hamstring injury, and United, with two full-backs actually playing in their rightful positions, gradually began to play as a team. When they beat Millwall 2-1 at the Den on 10 February 1990 — defeat would have put United into the bottom three — it ended a run of 11 League matches without a win, United's worst record for 18 years. A series of League wins helped United pull away from the relegation zone, and by the end of the season, players were looking for the ball, not hiding, and the team was showing a determination to win. The FA Cup had been Alex's lifeline, and he grabbed it with both hands.

United had been fortunate to pip Oldham in the semi-final, and their opponents in the Final, Crystal Palace — managed by Steve Coppell — were confident after having beaten Liverpool 4-3 in their semi-final. In front of Wembley's first all-seater crowd, United and Palace produced a magnificent game. Mark Hughes, who is as good as any player in Britain, was at his marauding, enterprising best.

The Final seesawed in both teams' favour, and with United 2-1 up, Coppell sent on substitute Ian Wright, who was like a bolt of lightning. Within three minutes of coming on, he turned Pallister inside out before equalising. In extra time, Wright scored again to leave United trailing 2-3, but Mark Hughes, scoring his second goal of the game, ensured that it would go to a replay.

The return encounter was scheduled for Thursday night, and Ferguson was worried because his players, and the supporters, had lost confidence in their goalkeeper. As a player, Ferguson had experienced the heartache of being dropped for a Final, when he was left out of the Dunfermline side that lost 2-3 to Celtic in the 1965 Scottish Cup Final. Would he have the courage to drop his number one goalkeeper in favour of Les Sealey, on loan from Luton, who had played only two games for United? A clue was provided in a description of Ferguson that Bryan Robson gave to the *Daily Mirror* in September 1987: 'Alex is hard and tough, and scrupulously dedicated to the whole team. The difference between him and Ron Atkinson is that Big Ron was a little too sentimental. He would stay loyal to his players and keep them in the team even when they weren't performing as they should have done. Alex *won't* do that. He thinks of the team, not sensibilities. Friendships and reputations count for nothing with him.' Leighton's reputation and friendship was put aside, and Les Sealey was selected for the replay. It was a turning-point for both men. United won a dour, bad-tempered game 1-0 with a goal from Lee Martin,

BELOW: Lee Martin, the 22-year-old full-back who joined United as a YTS trainee, fires home the winning goal against Crystal Palace in the 1990 FA Cup Final replay to give United their third FA Cup win in seven years.

the young full-back who had been United's most consistent player that season, and Ferguson's decision had been vindicated. Ferguson could now face the future with confidence. He said after the win: 'The Cup run has been a Godsend, because it's a visible reminder that we are not far away from getting it right.'

It had taken him a long time to blend his new players into a team (and McClair and Hughes, although individually successful, still do not operate as an effective striking partnership), and there had been numerous times during his first three years when key players were out with long-term injuries. Although many of his players were very talented, some found that their huge transfer fees were like an albatross. Players who had come from smaller clubs found the pressure and expectations at United a real burden — it was like making a jump from a small-town theatre to the London Palladium — and it took time to handle the transition.

Despite all his difficulties, Alex had weathered the storm, and he was very optimistic about the prospects of Lee Sharpe, who had made his debut against West Ham in 1988. Although he missed the Cup Final through injury, he is United's brightest prospect for the 1990s. United paid Torquay United £65,000 for Sharpe

(and an extra £120,000 after 30 full appearances) and for that money he was the steal of the decade. Alex should have got a gold medal for that signing.

During the height of his troubles in 1989, when the Knighton pantomime was in full swing and United were playing poorly, Alex Ferguson had said: 'I certainly don't regret for a moment asking Martin Edwards to go into the red to buy big in the summer. I said: "We have to go for broke, we have to show that we want to win the League, that we are not going to accept Liverpool's dominance."' So far, the words have been bolder than the deeds — in his first four seasons, United had finished 11th, 2nd, 11th and 13th and had played some mediocre, unattractive football — and I think Alex himself would recognise that he should have got a better return. However, the Cup win was a marvellous launching pad for the new decade. Would the 1990-91 season produce another lap of honour?

The 1990 FA Cup Final was a game of two 'keepers. In the first game, which ended 3-3, there were sharp criticisms of Jim Leighton's performance. In the replay, Alex Ferguson's gamble — he dropped Leighton (right, Unlucky Jim walks to his seat in the stand before the game), and played on-loan Les Sealey, paid off (below, Sealey and Fergie embrace). In May 1991, however, Sealey was given a free transfer.

CUP CHAMPIONS

In the years since my FA Cup win in 1977, Manchester United have become Britain's premier cup team, but their repeated failures to land the League Championship haunt the club. When United kicked off the 1991-92 season, it was exactly 25 years since they had started a successful title campaign.

Saturday 6 August 1966 was the last day that United kicked off a League Championship winning season. In the years since, United have finished as runners-up three times and their glory, such as it has been, has come in cup competitions. In those 25 years, they have won the European Cup, the European Cup Winners' Cup, the FA Cup four times — and been finalists twice more — and have been losing finalists in the League Cup on two occasions. Yet it is their failure to land British football's most challenging prize, the League title, that has been the chief talking point about the club's performance in the last quarter of a century. Winning that trophy has now become a fixation with the club's supporters, players and manager.

The yearly renewal of hope at United — that the forthcoming season will bring the desired success — has become somewhat farcical over the years. Interestingly, when the club issued their first *Official Yearbook*, in 1987, the advertisement for United's sponsors, Sharp, on the back cover, said: 'We're Backing United For The Title!' By 1990, this slogan had been given a more realistic hue: 'We're Backing United As A Winner!'.

BELOW: George Best (left), with a real sparkle in his eyes, and John Aston lead the parade around Wembley after winning the 1968 European Cup Final against Benfica. Best scored a dazzling goal in United's 4-1 win, which made Manchester United the first English club to win the trophy.

Under Matt Busby, of course, it was a different story. United won the Championship five times and were runners-up a further seven times. His teams possessed seminal qualities that their successors have lacked: consistency, self-belief and a guiding strategy. In 1966-67, Busby's team won the title four points ahead of Nottingham Forest. They lost only six times in 42 games, and their last defeat that season came in December. Their home record was awesome: played 21, won 17, drawn 4. Busby's strategy of winning at home and drawing away worked a treat.

'The Old Trafford filmstar image works against them'

Busby's teams contained some of the greatest players in the game, but they were determined to *prove* they were the best, as Tony Dunne put it: 'We realised that teams without as much ability were giving more effort. Ability on its own is not enough, but our consistent effort in 1966-67 was the key.' Since then, many United teams have been criticised for precisely this flaw: that they haven't given complete commitment. During Frank O'Farrell's reign, United were beaten 1-5 at Leeds United. Jack Charlton, who played for Leeds that day, said after the game: 'Some of the players Manchester United have got don't realise how lucky they are. They are the best crowd-pullers in the League. Why this massive public appeal isn't enough on its own to light a fire under every United player, I don't know. But it doesn't happen, and it's part of their problem.' Nearly 20 years later, Jimmy Case — who won four Championship medals with Liverpool — said after playing at Old Trafford for Southampton: 'United keep trying to match Liverpool in the League, but psychologically, they're not geared for it. The Old Trafford filmstar image works against them. They are simply not made to be Champions.' This allegation of complacency doesn't explain much in itself, however.

Too many signings have failed to fulfil their potential at Old Trafford

United's players have had it better than their fellow professionals in terms of the support they receive — and United players are hero-worshipped — and some of the players have, perhaps unwittingly, taken it for granted that there will be another 40,000 or more diehard fans at the next game, whatever the previous result. However, I think I can safely speak for all of the players who have pulled on the red shirt in the past 25 years when saying that every one of them would dearly have loved to bring back the title for those fans. The fans, having done their part, of course, have grown frustrated at the lack of success. Yet the intense pressure that sort of committed support creates can be a hindrance as well if you can't cope with pressure. If you are the

United's European Cup success was celebrated in a host of memorabilia. The cover of this official guide shows a joyful Nobby Stiles raising the trophy. That famous victory against Benfica, of course, was achieved in blue shirts.

right type of character, such as Bryan Robson, then that support will really fire you up, but many players — especially forwards — have buckled under the pressure of living up to the supporters' expectations. Old Trafford is a special stadium and a very difficult place to perform well in, and many players haven't been able to handle the transition from small clubs to Manchester United. Too many signings have failed to fulfil their potential at Old Trafford, and players bought to help win the Championship have let the club and themselves down.

United have also lacked key players in vital positions, none more so than in goal. Since 1966, only Alex Stepney has ranked as a top-class goalkeeper, and during the 1970s he was in his twilight years. In 1976, I tried to sign Stoke City's Peter Shilton. I had arranged a deal with their caretaker manager, George Eastham, whereby Stoke City would take either Stepney or Paddy Roche in return for Shilton and a cash settlement. Shilton was anxious to leave, because Stoke had just been relegated, but at the time, directors Denzil Haroun and Matt Busby wouldn't extend United's wage structure to meet Shilton's demand of £400 a week. It was a shortsighted decision, one that baffles me to this day. Shilton would have made a world of difference. He was then around 27, and he would probably have saved United about 20 goals a season — and made the difference between us being a club thereabouts in the League to being one that finished as Champions.

This goalkeeping problem outlived my reign, and although Gary Bailey, Chris Turner, Jim Leighton and Les Sealey have been reasonable 'keepers, they are not in the class of Shilton, Ray Clemence or David Seaman. If United are to win the league, it will have to be with a top-class goalkeeper.

All six of Busby's successors have realised that win-ning the League is what is really expected of them. I built a very attacking side, with a good defence, but we were more of a cup side than a League one. To win the FA Cup, you have to win only six games, but the League is a different type of challenge. As Bill Shankly once said: 'The League Championship is not a sprint, it's a marathon.' It is the team that plays consistently well throughout the season that comes out on top.

'Every time there was a knock-out contest, the adrenaline was flowing'

Dave Sexton led United to a runners-up spot, and he realised that the League required a different sort of strategy from cup campaigns. Sexton's problem was that he found it difficult to create a team that could score sufficient goals. In four League campaigns, his teams scored 67, 60, 65 and 51 goals — in 1966-67 United scored 84. Sexton explained the difficulties he faced: 'In terms of winning the League Championship, the United way of playing makes the task harder, because the fans don't want defensive tactics and cau-tion or a negative approach to aim for a point.'

Sexton's successor, however, managed to build two fantastic cup sides, who also challenged seriously for the title. Ron Atkinson led United to two FA Cup Final wins within three years and took United to the Final of the Milk Cup. Under Ron, United lost only 12 cup matches out of the 65 they played — and they won them in great attacking style, particularly in the high pressure games. Their whole way of playing showed a greater persistence and resourcefulness in attack that paid off in the critical games. A superb 4-0 victory against Nottingham Forest in the 1983 Milk Cup quar-ter-final was followed by a 4-2 win against Arsenal in the semi-final first leg. On a frozen Highbury pitch, United gave a devastating display of power football. Arnold Muhren picked out Frank Stapleton time after time with accurate, dangerous through balls, and Steve Coppell, who scored twice, tore the Arsenal defence to pieces. Ron Atkinson later described how: 'The sheer buoyancy of the team whenever cup contests came around betrayed the appetite of the players for glory. It seemed that every time there was a knock-out contest, the adrenaline was flowing. We gave some brilliant and memorable performances in 1983.'

Perhaps the finest performance was in the FA Cup semi-final against Arsenal, at Villa Park, which United won 2-1 after trailing to a Tony Woodcock goal. Bryan

Reaching a Cup Final is a wonderful achievement, and the atmosphere on the pitch at Wembley before the kickoff is something to really savour. Here, I'm applauding our sup-porters (below left) with the marvellous Greenhoff brothers — whose father played for Lincoln City — Jimmy (centre) and Brian. They were instrumental in our victory that day.

Robson scored a wonderful equaliser with one of his determined runs into the penalty box, and Norman Whiteside scored the winner with a superb volley. Later Bryan Robson described the game as one of the most enjoyable of his career: 'The Arsenal semi-final was a true test of the character and grit of the United team. Having good players or talented individuals is all very well, but you need a team of fighters to achieve success and that day we proved there was more to Manchester United than its glorious tradition.'

Luck plays a greater part in cup competitions than it does in the League

This character has been one of United's strongest advantages in the last 20 years. Since 1976, they have won all six FA Cup semi-finals they have played; both League Cup semi-finals and one European Cup Winners' Cup semi-final (they also lost one, in 1984, to Juventus). They really are a team for the big occasion. Motivating players for the big occasion isn't as demanding as it is for less glamorous League games. Another factor in cup competitions, though, is that luck plays a greater part than in the league. The ball might hit the post and stay out, or the referee give you a favourable

RIGHT: The now defunct *London Evening News* celebrates our victory against Liverpool in 1977. That victory meant that I became the first of Busby's successors to bring a major trophy back to Old Trafford (right, the match day programme, a ticket from the game and a celebratory first-day cover).

Goalscorer Stuart Pearson (left) and Gordon Hill raise the FA Cup in 1977. Pearson and Hill linked up wonderfully well on the pitch, and Pancho would always look for Hill's crosses.

decision, but you have to ride your luck in cups, and we did that on our way to the FA Cup Finals in 1976 and 1977. There were many occasions when we should have gone out. It is often hardest in the cup when you are faced by 'underdog' teams, when you are on a hiding to nothing. In their first game as FA Cup holders in 1984, United went out 0-2 away at Bournemouth. Atkinson's assistant, Mick Brown, recalled that shock

third-round defeat: 'That sort of upset doesn't happen very often to United. They have so many good players that somebody is always likely to save them.' That has been the story of United since 1967: great players who are unstoppable as a team *when* they really perform.

An ecstatic Bobby Charlton danced with delight in his seat

When United's players have really turned it on, they have been world beaters. One of the most glorious games of the last 25 years — indeed in the club's history — came on 21 March 1984, when United faced Barcelona at Old Trafford in the quarter-final second leg of the European Cup Winners' Cup. United trailed 0-2 from the first leg to Diego Maradona's team, but turned it round for a memorable 3-0 victory.

Bryan Robson was truly sensational that night. He scored United's first with a diving header, flying in among the boots, and scored another before Frank Stapleton netted United's third. Old Trafford that night was like a cauldron. At the end of the game, the roar from the 58,547 crowd was deafening and fans flooded on to the pitch to carry Robson off on their shoulders. A delighted Matt Busby said: 'The memories came flooding back; it took me back to the time we pulled two goals back against Bilbao at Maine Road in our first season in Europe in 1957.' An ecstatic Bobby Charlton, who danced with delight in his seat said: 'The immense joy resulting from that victory surpassed anything I have

Bryan Robson has rightly been dubbed Captain Marvel (above, being hoisted shoulder high by jubilant fans after United's win over Barcelona in 1984). Ron Atkinson, who signed him for United, said: 'Bryan is the most complete midfield player in the game. He can really inspire — he can take over any game, even when it's going against his team.'

ever experienced in the game. It was even better than winning the FA Cup at Wembley.' Manchester United thrive on that sort of drama.

Given time, Ron Atkinson would have brought the title to Old Trafford

Although Atkinson built this great cup side, he also came tantalisingly close to bringing the title back to Old Trafford in 1985-86. Despite a flying start, when United won their first 10 games and built up a 10-point lead at the top, their form collapsed and they finished in fourth place. It's important to remember, however, that United hadn't been in that position before. Liverpool have been over that territory — of being top and staying the course — season after season, and they know how to handle the pressure, particularly if they have a difficult patch. When they do lose a few games, they don't panic, they just go back to basics. United panicked and faltered. It was the same with George Graham's Arsenal when they won the title in 1991. Having been through it in 1989 definitely helped them cope with the pressure two years later. Given time, however, I believe

Under Ron Atkinson, Manchester United teams rose to the big occasion. When they played Barcelona in the second-leg of the 1984 Cup Winners' Cup quarter-final, they had to overcome a 0-2 deficit from the first leg in the Nou Camp Stadium. Barcelona, with Diego Maradona (left, Bryan Robson closes in on the soccer superstar of the 1980s), were favourites, but United won through with a 3-0 victory in front of 57,547 exhilarated fans at Old Trafford.

RIGHT: Kevin Moran (left), assistant manager Mick Brown (right) and Arthur Albiston leap to their feet after Norman Whiteside's shot had beaten Everton's goalkeeper Neville Southall to give United a decisive 1-0 lead in the 1985 FA Cup Final. United had been reduced to 10 men, after Kevin Moran had become the first player to be sent off in a Final.

Ron would have built a Championship winning side.

United's lack of consistency has been the chief reason for their lack of success in the League, and the success of their neighbours Liverpool (their title win in 1990 was their 10th in 15 years) has intensified the inquest at Old Trafford into United's lack of success in the hunt for the title. When United finished as runners-up in 1979-80, Steve Coppell said: 'While Liverpool had their usual cutting edge and streak of ruthlessness, we again lacked consistency.'

'United fell down against weaker sides. Liverpool didn't make that mistake'

Ray Wilkins, who made 160 League appearances for United, said that United's players knew they were compared unfavourably to their Merseyside rivals: 'People often made comparisons between Liverpool and United teams. United had so many skilful players, and as a team we were comparable in technique, but there was a difference in attitude. They were all trained to work as hard as possible for each other, and they were never complacent. United sometimes fell down against weaker sides. When it boils down to it, Liverpool didn't make that mistake.'

If there has been a big difference between United and Liverpool players in the 1970s and 1980s, it is that while United have possessed great stars, Liverpool players have always known that they are great players but they have always wanted to go out each week and prove it. As Bob Paisley said of United: 'They are one or

two players short, and some of those they've got need a good talking to!'. United's lack of singlemindedness is a fault that has to be laid at the door of the managers, myself included. There are other factors — does the ambition of the Board match that of the manager? Have you had the blessing of an injury-free squad? — but in the end it is all down to the steel of the manager and his team. Frankly, the teams that have won it in the

BELOW: Referee Peter Willis orders off United's Kevin Moran in the 1985 FA Cup Final, after Moran had collided with Peter Reid as he was running through on goal. Moran later recalled: 'When the referee called me over and gave me the red card, I couldn't believe it. Now, when I saw the tackle afterwards on television I thought it *looked* terrible, but at the time all I kept asking the ref was: "Why are you sending me off?" And he wouldn't say a thing. He just kept pointing. That's what was making me really mad, the fact that he was being obstinate and not saying anything.'

last 25 years have shown greater determination than United. It is the manager's job to keep a large squad motivated and hungry. The manager has to be able to carry a large squad and keep them all happy — the ones in *and* out of the team. All the great managers who have won the title in the past 25 years — such as Brian Clough, Bob Paisley, Kenny Dalglish and now George Graham — have kept their players right on their toes, looking over their shoulders at all times, knowing that if they aren't doing the job they are selected for then they will be replaced.

'Each new season brought a fresh wave of optimism'

When Alex Ferguson arrived, hopes were again raised that United had a manager who would bring the title to Old Trafford. To that end, he has spent nearly £16 million on players, but so far United have come close only once. Chris Turner, who was United's regular goalkeeper when they finished as runners-up in 1987-88, explained, in an interview for this book, what it's like for the players: 'We were all aware of the time lapse since the club had last won the title, and each new season brought a fresh wave of optimism, and the belief that "this will be the year!". The recent campaigns had brought disappointments, and even when we finished as runners-up, we felt that it was regarded as another failure. The problem for the players isn't motivation — every player who pulls on a Manchester United shirt should be motivated already — the problem is lack of consistency. United teams drop silly points against weak teams when they should bury them.'

On their day, Alex Ferguson's team can beat anyone

Alex Ferguson has gradually tried to assemble a team of winners, but they haven't been able to do it week in and week out; they have relied on cup competitions. As he said in August 1989: 'What I think has happened to United is that they have become a cup-tie club, regarding the Wembley trip as being on the cards.' In both the 1989-90 and 1990-91 seasons, under Ferguson's stewardship, United have become the premier cup team in Britain. United's European Cup Winners' Cup Final victory against Barcelona was Ferguson's 52nd cup game with United, out of which they have won 34, drawn 9 and lost 8. This ratio of winning 67 per cent of cup games is superb, and if transferred to the League would make them serious Championship contenders.

When Alex came down from Aberdeen, he found the transition particularly difficult to handle in the League — the way that there are so many more strong opponents in the First Division than in the Premier League, where Rangers, Celtic and Aberdeen are the only teams who realistically contest the Championship. His num-ber two then, Archie Knox — who left to become assistant manager at Rangers in May 1991 — was also unfamiliar with the English game.

Ferguson's United possess some of the finest players in Britain, and on their day they are capable of beating anyone. They have developed an element of steel to their game, shown in their 2-0 victory in the European Cup Winners' Cup quarter-final against Montpellier. It was a real test of character winning in a hostile atmosphere, particularly after the set-back of the 1-1 draw in the first leg. United also showed their grit in the Rumbelows League Cup semi-final victory against Leeds United, after which George Best said: 'United were absolutely brilliant. After the first game, they knew they'd have a physical battle, but they matched Leeds. In the past that's been a problem, but not now. Lee Sharpe looks better with every game. Most players would have shot early against John Lukic, but Lee took him on and scored from a tremendous angle.'

'Everyone at United badly wants the title. We're in a good position to give it a go'

Manchester United's players are going to have to show every ounce of that great character if they are to win the League in 1992. Winning the title is increasingly difficult. The sheer number of big cup matches can work against your League form, because there is the added chance of players picking up injury — and foreign travel is quite tiring — and the squad can get despondent if they have a set-back in an important cup tie.

All these factors make it critically important that you have a good enough squad to see you through a season in which you might play 60 or more games. Alex knew when he arrived at Old Trafford that the calibre of the squad wasn't good enough and that he had to buy players. As he said in 1988: 'Liverpool have bought the best and what sticks in my gullet is the difference between us and them. I respect them, but I don't like being second.'

I think that the squad who won the European Cup Winners' Cup is probably the strongest of the past decade, but it still needs some fine tuning. However, because of the massive outlay the club will have to pay out for the redevelopment of the Stretford End, the money that is available for new players will probably be limited. Chairman Martin Edwards said after the victory against Barcelona in Rotterdam that he didn't think that any new signings were necessary: 'We don't need to spend big, because we've already done that. We've spent a lot of money getting the average age of the squad down to 26, and the opportunity is now there for the players.'

Bryan Robson, however, did not agree with his Chairman, as he said: 'Everyone at United badly wants to win the title and we are in a good position to give it a real go. Winning in Europe has given the club money in the bank. Hopefully, it will be used to get the playing strength to compete with Arsenal and Liverpool next season. It just shows how far we've progressed when a player of the calibre of Neil Webb is left on the substitute's bench in a European Cup Winners' Cup Final, but we still have work to do.'

Alex Ferguson is the man to bring the title back to Old Trafford

Alex will certainly know the capabilities of the squad — and his decision to buy the Soviet forward Andrej Kontchelskis shows that he believes it does need strengthening — and despite his successes in the cup competitions, his League results have been, on the whole, disappointing. In his first five seasons, United finished as runners-up once, and their other positions: 11th, 11th, 13th and 6th is not Championship materi-

BELOW: United's players celebrate their first trophy win under Alex Ferguson, after beating Crystal Palace, managed by former United star Steve Coppell, 1-0 in the 1990 FA Cup Final replay. From left to right (back row): Paul Ince, Russell Beardsmore, Steve Bruce, Lee Sharpe, Mark Robins, Les Sealey, Michael Phelan, Brian McClair, Clayton Blackmore and Colin Gibson. Front row: Danny Wallace, Mark Hughes, Gary Pallister, Lee Martin, Bryan Robson and Neil Webb. That night, Bryan Robson became the first United captain to collect the FA Cup for a third time.

al. In too many games, United have lacked shape, pattern and imagination — and the wretched state of the pitch in 1990-91 certainly didn't help them develop a consistent passing game.

Over the last 25 years, a series of different United teams have failed to win the Championship, because they haven't been good enough to sustain a challenge. United have tried it a number of ways, including splashing out with the cheque book, yet their last title win was built on a rock-solid youth policy, and I believe their next win will be built on these foundations. Alex Ferguson knows that United must have a large, talented squad, with players who can last a 60-game season — and he knows that a core of players must come from the club's own youth system. In that respect the future looks good. There are a host of homegrown players — Ryan Giggs, Lee Martin, Darren Ferguson and Mark Robins among them — who will give the squad real depth.

Although the Cup success is glorious and enjoyable, for a club of United's stature it is secondary. On 1 January 1990, Alex Ferguson said: 'The monkey on our backs is the fact that it is over 23 years since we last won the Championship. It is something a succession of managers have been saddled with, and it's not something that gets any easier with the passage of time.' Wilf McGuinness, Frank O'Farrell, Dave Sexton, Ron Atkinson and I all struggled and failed with the quest to win the title. It certainly won't get easier, but I believe Alex is the man to bring the title back to Old Trafford.

GLORY, GLORY MAN UNITED

The 1990-91 season was the best United had produced since the days of Matt Busby. Alex Ferguson's team had superb cup victories over Liverpool, and champions Arsenal, reached the Rumbelows Cup Final and capped the season with a glorious victory in the European Cup Winners' Cup Final.

When Bryan Robson raised the European Cup Winners' Cup trophy in Feyenoord's Stadium in Rotterdam on 15 May 1991, more than 25,000 jubilant Manchester United fans danced jigs of delight in recognition of Alex Ferguson's team having just reclaimed the club's European heritage. Beating Johan Cruyff's Spanish Champions Barcelona capped a marvellous season for United, during which they had produced some dazzling performances and reached two cup finals.

United approached the 1990-91 season with justifiable optimism. They had recently won the FA Cup in fine style, and many of the 'new' signings were now established at the club. Alex Ferguson was happy with his squad — a mixture of long established senior players and some young, highly promising players. The squad also had a new full-back, in Cork-born Denis Irwin, who was bought for £700,000 from Oldham.

United opened the season with a 1-1 draw in the Charity Shield against Liverpool, but it became clear in September and October that there would again be a chasm between United's performances in the League and in the three cup competitions they were involved in.

BELOW: One of the finest displays of the season was the 3-1 victory against Legia Warsaw in the first leg of the Cup Winners' Cup semi-final. Here, Brian McClair forces the ball home for United's equaliser and his 20th goal of the season.

Some of United's best performances of the season came in the Rumbelows League Cup. United kicked off their campaign against Halifax Town on 26 September, winning 3-1. The game marked Jim Leighton's only appearance of the season. He turned down a move to Hull City, on loan, and later joined Arsenal as cover for David Seaman. To his credit, Alex Ferguson was big enough to admit that his decision to axe him for the FA Cup Final replay had effectively crippled Leighton's career. Alex made the decision for the good of the club, but it had disastrous consequences for the player.

'Lee was up against a first-class full-back in Steve Nicol and he *slaughtered* him'

After knocking out Halifax, United met Liverpool at Old Trafford on 31 October. In their League meeting at Anfield, six weeks earlier, United had been beaten 0-4, and it was the perfect chance to exact revenge. The game marked the third full appearance of the season by young winger Lee Sharpe, who was adding a new dimension to United's game. Together, that night, Sharpe and Hughes struck up their first real partnership and they tore the Liverpool defence to shreds. Hughes capped a fine display with a marvellous run and 25-yard drive past a bewildered Bruce Grobbelaar. After the game, captain Bryan Robson said: 'We've needed somebody with a bit of pace for some time. Lee has given us the option of playing the ball to Hughes

Lee Sharpe (above left) won the PFA 'Young Player of the Year' award in April 1991, while Mark Hughes (right) won the PFA 'Player of the Year' award — for the second time.

and using his strength or playing it out to Sharpe and using his pace. We always knew he had ability, and it started to come out in the game against Liverpool in the Rumbelows Cup. He was up against a first-class full-back in Steve Nicol, and he *slaughtered* him.'

A month later, United travelled to League leaders Arsenal, and produced their best playing performance of the season to reach the quarter-final. It was Arsenal's first defeat in 17 games that season, but it was the manner in which they were absolutely crushed, 6-2, that was so impressive. Lee Sharpe, who was preferred to Neil Webb, ran the Arsenal defence ragged and scored a marvellous hat-trick. United's passing game that night was so incisive and imaginative that the Gunners' defence spent the night chasing shadows — a defence that conceded only 18 goals in the League all season had six put past them in one night by a red-hot United. After the game, Alex Ferguson said: 'They were totally magnificent. It was my biggest victory at United. I saved it for a special occasion.'

In the quarter-final, Mark Hughes was on splendid form in both games. He saved United in the first match at the Dell with a late equaliser — a splendid volley. In the return at Old Trafford it was his hat-trick that put out Southampton in an exciting 3-2 win. The semi-final pitted Manchester United against their old adversaries

Leeds United and the two encounters were tense, niggling affairs. In the first match at Old Trafford, United were rescued by Lee Sharpe's pace, and he gave Mel Sterland a roasting in both games. United won the first leg 2-1, but it was their victory in the second leg that was most impressive. United went to Elland Road after they had been knocked out of the FA Cup at Norwich — United's first defeat in any cup competition for 22 matches — and earned a memorable 1-0 victory. They didn't try to sit on their lead, but took the game to Leeds and were rewarded with a splendid late winner from Lee Sharpe, his sixth goal in the competition.

In the Final, Ron Atkinson led Sheffield Wednesday to a well deserved 1-0 win. Before the game, Atkinson was confident about his chances: 'I'll tell you something,' Ron quipped. 'We're a better team than that "legover" Warsaw lot they beat in the Cup Winners' Cup.' United, who had virtually ensured themselves a place in the Cup Winners' Cup Final with a superb 3-1 away victory against Legia Warsaw, did not seem to have their minds fully on their task at Wembley.

On the day, Ferguson's men were painfully short of zest and imagination and Wednesday were the better team. Ron did his homework well and his defence

OPPOSITE: Clayton Blackmore, United's Welsh international, had his best season at the club in 1990-91. He played 57 times and scored nine goals — his most sustained run yet in the first team. Alex Ferguson's son, Darren, played five League games and looked a good prospect (below, he skips past Alan Smith during Arsenal's 3-1 win in May 1991).

closed down Hughes, Sharpe and United's midfield, and John Sheridan struck an excellent winner. Apart from Bryan Robson, Les Sealey and Steve Bruce, United's players absolutely stalled, but the experience may, in the long run, have strengthened their resilience.

'We have yet to emerge as a team in the true meaning of the word'

While United were cruising through in the early rounds of the European Cup Winners' Cup, and dazzling in the Rumbelows, in the FA Cup, however, it was a different story completely. United never really looked like they were going to retain the trophy, and after sneaking past Queen's Park Rangers and Bolton Wanderers, they went out after losing 1-2 to Norwich City at Carrow Road — an unhappy hunting ground for Alex Ferguson.

In addition, their League form was disappointing. A serious challenge for the title never really looked on. There were too many draws, and too many games when total commitment was missing. At one stage in the season, Alex Ferguson actually complained that the lack of commitment was unfair to the fans, and the team's lack of ambition in some League games betrayed a preoccupation with forthcoming important cup matches. United weren't helped by the rotten condition of the Old Trafford pitch, but the side never looked cohesive enough to be a Championship winning team. They were playing far too many high, aimless balls, and not feeding the ball out to the wings with sufficient accuracy or

intelligence. They were vulnerable to good counter-attacking and were haphazard in their use of dead-ball situations. They rarely appeared to be a side at ease with themselves tactically, as Alex Ferguson acknowledged in the *United Review* during the season: 'This team is still in the developing stage. There are a lot of talented individuals, but I am well aware that we have yet to emerge as a team in the true meaning of the word. We are capable of doing well in cup competitions, but it takes a well-rooted team to produce the kind of consistency that wins the Championship.'

The League is the ultimate challenge for Ferguson, and it is where he needs to improve the team most. His cup record is great, but in League terms it is average. In nearly five years at the club, he has presided over 186 games in the League, and the 1-1 draw against Tottenham in May 1991 was the 57th draw. They have lost another 53 and won 76 — a mere 41 per cent of them. As Alex said, however, a manager needs a well-rooted team, and this is slowly beginning to emerge.

The progress of the squad in 1990-91 was encouraging. In defence, Denis Irwin had a good season. He looked a better player at Oldham, because they played more to his strength at running forward. He's good at overlapping runs, but can be exposed by a good winger running at him. On the left, Clayton Blackmore had his best season at the club. It's been difficult for him, because he's been swapped around so much — he played in seven different positions during the season — but he's a handy player and his ability at free kicks is extremely valuable. The one nagging doubt I have about him is that, as a naturally right-footed player, he doesn't look totally comfortable as a left-back. Indeed, both full-backs look more comfortable at dead-ball situations in attack than when confronted by an agile opponent.

Steve Bruce's scoring record in 1990-91, netting 19 goals, was tremendous

In central defence, Steve Bruce had a magnificent season. He's a real winner and a born Manchester United player. He's very strong in the air and confident about bringing the ball out from defence. Added to that, his scoring record in 1990-91, when he netted 19 goals, was tremendous. It's a measure of his character that he scored 11 penalties — several in really tense, vital moments of important matches. His partner, Gary Pallister, is improving, but he still has moments of indecision and looked very vulnerable in the Rumbelows Cup Final. Nevertheless, he links well with Bruce and is good in set-pieces, both in attack and defence.

The midfield still looked very unsettled, and Neil Webb looked a fairweather player. Although Michael Phelan has little of Webb's technical expertise, the difference between them was highlighted by their two cup final performances. Against Sheffield Wednesday, Neil Webb looked lethargic and ineffective. He's good at moving with the ball, but when he loses an opponent —

and this is a flaw in Ince's game, too — he is slow at getting back to cover and tackle. Phelan, a wholly industrious player, did this throughout the game against Barcelona, and kept Michael Laudrup out of the game. In fairness, Webb was again unlucky with injuries, and he looked desperately short of confidence.

Nat Lofthouse described Mark Hughes as the best volleyer he'd *ever* seen

Paul Ince, meanwhile, looked good in fits and starts, but won't be really productive until he learns to keep concentrating throughout a whole game. I'm always reading in the papers what he says he'll do and then watching him fail to do it. This must be frustrating for his colleagues, something Ince himself admitted during the season: 'Bryan Robson told me to get grafting, and that I was not giving enough of myself. He told me I was the only one who could prove myself.'

Robson himself did superbly when he came back from injury, and he had an excellent testimonial year. He is slowing down, but it's not surprising that he was given an extension to his contract, as he is still able to do a good job for the team. In attack, Brian McClair had a steady season. He plays for the team and he plays to manager's instructions, and as a manager you can't argue with that. In terms of scoring, McClair had another good season, finishing with 21 goals — including a goal in every qualifying round of the Cup Winners' Cup.

Mark Hughes had a superb season, during which he won the PFA 'Player of the Year' award for the second time. Hughes is so intimidating; opponents just cannot knock him off the ball. Defenders often concede free kicks against him simply because they cannot get near the ball. He has learned to lead a forward line, and his volleying is as splendid as ever. He scored magnificent volleyed goals throughout the season, and after his one against Bolton in the FA Cup, Nat Lofthouse described him as the best volleyer he'd *ever* seen. His ability at shielding the ball is so important, and during his purple patch in the season, when he scored 15 goals in 17 matches, he was unstoppable. Hughes has also been pleased with the progress of the team during the season, as he put it: 'In some games in 1990-91, we played as well as any United team I've been involved with. People are moving quicker towards you, giving the ball exactly where you want it. It makes the job easier.'

One team-mate who made his job easier was, of course, winger Lee Sharpe, whose performances earned him the PFA 'Young Player of the Year' award. He's been a breath of fresh air to the whole game. Lee is brave, possesses a great temperament and is incredibly fast. Lee's got great composure and he is simply

OPPOSITE: Lee Sharpe begins to outpace Mel Sterland during the second leg of the Rumbelows Cup semi-final against Leeds United. Sharpe played superbly in both games, running Sterland ragged and scoring in both legs.

MANCHESTER UNITED
FC BARCELONA

MAY 15 - 1991 KICK-OFF 20.15
STADION FEIJENOORD ROTTERDAM

not put off by tough tackling. Lee Sharpe knows what to do with the ball when he gets it, and he does so without hesitating. His form was so good that in March he earned his first full international cap for England at the age of 19.

Significantly, Bryan Robson looked much happier with Sharpe there, because he had someone to look for on the wings. 'Sharpe', said Hughes, 'turns the key for us. His pace on the left tears up defences. With no one wide, Brian McClair and myself were cluttering up the midfield dropping back for possession. Now, we just knock the ball wide and head straight for the penalty area.'

Les Sealey had a good year, but Alex thought that Les was not the long-term solution to the goalkeeping problem at Old Trafford and gave him a free transfer at the end of the season. Danny Wallace had another poor, unproductive season; Mal Donaghy was a useful squad member; Lee Martin treaded water for a season and was unlucky with injuries; Russell Beardsmore and Mark Robins were given little opportunity to prove their worth; and Gary Walsh did well to come back from his injury problems and earned a new four-year contract.

There were also three departures — Viv Anderson, Colin Gibson and Jim Leighton — and there were also debuts for the new Soviet forward, Andrej Kontchelskis, whom Ferguson has praised highly; Ryan Giggs, who looked a fantastic prospect; Paul Wratten; defender Neil Whitworth, an England youth player; and Alex's own son, Darren, whom Brian Clough had tried to sign for Nottingham Forest, played five times during the season and looks a good prospect. It's very hard when your father is the manager, but Darren has handled it well. I've watched his development, and he looks like he's

Manchester United were worthy winners of the European Cup Winners' Cup (left, match-day programme and ticket). OPPOSITE ABOVE: Steve Bruce climbs high to head Bryan Robson's free kick goalbound. The header was kicked into the net by Mark Hughes, who grabbed a second with a solo goal. Put through by Robson, he rounded the 'keeper (opposite below), took the ball wide into the box and fired home a great drive. On the day, United prevented Barcelona from performing (below, Denis Irwin goes past Michael Laudrup).

modelled himself on Bryan Robson's style of play.

In all, it was an eventful, dramatic season for United, but unlike 1989-90, the drama was for the most part on the pitch. One incident spilled over from the pitch, however. In October, United players were involved in a brawl with Arsenal that ended with both clubs being fined and docked League points .

For United's fans it was the European competition that was always going to be the big one in 1990-91, and they did the club proud with the fantastic, exemplary support they gave the team during the away matches. The road to Rotterdam was certainly easier than might have been expected. First-round opponents Pecsi Munkas weren't very testing, and their next opponents, Wrexham, finished the season as the bottom team in the Football League. United's first real test came in the quarter-final against Montpellier. After faltering in the first-leg at Old Trafford, United went to Montpellier with the scores level at 1-1 and earned a great 2-0 victory. This performance was surpassed in the semi-final with a 3-1 away win against Legia Warsaw. The Poles were poor, admittedly, but United dominated the game, and attacked with purpose.

In the Final, Barcelona — who put out Dynamo Kiev and Juventus on their way to Rotterdam — were disappointing, but that doesn't detract from a superb United display. It was a tremendous, proud night for the club and its followers. Bryan Robson gave one of his finest displays for United, and Mark Hughes, who was relishing playing against his former club, gave a typically rugged performance. His first goal was a great piece of opportunism — following up Steve Bruce's excellent set-piece header. His second was extraordinary, and showed how confident he's become. After rounding the 'keeper, he looked as though he'd taken it far too wide, but he simply smashed the ball into the back of the net.

In Rotterdam, Manchester United added a memorable chapter to their long and proud European history when they won their first European Final on foreign soil. Throughout the season, Ferguson said that the team was a young, developing side 'on a learning curve', but winning is a habit and Alex has bred it into them.

In his first manager's column in the *United Review*, on 22 November 1986, Alex Ferguson wrote: 'I am not really interested in what has happened here in the past. The aim of this club must clearly be to win the Championship. This is the only way to lay to rest the ghosts of the past.' That aim looked a far-fetched one in Alex's first four years, but not anymore. He has assembled a fine squad, who have proved they can win cups. The European Cup Winners' Cup triumph is the perfect springboard to take Manchester United forward, and, hopefully, see those ghosts laid to rest.

THE STATISTICS

Manchester United's record season by season, from 1966/67 to 1990/91, inclusive, including details of all first-team matches

HONOURS LIST:

Football League Division One: Champions 1907-08, 1910-11, 1951-52, 1955-56, 1956-57, 1964-65, 1966-67
Runners-up: 1946-47, 1947-48, 1948-49, 1950-51, 1958-59, 1963-64, 1967-68, 1979-80, 1987-88
Football League Division Two: Champions 1935-36, 1974-75; runners-up 1896-97, 1905-06, 1924-25, 1937-38
FA Cup: Winners 1909, 1948, 1963, 1977, 1983, 1985, 1990; Losing finalists 1957, 1958, 1976, 1979
Football League Cup (now Rumbelows League Cup); Losing finalists 1983, 1991
European Cup: Winners 1968
European Cup Winners' Cup: Winners 1991
FA Youth Cup: Winners 1953, 1954, 1955, 1956, 1957, 1964; Losing finalists 1982, 1986

D1 — Division One match; **D2** — Division Two match; **FA** — FA Cup; **LC** League Cup (later Milk Cup, Littlewoods Cup and Rumbelows League Cup); **AI** — Anglo-Italian Tournament; **CS** — Charity Shield; **EC** — European Cup; **UC** — UEFA Cup; **ECWC** — European Cup Winners' Cup; **FAPO** — FA Cup third-place play off; **WC** — Watneys Cup; **WCC** — World Champions Cup; **SF** — Semi-final; **F** — Final; **A** — Away match; **H** — Home match; **N** — Neutral ground; **W** — Wembley

1966-67

Manager: Matt Busby
Played 45, **Won** 25, **Lost** 8, **Drawn** 12, **Goals for** 88, **Goals against** 57
Appearances (including as substitute): Best 45; Charlton 44; A. Dunne 43; Crerand 42; Stiles 40; Sadler 39; Law 38; Stepney 37; Foulkes 35; Aston, Herd, Noble 31; Brennan 17; Connelly 7; Ryan 6; Gaskell 5; Cantwell 4; Fitzpatrick 3; Gregg 2; Anderson, P. Dunne 1
Goals: Law 25 (2 pens); Herd 18; Charlton 12; Best 10 (1 pen); Aston, Sadler 5; Foulkes 4; Crerand, Stiles 3; Connelly 2; own goals 1

August
20 D1 West Bromwich Albion	H 5-3 Law 2, Best, Herd, Stiles
23 D1 Everton	A 2-1 Law 2
27 D1 Leeds United	A 1-3 Best
31 D1 Everton	H 3-0 Connelly, Foulkes, Law

September
2 LC Blackpool	A 1-5 Herd
3 D1 Newcastle United	H 3-2 Connelly, Law, Herd
7 D1 Stoke City	A 0-3
10 D1 Tottenham Hotspur	A 1-2 Law
17 D1 Manchester City	H 1-0 Law
24 D1 Burnley	H 4-1 Crerand, Law, Herd, Sadler

October
1 D1 Nottingham Forest	A 1-4 Charlton
8 D1 Blackpool	A 2-1 Law 2 (1 pen)
15 D1 Chelsea	H 1-1 Law
29 D1 Arsenal	H 1-0 Sadler

November
5 D1 Chelsea	A 3-1 Aston 2, Best
12 D1 Sheffield Wednesday	H 2-0 Charlton, Herd
19 D1 Southampton	A 2-1 Charlton 2
26 D1 Sunderland	H 5-0 Herd 4, Law
30 D1 Leicester City	A 2-1 Best, Law

December
3 D1 Aston Villa	A 1-2 Herd
10 D1 Liverpool	H 2-2 Best 2 (1 pen)
17 D1 West Bromwich Albion	A 4-3 Herd 3, Law
26 D1 Sheffield United	A 1-2 Herd
27 D1 Sheffield United	H 2-0 Crerand, Herd
31 D1 Leeds United	H 0-0

January
14 D1 Tottenham Hotspur	H 1-0 Herd
21 D1 Manchester City	A 1-1 Foulkes
28 FA Stoke City	H 2-0 Law, Herd

February
4 D1 Burnley	A 1-1 Sadler
11 D1 Nottingham Forest	H 1-0 Law

18 FA Norwich City	H 1-2 Law
25 D1 Blackpool	H 4-0 Charlton 2, Law, Hughes (og)

March
3 D1 Arsenal	A 1-1 Aston
11 D1 Newcastle United	A 0-0
18 D1 Leicester City	H 5-2 Aston, Charlton, Herd, Law, Sadler
25 D1 Liverpool	A 0-0
27 D1 Fulham	A 2-2 Best, Stiles
28 D1 Fulham	H 2-1 Foulkes, Stiles

April
1 D1 West Ham United	H 3-0 Best, Charlton, Law
10 D1 Sheffield Wednesday	A 2-2 Charlton 2
18 D1 Southampton	H 3-0 Charlton, Law, Sadler
22 D1 Sunderland	A 0-0
29 D1 Aston Villa	H 3-1 Aston, Best, Law

May
6 D1 West Ham United	A 6-1 Law 2 (1 pen), Best, Charlton, Crerand, Foulkes
13 D1 Stoke City	H 0-0

Final League position: Champions

1967-68

Manager: Matt Busby
Played 54, **Won** 29, **Lost** 12, **Drawn** 13, **Goals for** 112, **Goals against** 70
Appearances: Best, Charlton, Crerand, Stepney 54; Sadler 52; Dunne, Kidd 50; Aston 47; Burns 45; Foulkes 32; Law, Stiles 29; Fitzpatrick 21; Brennan 18; Herd, Ryan 8; Gowling 5; Kopel 2; Rimmer 1
Goals: Best 32 (2 pens); Charlton 22; Kidd 17; Aston, Law (2 pens) 11; Sadler 6; Burns, Foulkes, Ryan, own goals 2; Brennan, Crerand, Dunne, Gowling, Herd 1

August
12 CS Tottenham Hotspur	H 3-3 Charlton 2, Law
19 D1 Everton	A 1-3 Charlton
23 D1 Leeds United	H 1-0 Charlton
26 D1 Leicester City	H 1-1 Foulkes

September
2 D1 West Ham United	A 3-1 Kidd, Ryan, Sadler
6 D1 Sunderland	A 1-1 Kidd
9 D1 Burnley	H 2-2 Burns, Crerand
16 D1 Sheffield Wednesday	A 1-1 Best
20 EC Hibernians (Malta)	H 4-0 Sadler 2, Law 2
23 D1 Tottenham Hotspur	H 3-1 Best 2, Law
27 EC Hibernians (Malta)	A 0-0
30 D1 Manchester City	A 2-1 Charlton 2

October
7 D1 Arsenal	H 1-0 Aston
14 D1 Sheffield United	A 3-0 Aston, Kidd, Law (pen)
25 D1 Coventry City	H 4-0 Aston 2, Best, Charlton
28 D1 Nottingham Forest	A 1-3 Best

November
4 D1 Stoke City	H 1-0 Charlton
8 D1 Leeds United	A 0-1
11 D1 Liverpool	A 2-1 Best, Charlton
15 EC FK Sarajevo	A 0-0
18 D1 Southampton	H 3-2 Aston, Charlton, Kidd
25 D1 Chelsea	A 1-1 Kidd
29 EC FK Sarajevo	H 2-1 Best, Aston

December
2 D1 West Bromwich Albion	H 2-1 Best 2
9 D1 Newcastle United	A 2-2 Dunne, Kidd
16 D1 Everton	H 3-1 Aston, Law, Sadler
23 D1 Leicester City	A 2-2 Charlton, Law
26 D1 Wolves	H 4-0 Best 2, Charlton, Kidd
30 D1 Wolves	A 3-2 Aston, Charlton, Kidd

January
6 D1 West Ham United	H 3-1 Aston, Best, Charlton
20 D1 Sheffield Wednesday	H 4-2 Best 2, Charlton, Kidd
27 FA Tottenham Hotspur	H 2-2 Best, Charlton
31 FA Tottenham Hotspur	A 0-1 (aet)

February
3 D1 Tottenham Hotspur	A 2-1 Best, Charlton
17 D1 Burnley	A 1-2 Best
24 D1 Arsenal	A 2-0 Best, Storey (og)
28 EC Gornik Zabrze	H 2-0 Kidd, Florenski (og)

March
2 D1 Chelsea	H 1-3 Kidd
13 EC Gornik Zabrze	A 0-1
16 D1 Coventry City	A 0-2
23 D1 Nottingham Forest	H 3-0 Herd, Brennan, Burns
27 D1 Manchester City	H 1-3 Best
30 D1 Stoke City	A 4-2 Aston, Best, Gowling, Ryan

April
6 D1 Liverpool	H 1-2 Best
12 D1 Fulham	A 4-0 Best 2, Kidd, Law
13 D1 Southampton	A 2-2 Best, Charlton
15 D1 Fulham	H 3-0 Aston, Best, Charlton
20 D1 Sheffield United	H 1-0 Law
24 ECSF Real Madrid	H 1-0 Best
27 D1 West Bromwich Albion	A 3-6 Kidd 2, Law (pen)

May
4 D1 Newcastle United	H 6-0 Best 3 (2 pens), Kidd 2, Sadler
11 D1 Sunderland	A 1-2 Best
15 ECSF Real Madrid	A 3-3 Foulkes, Sadler, Zocco (og)
29 ECF Benfica	W 4-1 (aet) Charlton 2, Best, Kidd

Final League position: 2nd. **Won European Cup**

1968-69

Manager: Sir Matt Busby
Played 56, **Won** 23, **Lost** 18, **Drawn** 15, **Goals for** 89, **Goals against** 67
Appearances: Stiles 55; Best 53; Stepney 49; Crerand 47; Charlton 46; Dunne 45; Law 43; Fitzpatrick, Kidd 40; Morgan 38; Sadler 35; James 29; Burns 21; Foulkes 18; Brennan, Sartori 16; Aston 13; Kopel 10; Rimmer 8; Ryan 6; Gowling 2
Goals: Law 29 (2 pens); Best 23; Morgan 8; Charlton 7; Fitzpatrick, Kidd, own goals 4; Aston, Crerand, Stiles 2; Burns, James, Ryan, Sartori 1

August
10 D1 Everton	H 2-1 Best, Charlton
14 D1 West Bromwich Albion	A 1-3 Charlton
17 D1 Manchester City	A 0-0
21 D1 Coventry City	H 1-0 Ryan
24 D1 Chelsea	H 0-4
28 D1 Tottenham Hotspur	H 3-1 Fitzpatrick 2, Beal (og)
31 D1 Sheffield Wednesday	A 4-5 Law 2, Best, Charlton

September
7 D1 West Ham United	H 1-1 Law
14 D1 Burnley	A 0-1
18 EC Waterford	A 3-1 Law 3
21 D1 Newcastle United	H 3-1 Best 2, Law

October
2 EC Waterford	H 7-1 Law 4, Stiles, Burns, Charlton
5 D1 Arsenal	H 0-0
9 D1 Tottenham Hotspur	A 2-2 Crerand, Law
12 D1 Liverpool	A 0-2
19 D1 Southampton	H 1-2 Best
26 D1 Queen's Park Rangers	A 3-2 Best 2, Law

November
2 D1 Leeds United	H 0-0
9 D1 Sunderland	A 1-1 Hurley (og)
13 EC RSC Anderlecht	H 3-0 Law 2, Kidd
16 D1 Ipswich Town	H 0-0

23 D1 Stoke City	A 0-0
27 EC RSC Anderlecht	A 1-3 Sartori
30 D1 Wolves	H 2-0 Best, Law

December
7 D1 Leicester City	A 1-2 Law (pen)
14 D1 Liverpool	H 1-0 Law
21 D1 Southampton	H 1-2 Best
26 D1 Arsenal	A 0-3

January
4 FA Exeter City	A 3-1 Fitzpatrick, Kidd, Newman (og)
11 D1 Leeds United	A 1-2 Charlton
18 D1 Sunderland	H 4-1 Law 3 (1 pen), Best
25 FA Watford	H 1-1 Law

February
1 D1 Ipswich Town	A 0-1
3 FA Watford	A 2-0 Law 2
8 FA Birmingham City	A 2-2 Law, Best
15 D1 Wolves	A 2-2 Best, Charlton
24 FA Birmingham City	H 6-2 Law 3, Kidd, Morgan, Crerand
26 EC Rapid Vienna	H 3-0 Best 2 (1 pen), Morgan

March
1 FA Everton	H 0-1
5 EC Rapid Vienna	A 0-0
8 D1 Manchester City	H 0-1
10 D1 Everton	A 0-0
15 D1 Chelsea	A 2-3 James, Law
19 D1 Queen's Park Rangers	H 8-1 Morgan 3, Best 2, Aston, Kidd, Stiles
22 D1 Sheffield Wednesday	H 1-0 Best
24 D1 Stoke City	H 1-1 Aston
29 D1 West Ham United	A 0-0
31 D1 Nottingham Forest	A 1-0 Best

April
2 D1 West Bromwich Albion	H 2-1 Best 2
5 D1 Nottingham Forest	H 3-1 Morgan 2, Best
8 D1 Coventry City	A 1-2 Fitzpatrick
12 D1 Newcastle United	A 0-2
19 D1 Burnley	H 2-0 Best, Waldron (og)
23 ECSF AC Milan	A 0-2

May
15 ECSF AC Milan	H 1-0 Charlton
17 D1 Leicester City	H 3-2 Best, Law, Morgan

Final League position: 11th

1969-70

Chief Coach: Wilf McGuinness. **General Manager:** Sir Matt Busby
Played 59, **Won** 23, **Lost** 13, **Drawn** 23, **Goals for** 91, **Goals against** 70
Appearances: Charlton, Sadler 57; Stepney 54; Best 53; Kidd, Morgan 49; Dunne, Ure 48; Burns 42; Crerand 36; Aston 30; Fitzpatrick 29; Edwards 28; Sartori 27; Law 16; Brennan 11; Stiles 10; Givens 9; Gowling 8; Rimmer 5; Foulkes, James 3; Ryan 1
Goals: Best 23 (1 pen); Kidd 20; Charlton 14; Morgan 9 (3 pens); Burns, Fitzpatrick, Gowling, Law, Sadler, Sartori 3; own goals 2; Aston, Crerand, Edwards, Givens, Ure 1

August
9 D1 Crystal Palace	A 2-2 Charlton, Morgan
13 D1 Everton	H 0-2
16 D1 Southampton	H 1-4 Morgan
19 D1 Everton	A 0-3
23 D1 Wolves	A 0-0
27 D1 Newcastle United	H 0-0
30 D1 Sunderland	H 3-1 Best, Givens, Kidd

September
3 LC Middlesbrough	H 1-0 Sadler
6 D1 Leeds United	A 2-2 Best 2
13 D1 Liverpool	H 1-0 Morgan
17 D1 Sheffield Wednesday	A 3-1 Best 2, Kidd
20 D1 Arsenal	A 2-2 Best, Sadler
23 LC Wrexham	H 2-0 Best, Kidd
27 D1 West Ham United	H 5-2 Best 2, Burns, Charlton, Kidd

October
4 D1 Derby County	A 0-2
8 D1 Southampton	A 3-0 Best, Burns, Kidd
11 D1 Ipswich Town	H 2-1 Best, Kidd
14 LC Burnley	A 0-0
18 D1 Nottingham Forest	H 1-1 Best
20 LC Burnley	H 1-0 Best (pen)
25 D1 West Bromwich Albion	A 1-2 Kidd

November
1 D1 Stoke City	H 1-1 Charlton
8 D1 Coventry City	A 2-1 Aston, Law
12 LC Derby County	A 0-0
15 D1 Manchester City	A 0-4

19 LC Derby County   H 1-0 Kidd
22 D1 Tottenham Hotspur   H 3-1 Charlton 2, Burns
29 D1 Burnley   A 1-1 Best

December
3 LCSF Manchester City   A 1-2 Charlton
6 D1 Chelsea   H 0-2
13 D1 Liverpool   A 4-1 Charlton, Morgan, Ure, Yeats (og)
17 LCSF Manchester City   H 2-2 Edwards, Law
26 D1 Wolves   H 0-0
27 D1 Sunderland   A 1-1 Kidd

January
3 FA Ipswich Town   A 1-0 McNeil (og)
10 D1 Arsenal   H 2-1 Morgan, Sartori
17 D1 West Ham United   A 0-0
24 FA Manchester City   H 3-0 Kidd 2, Morgan (pen)
26 D1 Leeds United   H 2-2 Kidd, Sadler
31 D1 Derby County   H 1-0 Charlton

February
7 FA Northampton Town   A 8-2 Best 6, Kidd 2
10 D1 Ipswich Town   A 1-0 Kidd
14 D1 Crystal Palace   H 1-1 Kidd
21 FA Middlesbrough   A 1-1 Sartori
25 FA Middlesbrough   H 2-1 Charlton, Morgan (pen)
28 D1 Stoke City   A 2-2 Morgan (pen), Sartori

March
14 FASF Leeds United   N 0-0
17 D1 Burnley   H 3-3 Best, Crerand, Law
21 D1 Chelsea   A 1-2 Morgan
23 FASF Leeds United   N 0-0 (aet)
26 FASF Leeds United   N 0-1
28 D1 Manchester City   H 1-2 Kidd
30 D1 Coventry City   H 1-1 Kidd
31 D1 Nottingham Forest   A 2-1 Charlton, Gowling

April
4 D1 Newcastle United   A 1-5 Charlton
8 D1 West Bromwich Albion   H 7-0 Charlton 2, Fitzpatrick 2, Gowling 2, Best
10 FAPO Watford   N 2-0 Kidd
13 D1 Tottenham Hotspur   A 1-2 Fitzpatrick
15 D1 Sheffield Wednesday   H 2-2 Best, Charlton

Final League position: 8th

1970-71

Manager: Wilf McGuinness until December, then Sir Matt Busby
Played 53, **Won** 21, **Lost** 18, **Drawn** 14, **Goals for** 83, **Goals against** 82
Appearances: Charlton 53; Best 51; Dunne, Fitzpatrick 45; Sadler 42; Law 37; Edwards, Kidd 36; Morgan 32; Crerand 28; Rimmer 28; Stepney 25; Aston 24; Burns, Gowling 22; Stiles 21; Ure 20; James 17; Watson 10; Sartori 8; Donald, O'Neil, Young 1
Goals: Best 22 (1 pen); Law 17; Kidd 13; Charlton 10; Gowling 8; Aston, Fitzpatrick, Morgan 3 (2 pens); Sartori 2; Edwards, Sadler

August
1 WC Reading   A 3-1 Charlton 2, Edwards
5 WCSF Hull   A 1-1 Law (aet)
8 WCF Derby County   A 1-4 Best
15 D1 Leeds United   H 0-1
19 D1 Chelsea   H 0-0
22 D1 Arsenal   A 0-4
25 D1 Burnley   A 2-0 Law 2
29 D1 West Ham United   H 1-1 Fitzpatrick

September
2 D1 Everton   H 2-0 Best, Charlton
5 D1 Liverpool   A 1-1 Kidd
9 LC Aldershot   A 3-1 Law, Kidd, Best
12 D1 Coventry City   H 2-0 Best, Charlton
19 D1 Ipswich Town   A 0-4
26 D1 Blackpool   H 1-1 Best

October
3 D1 Wolves   A 2-3 Gowling, Kidd
7 LC Portsmouth   H 1-0 Charlton
17 D1 Leeds United   A 2-2 Charlton, Fitzpatrick
24 D1 West Bromwich Albion   H 2-1 Kidd, Law
28 LC Chelsea   H 2-1 Best, Charlton
31 D1 Newcastle United   A 0-1

November
7 D1 Stoke City   H 2-2 Sadler, Law
14 D1 Nottingham Forest   A 2-1 Gowling, Sartori
18 LC Crystal Palace   H 4-2 Kidd 2, Charlton, Fitzpatrick
21 D1 Southampton   A 0-1
28 D1 Huddersfield Town   H 1-1 Best

December
5 D1 Tottenham Hotspur   A 2-2 Best, Law
12 D1 Manchester City   H 1-4 Kidd
16 LCSF Aston Villa   H 1-1 Kidd
19 D1 Arsenal   H 1-3 Sartori
23 LCSF Aston Villa   A 1-2 Kidd
26 D1 Derby County   A 4-4 Law 2, Best, Kidd

January
2 FA Middlesbrough   H 0-0
5 FA Middlesbrough   A 1-2 Best
9 D1 Chelsea   A 2-1 Gowling, Morgan (pen)
16 D1 Burnley   H 1-1 Aston
30 D1 Huddersfield Town   A 2-1 Aston, Law

February
6 D1 Tottenham Hotspur   H 2-1 Best, Morgan (pen)
20 D1 Southampton   H 5-1 Gowling 4, Morgan
23 D1 Everton   A 0-1
27 D1 Newcastle United   H 1-0 Kidd

March
6 D1 West Bromwich Albion   A 3-4 Aston, Best, Kidd
13 D1 Nottingham Forest   H 2-0 Best, Law
20 D1 Stoke City   A 2-1 Best 2

April
3 D1 West Ham United   A 1-2 Best
10 D1 Derby County   H 1-2 Law
12 D1 Wolves   H 1-0 Gowling
13 D1 Coventry City   A 1-2 Best
17 D1 Crystal Palace   A 5-3 Law 3, Best 2
19 D1 Liverpool   H 0-2
24 D1 Ipswich Town   H 3-2 Charlton, Best (pen), Kidd

May
1 D1 Blackpool   A 1-1 Law
5 D1 Manchester City   A 4-3 Best 2, Charlton, Law

Final League position: 8th

1971-72

Manager: Frank O'Farrell
Played 56, **Won** 24, **Lost** 16, **Drawn** 16, **Goals for** 89, **Goals against** 73
Appearances: Best, Charlton 54; Stepney 53; Gowling 52; O'Neil, Sadler 50; James, Morgan 49; Kidd 44; Law 43; Dunne 42; Burns 26; McIlroy 21; Buchan 15; Aston 14; Storey-Moore 11; Young 7; Edwards 6; Connaughton, Sartori 3; Fitzpatrick 2; Crerand 1
Goals: Best 27 (2 pens); Law 13; Charlton 12; Kidd 10; Gowling 9; Storey-Moore 5; McIlroy 4; Morgan 3 (all pens); Sadler 2; Aston, Buchan, Burns, James 1

July
31 WC Halifax Town   A 1-2 Best

August
14 D1 Derby County   A 2-2 Gowling, Law
18 D1 Chelsea   A 3-2 Charlton, Kidd, Morgan (pen)
20 D1 Arsenal   H 3-1 Charlton, Gowling, Kidd
23 D1 West Bromwich Albion   H 3-1 Best 2, Gowling
28 D1 Wolves   A 1-1 Best
31 D1 Everton   A 0-1

September
4 D1 Ipswich Town   H 1-0 Best
7 LC Ipswich Town   A 3-1 Best 2, Morgan (pen)
11 D1 Crystal Palace   A 3-1 Law 2, Kidd
18 D1 West Ham United   H 4-2 Best 3, Charlton
25 D1 Liverpool   A 2-2 Charlton, Law

October
2 D1 Sheffield United   H 2-0 Best, Gowling
6 LC Burnley   H 1-1 Charlton
9 D1 Huddersfield Town   A 3-0 Best, Charlton, Law
16 D1 Derby County   H 1-0 Best
18 LC Burnley   A 1-0 Charlton
23 D1 Newcastle United   A 1-0 Best
27 LC Stoke City   H 1-1 Gowling
30 D1 Leeds United   H 0-1

November
6 D1 Manchester City   A 3-3 Gowling, Kidd, McIlroy
8 LC Stoke City   A 0-0 (aet)
13 D1 Tottenham Hotspur   H 3-1 Law 2, McIlroy
15 LC Stoke City   A 1-2 Best
20 D1 Leicester City   H 3-2 Law 2, Kidd
27 D1 Southampton   A 5-2 Best 3, Kidd, McIlroy

December

4 D1 Nottingham Forest	H 3-2	Kidd 2, Law
11 D1 Stoke City	A 1-1	Law
18 D1 Ipswich Town	A 0-0	
27 D1 Coventry City	H 2-2	James, Law

January

1 D1 West Ham United	A 0-3	
8 D1 Wolves	H 1-3	McIlroy
15 FA Southampton	A 1-1	Charlton
19 FA Southampton	H 4-1 (aet)	Best 2, Sadler, Aston
22 D1 Chelsea	H 0-1	
29 D1 West Bromwich Albion	A 1-2	Kidd

February

5 FA Preston North End	A 2-0	Gowling 2
12 D1 Newcastle United	H 0-2	
19 D1 Leeds United	A 1-5	Burns
26 FA Middlesbrough	H 0-0	
29 FA Middlesbrough	A 3-0	Morgan (pen), Charlton, Best

March

4 D1 Tottenham Hotspur	A 0-2	
8 D1 Everton	H 0-0	
11 D1 Huddersfield Town	H 2-0	Best, Storey-Moore
18 FA Stoke City	H 1-1	Best
22 FA Stoke City	A 1-2	Best
25 D1 Crystal Palace	H 4-0	Charlton, Gowling, Law, Storey-Moore

April

1 D1 Coventry City	A 3-2	Best, Charlton, Storey-Moore
3 D1 Liverpool	H 0-3	
4 D1 Sheffield United	A 1-1	Sadler
8 D1 Leicester City	A 0-2	
12 D1 Manchester City	H 1-3	Buchan
15 D1 Southampton	H 3-1	Best (pen), Kidd, Storey-Moore
22 D1 Nottingham Forest	A 0-0	
25 D1 Arsenal	A 0-3	
29 D1 Stoke City	H 3-0	Best (pen), Charlton, Storey-Moore

Final League position: 8th

1972-73

Manager: Frank O'Farrell to December, then Tommy Docherty
Played 51, **Won** 15, **Lost** 19, **Drawn** 17, **Goals for** 59, **Goals against** 70
Appearances: Buchan 50; Morgan 48; Stepney 45; Charlton 44; Young 33; Storey-Moore 31; Dunne, James 28; Kidd 24; Best 23; Graham, Sadler 22; Macari, Martin 19; Holton, MacDougall 18; Davies, O'Neil 17; Law 15; McIlroy 14; Forsyth 11; Anderson 10; Young 8; Fitzpatrick, Rimmer 6; Donald, Fletcher 5; Watson 4; Kidd, Sidebottom 3; Daly 2; Edwards, Olney, McGivern 1
Goals: Charlton 9; Storey-Moore 7; Best 6; Macari, MacDougall 5; Davies, Holton, Kidd, Morgan 4; Law, Martin 3; Anderson, Fletcher, Graham, McIlroy, Olney 1

August

12 D1 Ipswich Town	H 1-2	Law
15 D1 Liverpool	A 0-2	
19 D1 Everton	A 0-2	
23 D1 Leicester City	H 1-1	Best (pen)
26 D1 Arsenal	H 0-0	
30 D1 Chelsea	H 0-0	

September

2 D1 West Ham United	A 2-2	Best, Storey-Moore
6 LC Oxford United	A 2-2	Charlton, Law
9 D1 Coventry City	H 0-1	
12 LC Oxford United	H 3-1	Best 2 (1 pen), Storey-Moore
16 D1 Wolves	A 0-2	
23 D1 Derby County	H 3-0	Davies, Morgan, Storey-Moore
30 D1 Sheffield United	A 0-1	

October

3 LC Bristol Rovers	A 1-1	Morgan
7 D1 West Bromwich Albion	A 2-2	Best (pen), Storey-Moore
11 LC Bristol Rovers	H 1-2	McIlroy
14 D1 Birmingham City	H 1-0	MacDougall
21 D1 Newcastle United	A 1-2	Charlton
28 D1 Tottenham Hotspur	H 1-4	Charlton

November

4 D1 Leicester City	A 2-2	Best, Davies
11 D1 Liverpool	H 2-0	Davies, MacDougall
18 D1 Manchester City	A 0-3	
25 D1 Southampton	H 2-1	Davies, MacDougall

December

2 D1 Norwich City	A 2-0	MacDougall, Storey-Moore
9 D1 Stoke City	H 0-2	
16 D1 Crystal Palace	A 0-5	
23 D1 Leeds United	H 1-1	MacDougall
26 D1 Derby County	A 1-3	Storey-Moore

January

6 D1 Arsenal	A 1-3	Kidd
13 FA Wolves	A 0-1	
20 D1 West Ham United	H 2-2	Charlton (pen), Macari
24 D1 Everton	H 0-0	
27 D1 Coventry City	A 1-1	Holton

February

10 D1 Wolves	H 2-1	Charlton 2 (1 pen)
17 D1 Ipswich Town	A 1-4	Macari
21 AI Fiorentina	H 1-1	Holton

March

3 D1 West Bromwich Albion	H 2-1	Kidd, Macari
10 D1 Birmingham City	A 1-3	Macari
17 D1 Newcastle United	H 2-1	Holton, Martin
21 AI Lazio	A 0-0	
24 D1 Tottenham Hotspur	A 1-1	Graham
31 D1 Southampton	A 2-0	Charlton, Holton

April

4 AI Bari	H 3-1	Law, Storey-Moore, Martin
7 D1 Norwich City	H 1-0	Martin
11 D1 Crystal Palace	H 2-0	Kidd, Morgan
14 D1 Stoke City	A 2-2	Macari, Morgan
18 D1 Leeds United	A 1-0	Anderson
21 D1 Manchester City	H 0-0	
23 D1 Sheffield United	H 1-2	Kidd
28 D1 Chelsea	A 0-1	

May

2 AI Verona	A 4-1	Charlton 2, Olney, Fletcher

Final League position: 8th

1973-74

Manager: Tommy Docherty
Played 45, **Won** 11, **Lost** 22, **Drawn** 12, **Goals for** 39, **Goals against** 50
Appearances: M. Buchan, Stepney 45; Morgan 44; B. Greenhoff 39; Macari 38; Holton 37; Young 33; McIlroy 31; Graham 26; Kidd 24; James 23; Forsyth, Houston 20; Martin 18; Daly 17; Anderson, Best 12; McCalliog 11; Griffiths 7; Fletcher 5; Sadler 3; Bielby, Sidebottom, Storey-Moore 2
Goals: Macari, McIlroy 6; McCalliog 4; B. Greenhoff 3; Best, Bielby, Houston, James, Kidd, Morgan, Stepney (2 pens) 2; Anderson, Daly, Forsyth, Graham, Storey-Moore, Young 1

August

25 D1 Arsenal	A 0-3	
29 D1 Stoke City	H 1-0	James

September

1 D1 Queen's Park Rangers	H 2-1	Holton, McIlroy
5 D1 Leicester City	A 0-1	
8 D1 Ipswich Town	A 1-2	Anderson
12 D1 Leicester City	H 1-2	Stepney (pen)
15 D1 West Ham United	H 3-1	Kidd 2, Storey-Moore
22 D1 Leeds United	A 0-0	
29 D1 Liverpool	H 0-0	

October

6 D1 Wolves	A 1-2	McIlroy
8 LC Middlesbrough	H 0-1	
13 D1 Derby County	H 0-1	
20 D1 Birmingham City	H 1-0	Stepney (pen)
27 D1 Burnley	A 0-0	

November

3 D1 Chelsea	H 2-2	Greenhoff, Young
10 D1 Tottenham Hotspur	A 1-2	Best
17 D1 Newcastle United	A 2-3	Graham, Macari
24 D1 Norwich City	H 0-0	

December

8 D1 Southampton	H 0-0	
15 D1 Coventry City	H 2-3	Best, Morgan
22 D1 Liverpool	A 0-2	
26 D1 Sheffield United	H 1-2	Macari
29 D1 Ipswich Town	H 2-0	Macari, McIlroy

January

1 D1 Queen's Park Rangers	A 0-3	
5 FA Plymouth Argyle	H 1-0	Macari
12 D1 West Ham United	A 1-2	McIlroy
19 D1 Arsenal	H 1-1	James
26 FA Ipswich Town	H 0-1	

February

2 D1 Coventry City	A 0-1	
9 D1 Leeds United	H 0-2	
16 D1 Derby County	A 2-2	Greenhoff, Houston
23 D1 Wolves	H 0-0	

March

2 D1 Sheffield United	A 1-0 Macari	
13 D1 Manchester City	A 0-0	
16 D1 Birmingham City	A 0-1	
23 D1 Tottenham Hotspur	H 0-1	
30 D1 Chelsea	A 3-1 Daly, McIlroy, Morgan	

April

3 D1 Burnley	H 3-3 Forsyth, Holton, McIlroy	
6 D1 Norwich City	A 2-0 Greenhoff, Macari	
13 D1 Newcastle United	H 1-0 McCalliog	
15 D1 Everton	H 3-0 McCalliog 2, Houston	
20 D1 Southampton	A 1-1 McCalliog (pen)	
23 D1 Everton	A 0-1	
27 D1 Manchester City	H 0-1	
29 D1 Stoke City	A 0-1	

Final League position: 21st (relegated to Division Two)

1974-75

Manager: Tommy Docherty
Played 51, **Won** 30, **Lost** 9, **Drawn** 12, **Goals for** 82, **Goals against** 39
Appearances: McIlroy 51; Buchan 50; Stepney 49; B. Greenhoff 49; Houston, Macari 48; Daly 46; Forsyth 45; Morgan 42; Pearson 37; McCalliog 27; Young 22; Holton 18; James, Sidebottom 15; Coppell, R. Davies 10; Martin 9; Albiston 3; Baldwin, McCreery, Roche 2; Graham, Nicholl 1
Goals: Macari, Pearson 18; Daly 13 (9 pens); McIlroy 10; Houston 7; B. Greenhoff, Morgan 4; McCalliog (1 pen), own goals 3; Coppell, Forsyth 1

August

17 D2 Orient	A 2-0 Houston, Morgan	
24 D2 Millwall	H 4-0 Daly 3 (2 pens), Pearson	
28 D2 Portsmouth	H 2-1 Daly (pen), McIlroy	
31 D2 Cardiff City	A 1-0 Daly (pen)	

September

7 D2 Nottingham Forest	H 2-2 Greenhoff, McIlroy	
11 LC Charlton Athletic	H 5-1 Macari 2, Houston, McIlroy, Warman (og)	
14 D2 West Bromwich Albion	A 1-1 Pearson	
16 D2 Millwall	A 1-0 Daly (pen)	
21 D2 Bristol Rovers	H 2-0 Pearson, Prince (og)	
25 D2 Bolton Wanderers	H 3-0 Macari, Houston, McAllister (og)	
28 D2 Norwich City	A 0-2	

October

5 D2 Fulham	A 2-1 Pearson 2	
9 LC Manchester City	H 1-0 Daly (pen)	
12 D2 Notts County	H 1-0 McIlroy	
15 D2 Portsmouth	A 0-0	
19 D2 Blackpool	A 3-0 Forsyth, McCalliog, Macari	
26 D2 Southampton	H 1-0 Pearson	

November

2 D2 Oxford United	H 4-0 Pearson 3, Macari	
9 D2 Bristol City	A 0-1	
13 LC Burnley	H 3-2 Macari 2, Morgan	
16 D2 Aston Villa	H 2-1 Daly 2 (1 pen)	
23 D2 Hull City	A 0-2	
30 D2 Sunderland	H 3-2 Pearson, Morgan, McIlroy	

December

4 LC Middlesbrough	A 0-0	
7 D2 Sheffield Wednesday	A 4-4 Houston, Macari 2, Pearson	
14 D2 Orient	H 0-0	
18 LC Middlesbrough	H 3-0 McIlroy, Pearson, Macari	
21 D2 York City	A 1-0 Pearson	
26 D2 West Bromwich Albion	H 2-1 McIlroy, Daly (pen)	
28 D2 Oldham Athletic	A 0-1	

January

4 FA Walsall	H 0-0	
7 FA Walsall	A 2-3 Daly (pen), McIlroy	
11 D2 Sheffield Wednesday	H 2-0 McCalliog 2 (1 pen)	
15 LCSF Norwich City	H 2-2 Macari 2	
18 D2 Sunderland	A 0-0	
22 LCSF Norwich City	A 0-1	

February

1 D2 Bristol City	H 0-1	
8 D2 Oxford United	A 0-1	
15 D2 Hull City	H 2-0 Houston, Pearson	
22 D2 Aston Villa	A 0-2	

March

1 D2 Cardiff City	H 4-0 Houston, McIlroy, Macari, Pearson	
8 D2 Bolton Wanderers	A 1-0 Pearson	
15 D2 Norwich City	H 1-0 Pearson	
22 D2 Nottingham Forest	A 1-0 Daly	
28 D2 Bristol Rovers	A 1-1 Macari	
29 D2 York City	H 2-1 Morgan, Macari	
31 D2 Oldham Athletic	H 3-2 McIlroy, Macari, Coppell	

April

5 D2 Southampton	A 1-0 Macari	
12 D2 Fulham	H 1-0 Daly	
19 D2 Notts County	A 2-2 Greenhoff, Houston	
26 D2 Blackpool	H 4-0 Pearson 2, Macari, Greenhoff	

Final position: Division Two **Champions**, promoted to Division One

1975-76

Manager: Tommy Docherty
Played 52, **Won** 30, **Lost** 11, **Drawn** 11, **Goals for** 85, **Goals against** 55
Appearances: Buchan, Houston 52; Daly, McIlroy 51; B. Greenhoff 50; Coppell, Pearson 49; Stepney 47; Macari 45; Forsyth 35; Hill 33; McCreery 32; Nicholl 25; Jackson 20; Roche 5; Albiston 3; Coyne, Grimshaw 2; Kelly, Young 1
Goals: Macari 15; Pearson 14; McIlroy 13; Daly (4 pens) 11; Hill 10; own goals 6; Coppell 5; McCreery 4; Forsyth 3; Houston 2; Coyne, B. Greenhoff 1

August

16 D1 Wolves	A 2-0 Macari 2	
19 D1 Birmingham City	A 2-0 McIlroy 2	
23 D1 Sheffield United	H 5-1 Pearson 2, Badger (og), Daly, McIlroy	
27 D1 Coventry City	H 1-1 Pearson	
30 D1 Stoke City	A 1-0 Dodd (og)	

September

6 D1 Tottenham Hotspur	H 3-2 Pratt (og), Daly 2 (1 pen)	
10 LC Brentford	H 2-1 McIlroy, Macari	
13 D1 Queen's Park Rangers	A 0-1	
20 D1 Ipswich Town	H 1-0 Houston	
24 D1 Derby County	A 1-2 Daly	
27 D1 Manchester City	A 2-2 McCreery, Macari	

October

4 D1 Leicester City	H 0-0	
8 LC Aston Villa	A 2-1 Coppell, Macari	
11 D1 Leeds United	A 2-1 McIlroy 2	
18 D1 Arsenal	H 3-1 Coppell 2, Pearson	
25 D1 West Ham United	A 1-2 Macari	

November

1 D1 Norwich City	H 1-0 Pearson	
8 D1 Liverpool	A 1-3 Coppell	
12 LC Manchester City	A 0-4	
15 D1 Aston Villa	H 2-0 Coppell, McIlroy	
22 D1 Arsenal	A 1-3 Pearson	
29 D1 Newcastle United	H 1-0 Daly	

December

6 D1 Middlesbrough	A 0-0	
13 D1 Sheffield United	A 4-1 Pearson 2, Hill, Macari	
20 D1 Wolves	H 1-0 Hill	
23 D1 Everton	A 1-1 Macari	
27 D1 Burnley	H 2-1 Macari, McIlroy	

January

3 FA Oxford United	H 2-1 Daly 2 (2 pens)	
10 D1 Queen's Park Rangers	H 2-1 Hill, McIlroy	
17 D1 Tottenham Hotspur	A 1-1 Hill	
24 FA Peterborough United	H 3-1 Forsyth, McIlroy, Hill	
27 D1 Birmingham City	H 3-1 Forsyth, Macari, McIlroy	

February

7 D1 Coventry City	A 1-1 Macari	
14 FA Leicester City	A 2-1 Daly, Macari	
18 D1 Liverpool	H 0-0	
21 D1 Aston Villa	A 1-2 Macari	
25 D1 Derby County	H 1-1 Pearson	
28 D1 West Ham United	H 4-0 Forsyth, Macari, McCreery, Pearson	

March

6 FA Wolves	H 1-1 Daly	
9 FA Wolves	A 3-2 B. Greenhoff, McIlroy, Pearson	
13 D1 Leeds United	H 3-2 Houston, Pearson, Daly	
17 D1 Norwich City	A 1-1 Hill	
20 D1 Newcastle United	A 4-3 Pearson 2, Bird (og), Howard (og)	
27 D1 Middlesbrough	H 3-0 Daly (pen), McCreery, Hill	

April

3 FASF Derby County	N 2-0 Hill 2	
10 D1 Ipswich Town	A 0-3	
17 D1 Everton	H 2-1 McCreery, Kenyon (og)	
19 D1 Burnley	A 1-0 Macari	
21 D1 Stoke City	H 0-1	
24 D1 Leicester City	A 1-2 Coyne	

May

1 FAF Southampton	W 0-1	
4 D1 Manchester City	H 2-0 Hill, McIlroy	

Final League position: 3rd. FA Cup losing finalists

1976-77

Manager: Tommy Docherty
Played 59, **Won** 29, **Lost** 16, **Drawn** 14, **Goals for** 103, **Goals against** 81
Appearances: B.Greenhoff, McIlroy, Stepney 57; Coppell, Hill 56; Nicholl 55; Pearson 53; Macari 52; Houston 51; Buchan 46; McCreery 37; J. Greenhoff34; Daly 28; Albiston 24; C. McGrath 7; Forsyth 5; Waldron 4; Foggan, Jackson, Paterson 5; Roche 2; Clark 1
Goals: Hill 22 (2 pens); Pearson 19; Macari 14; J. Greenhoff 12 (1 pen); Coppell 8; Daly 7 (3 pens); B. Greenhoff, Houston, own goals 5; McCreery, McIlroy 3; Nicholl 1

August
21 D1 Birmingham City	H 2-2	Coppell, Pearson
24 D1 Coventry City	A 2-0	Macari, Hill
28 D1 Derby County	A 0-0	

September
1 LC Tranmere Rovers	H 5-0	Daly 2, Pearson, Macari, Hill
2 D1 Tottenham Hotspur	H 2-3	Coppell, Pearson
11 D1 Newcastle United	A 2-2	B. Greenhoff, Pearson
15 UC Ajax Amsterdam	A 0-1	
18 D1 Middlesbrough	H 2-0	McAndrew (og), Pearson
22 LC Sunderland	H 2-2	Pearson, Clark (og)
25 D1 Manchester City	A 3-1	Coppell, McCreery, Daly
29 UC Ajax Amsterdam	H 2-0	McIlroy, Macari

October
2 D1 Leeds United	A 2-0	Daly, Coppell
4 LC Sunderland	A 2-2 (aet)	Daly (pen), B. Greenhoff
6 LC Sunderland	H 1-0	B. Greenhoff
16 D1 West Bromwich Albion	A 0-4	
20 UC Juventus	H 1-0	Hill
23 D1 Norwich City	H 2-2	Daly (pen), Hill
27 LC Newcastle United	H 7-2	Hill 3, Nicholl, Houston, Coppell, Pearson
30 D1 Ipswich Town	H 0-1	

November
3 UC Juventus	A 0-3	
6 D1 Aston Villa	A 2-3	Pearson, Hill
10 D1 Sunderland	H 3-3	Pearson, Hill, B. Greenhoff
20 D1 Leicester City	A 1-1	Daly (pen)
27 D1 West Ham United	H 0-2	

December
1 LC Everton	H 0-3	
18 D1 Arsenal	A 1-3	McIlroy
27 D1 Everton	H 4-0	Pearson, J. Greenhoff, Hill, Macari

January
1 D1 Aston Villa	H 2-0	Pearson 2
3 D1 Ipswich Town	A 1-2	Pearson
8 FA Walsall	H 1-0	Hill
15 D1 Coventry City	H 2-0	Macari 2
19 D1 Bristol City	H 2-1	B. Greenhoff, Pearson
22 D1 Birmingham City	A 3-2	Houston, J. Greenhoff, Pearson
29 FA Queen's Park Rangers	H 1-0	Macari

February
5 D1 Derby County	H 3-1	Houston, Macari, Powell (og)
12 D1 Tottenham Hotspur	A 3-1	Hill, Macari, McIlroy
16 D1 Liverpool	H 0-0	
19 D1 Newcastle United	H 3-1	J. Greenhoff 3
26 FA Southampton	A 2-2	Macari, Hill

March
5 D1 Manchester City	H 3-1	Pearson, Coppell, Hill
8 FA Southampton	H 2-1	J. Greenhoff 2
12 D1 Leeds United	H 1-0	Cherry (og)
19 FA Aston Villa	H 2-1	Houston, Macari
23 D1 West Bromwich Albion	H 2-2	Coppell, Hill

April
2 D1 Norwich City	A 1-2	Powell (og)
5 D1 Everton	A 2-1	Hill 2
9 D1 Stoke City	H 3-0	Houston, Macari, Pearson
11 D1 Sunderland	A 1-2	Hill (pen)
16 D1 Leicester City	H 1-1	J. Greenhoff
19 D1 Queen's Park Rangers	A 0-4	
23 FASF Leeds United	N 2-1	Coppell, J. Greenhoff
26 D1 Middlesbrough	A 0-3	
30 D1 Queen's Park Rangers	H 1-0	Macari

May
3 D1 Liverpool	A 0-1	
7 D1 Bristol City	A 1-1	J. Greenhoff (pen)
11 D1 Stoke City	A 3-3	Hill 2, McCreery
14 D1 Arsenal	H 3-2	J. Greenhoff, Macari, Hill
16 D1 West Ham United	A 2-4	Hill, Pearson
21 FAF Liverpool	W 2-1	Pearson, J. Greenhoff

Final League position: 6th. **Won FA Cup**

1977-78

Manager: Dave Sexton
Played 52, **Won** 19, **Lost** 19, **Drawn** 14, **Goals for** 85, **Goals against** 80
Appearances: Coppell 52; McIlroy 48; Nicholl 47; Hill 45; Macari 40; Pearson 39; Albiston, Buchan 38; Houston 37; B. Greenhoff 36; J. Greenhoff, Stepney 29; C. McGrath, Roche, McCreery 23; Grimes 17; Jordan 16; McQueen 14; Forsyth, Ritchie 4; Rogers 1
Goals: Hill (7 pens) 19; Pearson (1 pen) 15; Macari 11; McIlroy 9; Coppell 8; J. Greenhoff 6; Jordan, Nicholl 3; Grimes (1 pen), McCreery 2; Buchan, B. Greenhoff, C. McGrath, McQueen, own goal 1

August
13 CS Liverpool	W 0-0	
20 D1 Birmingham City	A 4-1	Macari 3, Hill
24 D1 Coventry City	H 2-1	Hill (pen), McCreery
27 D1 Ipswich Town	H 0-0	
30 LC Arsenal	A 2-3	McCreery, Pearson

September
3 D1 Derby County	A 1-0	Macari
10 D1 Manchester City	A 1-3	Nicholl
14 ECWC St. Etienne	A 1-1	Hill
17 D1 Chelsea	H 0-1	
24 D1 Leeds United	A 1-1	Hill

October
1 D1 Liverpool	H 2-0	Macari, McIlroy
5 ECWC St. Etienne	N 2-0	Coppell, Pearson
8 D1 Middlesbrough	A 1-2	Coppell
15 D1 Newcastle United	H 3-2	Coppell, J. Greenhoff, Pearson
19 ECWC FC Porto	A 0-4	
22 D1 West Bromwich Albion	A 0-4	
29 D1 Aston Villa	A 1-2	Nicholl

November
2 ECWC FC Porto	H 5-2	Coppell 2, Nicholl, Murca 2 (2 og)
5 D1 Arsenal	H 1-2	Hill
12 D1 Nottingham Forest	A 1-2	Pearson
19 D1 Norwich City	H 1-0	Pearson
26 D1 Queen's Park Rangers	A 2-2	Hill 2

December
3 D1 Wolves	H 3-1	McIlroy, J. Greenhoff, Pearson
10 D1 West Ham United	A 1-2	McGrath
17 D1 Nottingham Forest	H 0-4	
26 D1 Everton	A 6-2	Macari 2, Hill, J. Greenhoff, Ross (og), McIlroy
27 D1 Leicester City	H 3-1	J. Greenhoff, Coppell, Hill
31 D1 Coventry City	A 0-3	

January
2 D1 Birmingham City	H 1-2	J. Greenhoff
7 FA Carlisle United	A 1-1	Macari
11 FA Carlisle United	H 4-2	Pearson 2, Macari 2
14 D1 Ipswich Town	A 2-1	Pearson, McIlroy
21 D1 Derby County	H 4-0	Pearson, Hill 2 (1 pen), Buchan
28 FA West Bromwich Albion	H 1-1	Coppell

February
1 FA West Bromwich Albion	A 2-3	Pearson, Hill
8 D1 Bristol City	H 1-1	Hill (pen)
11 D1 Chelsea	A 2-2	McIlroy, Hill (pen)
25 D1 Liverpool	A 1-3	McIlroy

March
1 D1 Leeds United	H 0-1	
4 D1 Middlesbrough	H 0-0	
11 D1 Newcastle United	A 2-2	Jordan, Hill
15 D1 Manchester City	H 2-2	Hill 2 (2 pens)
18 D1 West Bromwich Albion	H 1-1	McQueen
25 D1 Leicester City	A 3-2	Pearson, Hill, J. Greenhoff
27 D1 Everton	H 1-2	Hill (pen)
29 D1 Aston Villa	H 1-1	McIlroy

April
1 D1 Arsenal	A 1-3	Jordan
8 D1 Queen's Park Rangers	H 3-1	Pearson 2 (1 pen), Grimes
15 D1 Norwich City	A 3-1	Jordan, McIlroy, Coppell
22 D1 West Ham United	H 3-0	Grimes (pen), McIlroy, Pearson
25 D1 Bristol City	A 1-0	Pearson
29 D1 Wolves	A 1-2	B. Greenhoff

Final League position: 10th

1978-79

Manager: Dave Sexton
Played 53, **Won** 21, **Lost** 14, **Drawn** 18, **Goals for** 78, **Goals against** 74
Appearances: Coppell 53; McIlroy 51; Buchan 48; McQueen 47; J. Greenhoff 44; Albiston 42; B. Greenhoff 40; Macari 38; Bailey, Jordan 37; Thomas 34; Nicholl 29; Houston 25; Grimes, Ritchie 21; McCreery, Roche 16; Sloan 4; Paterson 3; Connell, C. McGrath, Pearson 2; Moran 1
Goals: J. Greenhoff (2 pens) 17; Coppell 12; Jordan, Ritchie 10; McIlroy 8; McQueen 7; Macari 6; B. Greenhoff 3; Buchan, Thomas 2; Grimes 1

August
19 D1 Birmingham City	H 1-0 Jordan	
23 D1 Leeds United	A 3-2 McQueen, McIlroy, Macari	
26 D1 Ipswich Town	A 0-3	
30 LC Stockport County	H 3-2 McIlroy, J. Greenhoff (pen), Jordan	

September
2 D1 Everton	H 1-1 Buchan	
9 D1 Queen's Park Rangers	A 1-1 J. Greenhoff	
16 D1 Nottingham Forest	H 1-1 J. Greenhoff	
23 D1 Arsenal	A 1-1 Coppell	
30 D1 Manchester City	H 1-0 Jordan	

October
4 LC Watford	H 1-2 Jordan	
7 D1 Middlesbrough	H 3-2 Macari 2, Jordan	
14 D1 Aston Villa	A 2-2 Macari, McIlroy	
23 D1 Bristol City	H 1-3 J. Greenhoff	
28 D1 Wolves	A 4-2 J. Greenhoff 2, Jordan, B. Greenhoff	

November
4 D1 Southampton	H 1-1 J. Greenhoff	
11 D1 Birmingham City	A 1-5 Jordan	
18 D1 Ipswich Town	H 2-0 Coppell, J. Greenhoff	
21 D1 Everton	A 0-3	
25 D1 Chelsea	A 1-0 J. Greenhoff	

December
9 D1 Derby County	A 3-1 Ritchie 2, J. Greenhoff	
16 D1 Tottenham Hotspur	H 2-0 Ritchie, McIlroy	
22 D1 Bolton Wanderers	A 0-3	
26 D1 Liverpool	H 0-3	
30 D1 West Bromwich Albion	H 3-5 B. Greenhoff, McQueen, McIlroy	

January
15 FA Chelsea	H 3-0 Coppell, J. Greenhoff, Grimes	
31 FA Fulham	A 1-1 J. Greenhoff	

February
3 D1 Arsenal	H 0-2	
10 D1 Manchester City	A 3-0 Coppell 2, Ritchie	
12 FA Fulham	H 1-0 J. Greenhoff	
20 FA Colchester United	A 1-0 J. Greenhoff	
24 D1 Aston Villa	H 1-1 J. Greenhoff (pen)	
28 D1 Queen's Park Rangers	H 2-0 J. Greenhoff, Coppell	

March
3 D1 Bristol City	A 2-1 Ritchie, McQueen	
10 FA Tottenham Hotspur	A 1-1 Thomas	
14 FA Tottenham Hotspur	H 2-0 McIlroy, Jordan	
20 D1 Coventry City	A 3-4 Coppell 2, McIlroy	
24 D1 Leeds United	H 4-1 Ritchie 3, Thomas	
27 D1 Middlesbrough	A 2-2 McQueen, Coppell	
31 FASF Liverpool	N 2-2 Jordan, B. Greenhoff	

April
4 FASF Liverpool	N 1-0 J. Greenhoff	
7 D1 Norwich City	A 2-2 McQueen, Macari	
11 D1 Bolton Wanderers	H 1-2 Buchan	
14 D1 Liverpool	A 0-2	
16 D1 Coventry City	H 0-0	
18 D1 Nottingham Forest	A 1-1 Jordan	
21 D1 Tottenham Hotspur	A 1-1 McQueen	
25 D1 Norwich City	H 1-0 Macari	
28 D1 Derby County	H 0-0	
30 D1 Southampton	A 1-1 Ritchie	

May
5 D1 West Bromwich Albion	A 0-1	
7 D1 Wolves	H 3-2 Ritchie, Coppell 2	
12 FAF Arsenal	W 2-3 McQueen, McIlroy	
16 D1 Chelsea	H 1-1 Coppell	

Final League position: 9th. FA Cup losing finalists

1979-80

Manager: Dave Sexton
Played 47, **Won** 25, **Lost** 11, **Drawn** 11, **Goals for** 71, **Goals against** 44
Appearances: Bailey, Buchan, Coppell, Nicholl, Macari 47; Macari 44; McIlroy 43; Wilkins 42; Thomas 40; McQueen 37; Jordan 36; Albiston 28; Grimes 27; Houston 17; Ritchie 11; Moran 9; J. Greenhoff, Sloan 5; Jovanovic 2; C. McGrath, Paterson 1
Goals: Jordan 13; Thomas (1 pen) 10; Coppell, Macari, McQueen 9; McIlroy 8 (3 pens); Grimes, own goals, Ritchie 3; Wilkins 2; J. Greenhoff, Moran 1

August
18 D1 Southampton	A 1-1 McQueen	
22 D1 West Bromwich Albion	H 2-0 McQueen, Coppell	
25 D1 Arsenal	A 0-0	
29 LC Tottenham Hotspur	A 1-2 Thomas	

September
1 D1 Middlesbrough	H 2-1 Macari 2	
5 LC Tottenham Hotspur	H 3-1 Coppell, Thomas, Miller (og)	
8 D1 Aston Villa	A 3-0 Coppell, Thomas (pen), Grimes	
15 D1 Derby County	H 1-0 Grimes	
22 D1 Wolves	A 1-3 Macari	
26 LC Norwich City	A 1-4 McIlroy	
29 D1 Stoke City	H 4-0 Wilkins, McQueen 2, McIlroy	

October
6 D1 Brighton	H 2-0 Coppell, Macari	
10 D1 West Bromwich Albion	A 0-2	
13 D1 Bristol City	A 1-1 Macari	
20 D1 Ipswich Town	H 1-0 Grimes	
27 D1 Everton	A 0-0	

November
3 D1 Southampton	H 1-0 Macari	
10 D1 Manchester City	A 0-2	
17 D1 Crystal Palace	H 1-1 Jordan	
24 D1 Norwich City	H 5-0 Macari, Moran, Coppell, Jordan 2	

December
1 D1 Tottenham Hotspur	A 2-1 Macari, Coppell	
8 D1 Leeds United	H 1-1 Thomas	
15 D1 Coventry City	A 2-1 McQueen, Macari	
22 D1 Nottingham Forest	H 3-0 Jordan 2, McQueen	
26 D1 Liverpool	A 0-2	
29 D1 Arsenal	H 3-0 McQueen, Jordan, McIlroy (pen)	

January
5 FA Tottenham Hotspur	A 1-1 McIlroy (pen)	
9 FA Tottenham Hotspur	H 0-1 (aet)	
12 D1 Middlesbrough	A 1-1 Thomas	

February
2 D1 Derby County	A 3-1 Thomas, McIlroy, B. Powell (og)	
9 D1 Wolves	H 0-1	
16 D1 Stoke City	A 1-1 Coppell	
23 D1 Bristol City	H 4-0 Jordan 2, McIlroy, Merrick (og)	
27 D1 Bolton Wanderers	H 2-0 McQueen, Coppell	

March
1 D1 Ipswich Town	A 0-6	
12 D1 Everton	H 0-0	
15 D1 Brighton	A 0-0	
22 D1 Manchester City	H 1-0 Thomas	
29 D1 Crystal Palace	A 2-0 Jordan, Thomas	

April
2 D1 Nottingham Forest	A 0-2	
5 D1 Liverpool	H 2-1 Thomas, J. Greenhoff	
7 D1 Bolton Wanderers	A 3-1 McQueen, Thomas, Coppell	
12 D1 Tottenham Hotspur	H 4-1 Ritchie 3, Wilkins	
19 D1 Norwich City	A 2-0 Jordan 2	
23 D1 Aston Villa	H 2-1 Jordan 2	
26 D1 Coventry City	H 2-1 McIlroy 2 (1 pen)	

May
3 D1 Leeds United	A 0-2	

Final League position: 2nd

1980-81

Manager: Dave Sexton
Played 47, **Won** 16, **Lost** 12, **Drawn** 19, **Goals for** 55, **Goals against** 41
Appearances: Albiston, Coppell 47; Bailey 45; Macari 43; Nicholl 41; Jordan 36; Duxbury, McIlroy, Thomas 35; Moran 33; Buchan 30; Birtles 28; Jovanovic 22; Wilkins 15; McQueen 13; J. Greenhoff 11; Grimes 8; Ritchie 6; Sloan 3; McGarvey, Roche 2; C. McGrath, Whelan 1
Goals: Jordan 15; Macari 9; Coppell 6; McIlroy (3 pens) 5; Jovanovic 4; Duxbury, Thomas 3; Grimes, McQueen, Nicholl, own goals 2; Albiston, Birtles 1

August
16 D1 Middlesbrough	H 3-0 Macari, Grimes, Thomas	
19 D1 Wolves	A 0-1	

23 D1 Birmingham City	A 0-0	
27 LC Coventry City	H 0-1	
30 D1 Sunderland	H 1-1 Jovanovic	

September

2 LC Coventry City	A 0-1	
6 D1 Tottenham Hotspur	A 0-0	
13 D1 Leicester City	H 5-0 Coppell, Grimes, Jovanovic 2, Macari	
20 D1 Leeds United	A 0-0	
27 D1 Manchester City	H 2-2 Coppell, Albiston	

October

4 D1 Nottingham Forest	A 2-1 Coppell, Macari	
8 D1 Aston Villa	H 3-3 Coppell, McIlroy 2 (1 pen)	
11 D1 Arsenal	H 0-0	
18 D1 Ipswich Town	A 1-1 McIlroy (pen)	
22 D1 Stoke City	A 2-1 Jordan, Macari	
25 D1 Everton	H 2-0 Jordan, Coppell	

November

1 D1 Crystal Palace	A 0-1	
8 D1 Coventry City	H 0-0	
12 D1 Wolves	H 0-0	
15 D1 Middlesbrough	A 1-1 Jordan	
22 D1 Brighton	A 4-1 Jordan 2, McIlroy, Duxbury	
29 D1 Southampton	H 1-1 Jordan	

December

6 D1 Norwich City	A 2-2 Bond (og), Coppell	
13 D1 Stoke City	H 2-2 Macari, Jordan	
20 D1 Arsenal	A 1-2 Macari	
26 D1 Liverpool	H 0-0	
27 D1 West Bromwich Albion	A 1-3 Jovanovic	

January

3 FA Brighton	H 2-2 Duxbury, Thomas	
7 FA Brighton	A 2-0 Nicholl, Birtles	
10 D1 Brighton	H 2-1 McQueen, Macari	
24 D1 Nottingham Forest	A 0-1	
28 D1 Sunderland	A 0-2	
31 D1 Birmingham City	H 2-0 Jordan, Macari	

February

7 D1 Leicester City	A 0-1	
17 D1 Tottenham Hotspur	H 0-0	
21 D1 Manchester City	A 0-1	
28 D1 Leeds United	H 0-1	

March

7 D1 Southampton	A 0-1	
14 D1 Aston Villa	A 3-3 Jordan 2, McIlroy (pen)	
18 D1 Nottingham Forest	H 1-1 Burns (og)	
21 D1 Ipswich Town	H 2-1 Thomas, Nicholl	
28 D1 Everton	A 1-0 Jordan	

April

4 D1 Crystal Palace	H 1-0 Duxbury	
11 D1 Coventry City	A 2-0 Jordan 2	
14 D1 Liverpool	A 1-0 McQueen	
18 D1 West Bromwich Albion	H 2-1 Jordan, Macari	
25 D1 Norwich City	H 1-0 Jordan	

Final League position: 8th

1981-82

Manager: Ron Atkinson
Played 45, **Won** 22, **Lost** 11, **Drawn** 12, **Goals for** 59, Goals **against** 32
Appearances: Albiston, Wilkins 42; Stapleton 44; Bailey 42; Gidman 40; Coppell 38; Birtles 36; Robson 35; Moran 33; Buchan 30; Duxbury 25; Moses 23; McQueen 21; McGarvey 16; McIlroy 14; Macari 12; Grimes 11; Roche 3; Whiteside 2; Davies, Nicholl 1
Goals: Stapleton (1 pen) 13; Birtles 11; Coppell (1 pen) 9; Moran 7; Robson 5; McIlroy 3; Macari, McGarvey, Moses 2; Albiston, Gidman, Grimes, Whiteside, Wilkins 1

August

29 D1 Coventry City	A 1-2 Macari	
31 D1 Nottingham Forest	H 0-0	

September

5 D1 Ipswich Town	H 1-2 Stapleton	
12 D1 Aston Villa	A 1-1 Stapleton	
19 D1 Swansea City	H 1-0 Birtles	
22 D1 Middlesbrough	A 2-0 Stapleton, Birtles	
26 D1 Arsenal	A 0-0	
30 D1 Leeds United	H 1-0 Stapleton	

October

3 D1 Wolves	H 5-0 Stapleton, Birtles, McIlroy 3	
7 LC Tottenham Hotspur	A 0-1	
10 D1 Manchester City	A 0-0	
17 D1 Birmingham City	H 1-1 Coppell	
21 D1 Middlesbrough	H 1-0 Moses	
24 D1 Liverpool	A 2-1 Moran, Albiston	
28 LC Tottenham Hotspur	H 0-1	

31 D1 Notts County	H 2-1 Birtles, Moses	

November

7 D1 Sunderland	A 5-1 Moran, Robson, Stapleton 2, Birtles	
21 D1 Tottenham Hotspur	A 1-3 Birtles	
28 D1 Brighton	H 2-1 Birtles, Stapleton	

December

5 D1 Southampton	A 2-3 Stapleton, Robson	

January

2 FA Watford	A 0-1	
6 D1 Everton	H 1-1 Stapleton	
23 D1 Stoke City	A 3-0 Stapleton (pen), Coppell, Birtles	
27 D1 West Ham United	H 1-0 Macari	
30 D1 Swansea City	A 0-2	

February

6 D1 Aston Villa	H 4-1 Moran 2, Robson, Coppell	
13 D1 Wolves	A 1-0 Birtles	
20 D1 Arsenal	H 0-0	
27 D1 Manchester City	H 1-1 Moran	

March

6 D1 Birmingham City	A 1-0 Birtles	
17 D1 Coventry City	H 0-1	
20 D1 Notts County	A 3-1 Coppell 2, Stapleton	
27 D1 Sunderland	H 0-0	

April

3 D1 Leeds United	A 0-0	
7 D1 Liverpool	H 0-1	
10 D1 Everton	A 3-3 Coppell 2, Grimes	
12 D1 West Bromwich Albion	H 1-0 Moran	
17 D1 Tottenham Hotspur	H 2-0 Coppell (pen), McGarvey	
20 D1 Ipswich Town	A 1-2 Gidman	
24 D1 Brighton	A 1-0 Wilkins	

May

1 D1 Southampton	H 1-0 McGarvey	
5 D1 Nottingham Forest	A 1-0 Stapleton	
8 D1 West Ham United	A 1-1 Moran	
12 D1 West Bromwich Albion	A 3-0 Robson, Birtles, Coppell	
15 D1 Stoke City	H 2-0 Robson, Whiteside	

Final League position: 3rd

1982-83

Manager: Ron Atkinson
Played 60, **Won** 31, **Lost** 12, **Drawn** 17, **Goals for** 92, **Goals against** 51
Appearances: Duxbury 60; Stapleton 59; Whiteside 57; Albiston 56; Bailey 55; McQueen 53; Robson 49; Muhren 46; Moran 44; Coppell, Moses 43; Wilkins 36; Grimes 21; McGrath 16; Macari1 14; McGarvey 8; Buchan 6; Cunningham, Davies, Wealands 5; Gidman 3; Beardsley 1
Goals: Stapleton 19; Robson 15; Whiteside 14; Coppell (2 pens) 11; Muhren (1 pen) 7; Moran 5; McGrath, McQueen 3; Albiston, Grimes (1 pen), Macari, Moses, own goals, Wilkins 2; Cunningham, Duxbury, McGarvey 1

August

28 D1 Birmingham City	H 3-0 Moran, Stapleton, Coppell	

September

1 D1 Nottingham Forest	A 3-0 Wilkins, Whiteside, Robson	
4 D1 West Bromwich Albion	A 1-3 Robson	
8 D1 Everton	H 2-1 Whiteside, Robson	
11 D1 Ipswich Town	H 3-1 Whiteside 2, Coppell	
15 UC Valencia	H 0-0	
18 D1 Southampton	A 1-0 Macari	
25 D1 Arsenal	H 0-0	
29 UC Valencia	A 1-2 Robson	

October

2 D1 Luton Town	A 1-1 Grimes	
6 LC Bournemouth	H 2-0 Redknapp (og), Stapleton	
9 D1 Stoke City	H 1-0 Robson	
16 D1 Liverpool	A 0-0	
23 D1 Manchester City	H 2-2 Stapleton 2	
26 LC Bournemouth	A 2-2 Muhren, Coppell (pen)	
30 D1 West Ham United	A 1-3 Moran	

November

6 D1 Brighton	A 0-1	
10 LC Bradford City	A 0-0	
13 D1 Tottenham Hotspur	H 1-0 Muhren	
20 D1 Aston Villa	A 1-2 Stapleton	
24 LC Bradford City	H 4-1 Moses, Albiston, Moran, Coppell	
27 D1 Norwich City	H 3-0 Muhren, Robson 2	

December

1 LC Southampton	H 2-0 McQueen, Whiteside	
4 D1 Watford	A 1-0 Whiteside	
11 D1 Notts County	H 4-0 Whiteside, Stapleton, Robson, Duxbury	

18 D1 Swansea City	A 0-0	
27 D1 Sunderland	H 0-0	
28 D1 Coventry City	A 0-3	

January

1 D1 Aston Villa	H 3-1 Stapleton 2, Coppell	
3 D1 West Bromwich Albion	H 0-0	
8 FA West Ham United	H 2-0 Stapleton, Coppell	
15 D1 Birmingham City	A 2-1 Whiteside, Robson	
19 LC Nottingham Forest	H 4-0 McQueen 2, Coppell, Robson	
22 D1 Nottingham Forest	H 2-0 Coppell (pen), Muhren	
29 FA Luton Town	A 2-0 Moses, Moran	

February

5 D1 Ipswich Town	A 1-1 Stapleton
15 LCSF Arsenal	A 4-2 Whiteside, Stapleton, Coppell 2
19 FA Derby County	A 1-0 Whiteside
22 LCSF Arsenal	H 2-1 Coppell, Moran
26 D1 Liverpool	H 1-1 Muhren

March

2 D1 Stoke City	A 0-1
5 D1 Manchester City	A 2-1 Stapleton 2
12 FA Everton	H 1-0 Stapleton
19 D1 Brighton	H 1-1 Albiston
22 D1 West Ham United	H 2-1 Stapleton, McGarvey
26 LCF Liverpool	W 1-2 Whiteside

April

2 D1 Coventry City	H 3-0 Stapleton, Gillespie (og), Macari
4 D1 Sunderland	A 0-0
9 D1 Southampton	H 1-1 Robson
16 FASF Arsenal	N 2-1 Robson, Whiteside
19 D1 Everton	A 0-2
23 D1 Watford	H 2-0 Cunningham, Grimes (pen)
30 D1 Norwich City	A 1-1 Whiteside

May

2 D1 Arsenal	A 0-3
7 D1 Swansea City	H 2-1 Robson, Stapleton
9 D1 Luton Town	H 3-0 McGrath 2, Stapleton
11 D1 Tottenham Hotspur	A 0-2
14 D1 Notts County	A 2-3 McGrath, Moran
21 FAF Brighton	W 2-2 Stapleton, Wilkins
26 FAF (replay) Brighton	W 4-0 Robson 2, Whiteside, Muhren

Final League position: 3rd. **Won FA Cup.** Losing finalists Milk Cup

1983-84

Manager: Ron Atkinson
Played 58, **Won** 27, **Lost** 12, **Drawn** 19, **Goals for** 93, **Goals against** 56
Appearances: Stapleton 58; Albiston, Wilkins 56; Bailey, Duxbury 55; Moran 52; Graham, Whiteside 51; Moses, Robson 47; Muhren 35; McQueen 29; Hughes 17; McGrath 13; Gidman, Macari 10; Crooks 7; Hogg 6; Davies 4; Wealands 3; Blackmore 1
Goals: Stapleton 19, Robson 18; Whiteside 12; Muhren 8; Graham, Moran 7; Hughes, Wilkins 5; Moses 3; Albiston, Crooks, McQueen 2; Davies, Hogg, McGrath 1

August

20 CS Liverpool	W 2-0 Robson 2
27 D1 Queen's Park Rangers	H 3-1 Muhren 2 (1 pen), Stapleton
29 D1 Nottingham Forest	H 1-2 Moran

September

3 D1 Stoke City	A 1-0 Muhren
6 D1 Arsenal	A 3-2 Moran, Robson, Stapleton
10 D1 Luton Town	H 2-0 Muhren (pen), Albiston
14 ECWC Dulka Prague	H 1-1 Wilkins
17 D1 Southampton	A 0-3
24 D1 Liverpool	H 1-0 Stapleton
27 ECWC Dulka Prague	A 2-2 Stapleton, Robson

October

1 D1 Norwich City	A 3-3 Whiteside 2, Stapleton
3 LC Port Vale	A 1-0 Stapleton
15 D1 West Bromwich Albion	H 3-0 Albiston, Graham, Whiteside
19 ECWC JSK Spartak Varna	A 2-1 Robson, Graham
22 D1 Sunderland	A 1-0 Wilkins (pen)
26 LC Port Vale	H 2-0 Wilkins (pen), Whiteside
29 D1 Wolves	H 3-0 Stapleton 2, Robson

November

2 ECWC JSK Spartak Varna	H 2-0 Stapleton 2
5 D1 Aston Villa	H 1-2 Robson
8 LC Colchester United	A 2-0 McQueen, Moses
12 D1 Leicester City	A 1-1 Robson
19 D1 Watford	H 4-1 Stapleton 3, Robson
27 D1 West Ham United	A 1-1 Wilkins
30 LC Oxford United	A 1-1 Hughes

December

3 D1 Everton	H 0-1

7 LC Oxford United	H 1-1 Stapleton
10 D1 Ipswich Town	A 2-0 Graham, Crooks
16 D1 Tottenham Hotspur	H 4-2 Moran 2, Graham 2
19 LC Oxford United	A 1-2 Graham
26 D1 Coventry City	A 1-1 Muhren (pen)
27 D1 Notts County	H 3-3 Crooks, McQueen, Moran
31 D1 Stoke City	H 1-0 Graham

January

2 D1 Liverpool	A 1-1 Whiteside
7 FA Bournemouth	A 0-2
13 D1 Queen's Park Rangers	A 1-1 Robson
21 D1 Southampton	H 3-2 Robson, Stapleton, Muhren

February

4 D1 Norwich City	H 0-0
7 D1 Birmingham City	A 2-2 Whiteside, Hogg
12 D1 Luton Town	A 5-0 Robson 2, Whiteside 2, Stapleton
18 D1 Wolves	A 1-1 Whiteside
25 D1 Sunderland	H 2-1 Moran 2

March

3 D1 Aston Villa	A 3-0 Moses, Whiteside, Robson
7 ECWC FC Barcelona	A 0-2
10 D1 Leicester City	H 2-0 Moses, Hughes
17 D1 Arsenal	H 4-0 Muhren 2 (1 pen), Stapleton, Robson
21 ECWC FC Barcelona	H 3-0 Robson 2, Stapleton
31 D1 West Bromwich Albion	A 0-2

April

7 D1 Birmingham City	H 1-0 Robson
11 ECWCSF Juventus	H 1-1 Davies
14 D1 Notts County	A 0-1
17 D1 Watford	A 0-0
21 D1 Coventry City	H 4-1 Hughes 2, McGrath, Wilkins
25 ECWCSF Juventus	A 1-2 Whiteside
28 D1 West Ham United	H 0-0

May

5 D1 Everton	A 1-1 Stapleton
7 D1 Ipswich Town	H 1-2 Hughes
12 D1 Tottenham Hotspur	A 1-1 Whiteside
16 D1 Nottingham Forest	A 0-2

Final League position: 4th

1984-85

Manager: Ron Atkinson
Played 60, **Won** 24, **Lost** 12, **Drawn** 14, **Goals for** 113, **Goals against** 62
Appearances: Albiston 57; Strachan 56; Bailey, Hughes 55; Olsen 51; Robson 46; Duxbury, Hogg 43; Gidman 41; Whiteside 39; Moses 38; Stapleton 37; McGrath 32; Moran 28; Brazil 27; Muhren 18; McQueen 15; Garton 9; Pears 5; Blackmore 2; Davies, Graham 1
Goals: Hughes 25; Strachan (7 pens) 20; Robson 13; Brazil, Whiteside (1 pen) 9; Stapleton 8; Olsen 6; Moran 4; Gidman, Moses, Muhren (1 pen) 3; McGrath, McQueen 2; Duxbury, own goal 1

August

25 D1 Watford	H 1-1 Strachan (pen)
28 D1 Southampton	A 0-0

September

1 D1 Ipswich Town	A 1-1 Hughes
5 D1 Chelsea	H 1-1 Olsen
8 D1 Newcastle United	H 5-0 Hughes, Moses, Olsen, Strachan 2 (1 pen)
15 D1 Coventry City	A 3-0 Robson, Whiteside 2
19 UC Raba Vasa Eto Gyor	H 3-0 Robson, Muhren, Hughes
22 D1 Liverpool	H 1-1 Strachan (pen)
26 LC Burnley	H 4-0 Hughes 3, Robson
29 D1 West Bromwich Albion	A 2-1 Robson, Strachan (pen)

October

3 UC Raba Vasa Eto Gyor	A 2-2 Brazil, Muhren (pen)
6 D1 Aston Villa	A 0-3
9 LC Burnley	A 3-0 Brazil 2, Olsen
13 D1 West Ham United	H 5-1 Brazil, Hughes, McQueen, Moses, Strachan
20 D1 Tottenham Hotspur	H 1-0 Hughes
24 UC PSV Eindhoven	A 0-0
27 D1 Everton	A 0-5
30 LC Everton	H 1-2 Brazil

November

2 D1 Arsenal	H 4-2 Hughes, Robson, Strachan 2
7 UC PSV Eindhoven	H 1-0 (aet) Strachan (pen)
10 D1 Leicester City	A 3-2 Brazil, Hughes, Strachan (pen)
17 D1 Luton Town	H 2-0 Whiteside 2
24 D1 Sunderland	A 2-3 Hughes, Robson
28 UC Dundee United	H 2-2 Strachan (pen), Robson

December

1 D1 Norwich City	H 2-0 Hughes, Robson
8 D1 Nottingham Forest	A 2-3 Strachan 2 (1 pen)
12 UC Dundee United	A 3-2 Hughes, Muhren, McGinnis (og)

15 D1 Queen's Park Rangers	H 3-0 Brazil, Duxbury, Gidman
22 D1 Ipswich Town	H 3-0 Gidman, Robson, Strachan (pen)
26 D1 Stoke City	A 1-2 Stapleton
29 D1 Chelsea	A 3-1 Hughes, Moses, Stapleton

January

1 D1 Sheffield Wednesday	H 1-2 Hughes
5 FA Bournemouth	H 3-0 Strachan, McQueen, Stapleton
12 D1 Coventry City	H 0-1
26 FA Coventry City	H 2-1 Hughes, McGrath

February

2 D1 West Bromwich Albion	H 2-0 Strachan 2
9 D1 Newcastle United	A 1-1 Moran
15 FA Blackburn Rovers	H 2-0 Strachan, McGrath
23 D1 Arsenal	A 1-0 Whiteside

March

2 D1 Everton	H 1-1 Olsen
6 UC Videoton	H 1-0 Stapleton
9 FA West Ham United	H 4-2 Whiteside 3 (1 pen), Hughes
12 D1 Tottenham Hotspur	A 2-1 Hughes, Whiteside
15 D1 West Ham United	A 2-2 Robson, Stapleton
20 UC Videoton	A 0-1 (aet) [Videoton won 6-4 on penalties]
23 D1 Aston Villa	H 4-0 Hughes 3, Whiteside
31 D1 Liverpool	A 1-0 Stapleton

April

3 D1 Leicester City	H 2-1 Robson, Stapleton
6 D1 Stoke City	H 5-0 Hughes 2, Olsen 2, Whiteside
9 D1 Sheffield Wednesday	A 0-1
13 FASF Liverpool	N 2-2 (aet) Hughes, Stapleton
17 FASF Liverpool	N 2-1 Robson, Hughes
21 D1 Luton Town	A 1-2 Whiteside
24 D1 Southampton	H 0-0
27 D1 Sunderland	H 2-2 Moran, Robson

May

4 D1 Norwich City	A 1-0 Moran
6 D1 Nottingham Forest	H 2-0 Gidman, Stapleton
11 D1 Queen's Park Rangers	A 3-1 Brazil 2, Strachan
13 D1 Watford	A 1-5 Moran
18 FAF Everton	W 1-0 Whiteside

Final League position: 4th. **Won FA Cup**

1985-86

Manger: Ron Atkinson
Played 52, **Won** 27, **Lost** 13, **Drawn** 12, **Goals for** 80, **Goals against** 42
Appearances: Stapleton 51; McGrath 49; Whiteside 47; Albiston, Hughes 46; Olsen 37; Strachan 34; Bailey 32; Duxbury 30; Gidman 28; Robson 27; Moran 26; C. Gibson 22; Hogg, Turner 20; Blackmore 17; Barnes, Brazil 15; Davenport, Garton 11; Higgins 8; T. Gibson 7; Moses 5; Sivebaek 3; Dempsey, Wood 1
Goals: Hughes 18; Olsen (5 pens) 13; Stapleton 9; Robson (2 pens), Whiteside 7; C. Gibson, Strachan (1 pen) 5; McGrath 4; Barnes, Blackmore, Brazil 3; Albiston, Davenport (pen), Duxbury 1

August

10 CS Everton	W 0-2
17 D1 Aston Villa	H 4-0 Whiteside, Hughes 2, Olsen
20 D1 Ipswich Town	A 1-0 Robson
24 D1 Arsenal	A 2-1 Hughes, McGrath
26 D1 West Ham United	H 2-0 Hughes, Strachan
31 D1 Nottingham Forest	A 3-1 Hughes, Barnes, Stapleton

September

4 D1 Newcastle United	H 3-0 Hughes, Stapleton 2
7 D1 Oxford United	H 3-0 Whiteside, Robson, Barnes
14 D1 Manchester City	A 3-0 Robson (pen), Albiston, Duxbury
21 D1 West Bromwich Albion	A 5-1 Brazil 2, Strachan, Stapleton, Blackmore
24 LC Crystal Palace	A 1-0 Barnes
28 D1 Southampton	H 1-0 Hughes

October

5 D1 Luton Town	A 1-1 Hughes
9 LC Crystal Palace	H 1-0 Whiteside
12 D1 Queen's Park Rangers	H 2-0 Hughes, Olsen
19 D1 Liverpool	H 1-1 McGrath
26 D1 Chelsea	A 2-1 Olsen, Hughes
29 LC West Ham United	H 1-0 Whiteside

November

2 D1 Coventry City	H 2-0 Olsen 2
9 D1 Sheffield Wednesday	A 0-1
16 D1 Tottenham Hotspur	H 0-0
23 D1 Leicester City	A 0-3
26 LC Liverpool	A 1-2 McGrath
30 D1 Watford	H 1-1 Brazil

December

7 D1 Ipswich Town	H 1-0 Stapleton
14 D1 Aston Villa	A 3-1 Blackmore, Strachan, Hughes

21 D1 Arsenal	H 0-1
26 D1 Everton	A 1-3 Stapleton

January

1 D1 Birmingham City	H 1-0 C. Gibson
9 FA Rochdale	H 2-0 Stapleton, Hughes
11 D1 Oxford United	A 3-1 Whiteside, Hughes, C. Gibson
18 D1 Nottingham Forest	H 2-3 Olsen 2 (1 pen)
25 FA Sunderland	A 0-0
29 FA Sunderland	H 3-0 Olsen 2, Whiteside

February

2 D1 West Ham United	A 1-2 Robson
9 D1 Liverpool	A 1-1 C. Gibson
22 D1 West Bromwich Albion	H 3-0 Olsen 3 (2 pens)

March

1 D1 Southampton	A 0-1
5 FA West Ham United	A 1-1 Stapleton
9 FA West Ham United	H 0-2
15 D1 Queen's Park Rangers	A 0-1
19 D1 Luton Town	H 2-0 Hughes, McGrath
22 D1 Manchester City	H 2-2 C. Gibson, Strachan (pen)
29 D1 Birmingham City	A 1-1 Robson
31 D1 Everton	H 0-0

April

5 D1 Coventry City	A 3-1 C. Gibson, Robson, Strachan
9 D1 Chelsea	H 1-2 Olsen (pen)
13 D1 Sheffield Wednesday	H 0-2
16 D1 Newcastle United	A 4-2 Robson (pen), Hughes 2, Whiteside
19 D1 Tottenham Hotspur	A 0-0
26 D1 Leicester City	H 4-0 Stapleton, Hughes, Blackmore, Davenport (pen)

May

3 D1 Watford	A 1-1 Hughes

Final League position: 4th

1986-87

Manager: Ron Atkinson until November, then Alex Ferguson
Played 48, **Won** 17, **Lost** 16, **Drawn** 15, **Goals for** 61, **Goals against** 52
Appearances: Davenport 45; McGrath, Stapleton 40; Moran, Strachan 38; Duxbury, Whiteside 37; Robson 33; Olsen 32; Sivebaek 31; Turner 29; Albiston, C. Gibson 26; Moses 22; T. Gibson 20; Walsh 14; Blackmore, Hogg 13; Garton, O'Brien 11; Barnes 9; Bailey 5; Wood 3; Gill 1
Goals: Davenport (5 pens) 16; Whiteside 10; Stapleton 9; Robson 7; Strachan 4; Olsen (1 pen) 3; McGrath, Moses, own goals 2; Barnes, Blackmore, Duxbury, C. Gibson, T. Gibson, Sivebaek 1

August

23 D1 Arsenal	A 0-1
25 D1 West Ham United	H 2-3 Stapleton, Davenport
30 D1 Charlton Athletic	H 0-1

September

6 D1 Leicester City	A 1-1 Whiteside
13 D1 Southampton	H 5-1 Olsen (pen), Davenport, Stapleton 2, Whiteside
16 D1 Watford	A 0-1
21 D1 Everton	A 1-3 Robson
24 LC Port Vale	H 2-0 Stapleton, Whiteside
28 D1 Chelsea	H 0-1

October

4 D1 Nottingham Forest	A 1-1 Robson
7 LC Port Vale	A 5-2 Moses 2, Stapleton, Barnes, Davenport
11 D1 Sheffield Wednesday	H 3-1 Davenport 2 (1 pen), Whiteside
18 D1 Luton Town	H 1-0 Whiteside
26 D1 Manchester City	A 1-1 Stapleton
29 LC Southampton	H 0-0

November

1 D1 Coventry City	H 1-1 Davenport
4 LC Southampton	A 1-4 Davenport
8 D1 Oxford United	A 0-2
15 D1 Norwich City	A 0-0
22 D1 Queen's Park Rangers	H 1-0 Sivebaek
29 D1 Wimbledon	A 0-1

December

7 D1 Tottenham Hotspur	H 3-3 Whiteside, Davenport 2 (1 pen)
13 D1 Aston Villa	A 3-3 Davenport 2, Whiteside
20 D1 Leicester City	H 2-0 C. Gibson, Stapleton
26 D1 Liverpool	A 1-0 Stapleton
27 D1 Norwich City	H 0-1

January

1 D1 Newcastle United	H 4-1 Jackson (og), Whiteside, Stapleton, Olsen
3 D1 Southampton	A 1-1 Olsen
10 FA Manchester City	H 1-0 Whiteside
24 D1 Arsenal	H 2-0 Strachan, T. Gibson
31 FA Coventry City	H 0-1

February
7 D1 Charlton Athletic — A 0-0
14 D1 Watford — H 3-1 McGrath, Davenport (pen), Strachan
21 D1 Chelsea — A 1-1 Davenport (pen)
28 D1 Everton — H 0-0

March
7 D1 Manchester City — H 2-0 Reid (og), Robson
14 D1 Luton Town — A 1-2 Robson
21 D1 Sheffield Wednesday — A 0-1
28 D1 Nottingham Forest — H 2-0 McGrath, Robson

April
4 D1 Oxford United — H 3-2 Davenport 2, Robson
14 D1 West Ham United — A 0-0
18 D1 Newcastle United — A 1-2 Strachan
20 D1 Liverpool — H 1-0 Davenport
25 D1 Queen's Park Rangers — A 1-1 Strachan

May
2 D1 Wimbledon — H 0-1
4 D1 Tottenham Hotspur — A 0-4
6 D1 Coventry City — A 1-1 Whiteside
9 D1 Aston Villa — H 3-1 Blackmore, Duxbury, Robson

Final League position: 11th

1987-88

Manager: Alex Ferguson
Played 48, **Won** 29, **Lost** 7, **Drawn** 12, **Goals for** 86, **Goals against** 40
Appearances: McClair 48; Duxbury 47; Olsen, Strachan 44; Robson 43; Davenport 40; Anderson 38; C. Gibson 36; Whiteside 35; Turner 30; Blackmore 28; Bruce, McGrath, Moran 24; O'Brien 21; Moses 20; Walsh 18; Hogg 13; Albiston 11; Garton 9; Graham 2; Martin 1
Goals: McClair (6 pens) 31; Robson 11; Whiteside 10; Strachan 9; Davenport 6; Anderson, Blackmore, McGrath 3; Bruce, C. Gibson, O'Brien, Olsen, own goals 2

August
15 D1 Southampton — A 2-2 Whiteside 2
19 D1 Arsenal — H 0-0
22 D1 Watford — H 2-0 McGrath, McClair
29 D1 Charlton Athletic — A 3-1 McGrath, McClair, Robson
31 D1 Chelsea — H 3-1 McClair, Strachan, Whiteside

September
5 D1 Coventry City — A 0-0
12 D1 Newcastle United — H 2-2 Olsen, McClair (pen)
19 D1 Everton — A 1-2 Whiteside
23 LC Hull City — H 5-0 McGrath, Davenport, Whiteside, Strachan, McClair
26 D1 Tottenham Hotspur — H 1-0 McClair (pen)

October
3 D1 Luton Town — A 1-1 McClair
7 LC Hull City — A 1-0 McClair
10 D1 Sheffield Wednesday — A 4-2 Robson, McClair 2, Blackmore
17 D1 Norwich City — H 2-1 Davenport, Robson
25 D1 West Ham United — A 1-1 C. Gibson
28 LC Crystal Palace — H 2-1 McClair 2

November
15 D1 Liverpool — H 1-1 Whiteside
18 LC Bury — H 2-1 Whiteside, McClair
21 D1 Wimbledon — A 1-2 Blackmore

December
5 D1 Queen's Park Rangers — A 2-0 Davenport, Robson
12 D1 Oxford United — H 3-1 Strachan 2, Olsen
19 D1 Portsmouth — A 2-1 Robson, McClair
26 D1 Newcastle United — A 0-1
28 D1 Everton — H 2-1 McClair 2 (1 pen)

January
1 D1 Charlton Athletic — H 0-0
2 D1 Watford — A 1-0 McClair
10 FA Ipswich Town — A 2-1 D'Avray (og), Anderson
16 D1 Southampton — H 0-2
20 LC Oxford United — A 0-2
24 D1 Arsenal — A 2-1 Strachan, McClair
30 FA Chelsea — H 2-0 Whiteside, McClair

February
6 D1 Coventry City — H 1-0 O'Brien
10 D1 Derby County — A 2-1 Whiteside, Strachan
13 D1 Chelsea — A 2-1 Bruce, O'Brien
20 FA Arsenal — A 1-2 McClair
23 D1 Tottenham Hotspur — A 1-1 McClair

March
5 D1 Norwich City — A 0-1
12 D1 Sheffield Wednesday — H 4-1 Blackmore, McClair 2, Davenport
19 D1 Nottingham Forest — A 0-0
26 D1 West Ham United — H 3-1 Strachan, Anderson, Robson

April
2 D1 Derby County — H 4-1 McClair 3, C. Gibson
4 D1 Liverpool — A 3-3 Robson 2, Strachan
12 D1 Luton Town — H 3-0 McClair, Robson, Davenport
30 D1 Queen's Park Rangers — H 2-1 Bruce, Parker (og)

May
2 D1 Oxford United — A 2-0 Anderson, Strachan
7 D1 Portsmouth — H 4-1 McClair 2 (1 pen), Davenport, Robson
9 D1 Wimbledon — H 2-1 McClair 2 (1 pen)

Final League position: 2nd

1988-89

Manager Alex Ferguson
Played 48, **Won** 18, **Lost** 15, **Drawn** 15, **Goals for** 62, **Goals against** 41
Appearances: Bruce, Hughes, Leighton, McClair 48; Robson 43; Blackmore, Donaghy 37; Beardsmore, Sharpe 30; Martin, Milne, Strachan 29; McGrath 26; Duxbury 21; Garton 16; Gill 13; Olsen 12; Robins, Davenport 10; Anderson 7; Maiorana, Whiteside, Wilson 6; O'Brien, C. Gibson 3; D. Brazil, Graham 1
Goals: Hughes, McClair (1 pen) 16; Robson 8; Bruce 4; Blackmore, Davenport, Milne 3; Beardsmore, Gill, own goals 2; Graham, Martin, McGrath, Strachan 1

August
27 D1 Queen's Park Rangers — H 0-0

September
3 D1 Liverpool — A 0-1
10 D1 Middlesbrough — H 1-0 Robson
17 D1 Luton Town — A 2-0 Davenport, Robson
24 D1 West Ham United — H 2-0 Davenport, Hughes
28 LC Rotherham United — A 1-0 Davenport

October
1 D1 Tottenham Hotspur — A 2-2 Hughes, McClair
12 LC Rotherham United — H 5-0 McClair 3, Robson, Bruce
22 D1 Wimbledon — A 1-1 Hughes
26 D1 Norwich City — H 1-2 Hughes
30 D1 Everton — A 1-1 Hughes

November
2 LC Wimbledon — A 1-2 Robson
5 D1 Aston Villa — H 1-1 Bruce
12 D1 Derby County — A 2-2 Hughes, McClair
19 D1 Southampton — H 2-2 Robson, Hughes
23 D1 Sheffield Wednesday — H 1-1 Hughes
27 D1 Newcastle United — A 0-0

December
3 D1 Charlton Athletic — H 3-0 Milne, McClair, Hughes
10 D1 Coventry City — A 0-1
17 D1 Arsenal — A 1-2 Hughes
26 D1 Nottingham Forest — H 2-0 Milne, Hughes

January
1 D1 Liverpool — H 3-1 McClair, Hughes, Beardsmore
2 D1 Middlesbrough — A 0-1
7 FA Queen's Park Rangers — H 0-0
11 FA Queen's Park Rangers — A 2-2 (aet) Gill, Graham
14 D1 Millwall — H 3-0 Blackmore, Gill, Hughes
21 D1 West Ham United — A 3-1 Strachan, Martin, McClair
23 FA Queen's Park Rangers — H 3-0 McClair 2 (1 pen), Robson
28 FA Oxford United — H 4-0 Hughes, Bruce, Phillips (og), Robson

February
5 D1 Tottenham Hotspur — H 1-0 McClair
11 D1 Sheffield Wednesday — A 2-0 McClair 2
18 FA Bournemouth — A 1-1 Hughes
22 FA Bournemouth — H 1-0 McClair
25 D1 Norwich City — A 1-2 McGrath

March
12 D1 Aston Villa — A 0-0
18 FA Nottingham Forest — H 0-1
25 D1 Luton Town — H 2-0 Milne, Blackmore
27 D1 Nottingham Forest — A 0-2

April
2 D1 Arsenal — H 1-1 Adams (og)
8 D1 Millwall — A 0-0
15 D1 Derby County — H 0-2
22 D1 Charlton Athletic — A 0-1
29 D1 Coventry City — H 0-1

May
2 D1 Wimbledon — H 1-0 McClair
6 D1 Southampton — A 1-2 Beardsmore
8 D1 Queen's Park Rangers — A 2-3 Bruce, Blackmore
10 D1 Everton — H 1-2 Hughes
13 D1 Newcastle United — H 2-0 McClair, Robson

Final League position: 11th

1989-90

Manager: Alex Ferguson
Played 49, **Won** 20, **Lost** 17, **Drawn** 12, **Goals for** 64, **Goals against** 61
Appearances: Hughes, McClair, Phelan 48; Pallister 46; Leighton 45; Bruce 43; Martin 41; Ince 36; Wallace 35; Blackmore 31; Robson 27; Beardsmore, Duxbury 25; Robins 23; Anderson 21; Sharpe 20; Donaghy 18; Webb 15; C. Gibson 8; Sealey 3; Maiorana 2; Bosnich, Brazil, Graham, Milne 1
Goals: Hughes 15; Robins, McClair 8; Wallace 6; Robson 4; Blackmore, Bruce (1 pen), Pallister, Webb 3; Beardsmore, Ince 2; Gibson, Martin, own goal, Phelan, Sharpe 1

August

19 D1 Arsenal	H 4-1	Bruce, Hughes, Webb, McClair
22 D1 Crystal Palace	A 1-1	Robson
26 D1 Derby County	A 0-2	
30 D1 Norwich City	H 0-2	

September

9 D1 Everton	A 2-3	Beardsmore, McClair
16 D1 Millwall	H 5-1	Hughes 3, Robson, Sharpe
20 LC Portsmouth	A 3-2	Ince 2, Wallace
23 D1 Manchester City	A 1-5	Hughes

October

3 LC Portsmouth	H 0-0	
14 D1 Sheffield Wednesday	H 0-0	
21 D1 Coventry City	A 4-1	Bruce, Hughes 2, Phelan
25 D1 Tottenham Hotspur	H 0-3	
28 D1 Southampton	H 2-1	McClair 2

November

4 D1 Charlton Athletic	A 0-2	
12 D1 Nottingham Forest	H 1-0	Pallister
18 D1 Luton Town	A 3-1	Wallace, Blackmore, Hughes
25 D1 Chelsea	H 0-0	

December

3 D1 Arsenal	A 0-1	
9 D1 Crystal Palace	H 1-2	Beardsmore
16 D1 Tottenham Hotspur	H 0-1	
23 D1 Liverpool	A 0-0	
26 D1 Aston Villa	A 0-3	
30 D1 Wimbledon	A 2-2	Hughes, Robins

January

1 D1 Queen's Park Rangers	H 0-0	
7 FA Nottingham Forest	A 1-0	Robins
13 D1 Derby County	H 1-2	Pallister
21 D1 Norwich City	A 0-2	
28 FA Hereford United	A 1-0	Blackmore

February

3 D1 Manchester City	H 1-1	Blackmore
10 D1 Millwall	A 2-1	Wallace, Hughes
18 FA Newcastle United	A 3-2	Robins, Wallace, McClair
24 D1 Chelsea	A 0-1	

March

3 D1 Luton Town	H 4-1	McClair, Hughes, Wallace, Robins
11 FA Sheffield United	A 1-0	McClair
14 D1 Everton	H 0-0	
18 D1 Liverpool	H 1-2	Whelan (og)
21 D1 Sheffield Wednesday	A 0-1	
24 D1 Southampton	A 2-0	C. Gibson, Robins
31 D1 Coventry City	H 3-0	Hughes 2, Robins

April

8 FASF Oldham Athletic	N 3-3 (aet)	Robson, Webb, Wallace
11 FASF Oldham Athletic	N 2-1 (aet)	McClair, Robins
14 D1 Queen's Park Rangers	A 2-1	Robins, Webb
17 D1 Aston Villa	H 2-0	Robins 2
21 D1 Tottenham Hotspur	A 1-2	Bruce (pen)
30 D1 Wimbledon	H 0-0	

May

2 D1 Nottingham Forest	A 0-4	
5 D1 Charlton Athletic	H 1-0	Pallister
12 FAF Crystal Palace	W 3-3 (aet)	Hughes 2, Robson
17 FAF Crystal Palace	W 1-0	Martin

Final League position: 13th. **Won FA Cup**

1990-91

Manager: Alex Ferguson
Played 60, **Won** 32, **Lost** 12, **Drawn** 16 **Goals for** 101, **Goals against** 63
Appearances: Pallister 59; McClair 58; Blackmore 57; Hughes, Irwin 53; Sealey 52; Bruce, Phelan 51; Ince 48; Webb 47; Sharpe 42; Donaghy 38; Robson 30; Wallace 29; Robins 27; Martin 25; Beardsmore 15; Walsh 6; Ferguson 5; Anderson 3; Giggs, Wratten 2; Bosnich, Kontchelskis, Leighton, Whitworth 1
Goalscorers: Hughes, McClair 21; Bruce 19 (11 pens); Blackmore, Sharpe 9; Robins, Webb 5; Wallace 4; Ince 3; Anderson, Giggs, Pallister, Phelan, Robson 1

August

18 CS Liverpool	W 1-1	Blackmore
25 D1 Coventry City	H 2-0	Bruce, Webb
28 D1 Leeds United	A 0-0	

September

1 D1 Sunderland	A 1-2	McClair
4 D1 Luton Town	A 1-0	Robins
8 D1 Queen's Park Rangers	H 3-1	Robins 2, McClair
16 D1 Liverpool	A 0-4	
19 ECWC Pecsi Munkas	H 2-0	Blackmore, Webb
22 D1 Southampton	H 3-2	McClair, Hughes, Blackmore
26 LC Halifax Town	A 3-1	Blackmore, McClair, Webb
29 D1 Nottingham Forest	H 0-1	

October

3 ECWC Pecsi Munkas	A 1-0	McClair
10 LC Halifax Town	H 2-1	Anderson, Bruce (pen)
20 D1 Arsenal	H 0-1	
23 ECWC Wrexham	H 3-0	Bruce (pen), McClair, Pallister
27 D1 Manchester City	A 3-3	Hughes, McClair 2
31 LC Liverpool	H 3-1	Bruce (pen), Hughes, Sharpe

November

3 D1 Crystal Palace	H 2-0	Webb, Wallace
7 ECWC Wrexham	A 2-0	Bruce, Robins
10 D1 Derby County	A 0-0	
17 D1 Sheffield United	H 2-0	Hughes, Bruce
25 D1 Chelsea	H 2-3	Hughes, Wallace
28 LC Arsenal	A 6-2	Blackmore, Hughes, Sharpe 3, Wallace

December

1 D1 Everton	A 1-0	Sharpe
8 D1 Leeds United	H 1-1	Webb
15 D1 Coventry City	A 2-2	Hughes, Wallace
22 D1 Wimbledon	A 3-1	Bruce 2 (2 pens) Hughes
26 D1 Norwich City	H 3-0	McClair 2, Hughes
29 D1 Aston Villa	H 1-1	Bruce (pen)

January

1 D1 Tottenham Hotspur	A 2-1	Bruce (pen), McClair
7 FA Queen's Park Rangers	H 2-1	Hughes, McClair
12 D1 Sunderland	H 3-0	Hughes 2, McClair
16 LC Southampton	A 1-1	Hughes
19 D1 Queen's Park Rangers	A 1-1	Phelan
23 D1 Southampton	H 3-2	Hughes 3
26 FA Bolton Wanderers	H 1-0	Hughes

February

3 D1 Liverpool	H 1-1	Bruce (pen)
10 LCSF Leeds United	H 2-1	Sharpe, McClair
18 FA Norwich City	A 1-2	McClair
24 LCSF Leeds United	A 1-0	Sharpe
26 D1 Sheffield United	A 1-2	Blackmore (pen)

March

2 D1 Everton	H 0-2	
6 ECWC Montpellier	H 1-1	McClair
9 D1 Chelsea	A 2-3	Hughes, McClair
13 D1 Southampton	A 1-1	Ince
16 D1 Nottingham Forest	A 1-1	Blackmore
19 ECWC Montpellier	A 2-0	Blackmore, Bruce (pen)
23 D1 Luton Town	H 4-1	Bruce 2, Robins, McClair
30 D1 Norwich City	A 3-0	Bruce 2 (1 pen), Ince

April

2 D1 Wimbledon	H 2-1	Bruce, McClair
6 D1 Aston Villa	A 1-1	Sharpe
10 ECWCSF Legia Warsaw	A 3-1	McClair, Hughes, Bruce
16 D1 Derby County	H 3-1	Blackmore, McClair, Robson
21 LCF Sheffield Wednesday	W 0-1	
24 ECWCSF Legia Warsaw	H 1-1	Sharpe

May

4 D1 Manchester City	H 1-0	Giggs
6 D1 Arsenal	A 1-3	Bruce (pen)
11 D1 Crystal Palace	A 0-3	
15 ECWCF Barcelona	N 2-1	Hughes 2
20 D1 Tottenham Hotspur	H 1-1	Ince

Final League position: Sixth. **Won European Cup Winners' Cup.**
Losing Finalists Rumbelows League Cup.